Authoritarian Brazil

Authoritarian Brazil

Origins, Policies, and Future

edited by Alfred Stepan

New Haven and London, Yale University Press

Originally published with assistance from the foundation established
in memory of William McKean Brown.

Library of Congress catalog card number: 73–77167
International standard book number: 0–300–01622–0 (cloth)
0–300–01991–2 (paper)

Designed by John O. C. McCrillis
and set in Baskerville type.

Printed in the United States of America by
BookCrafters, Inc., Fredericksburg, Virginia.

Published in Great Britain, Europe, Africa, and Asia (except Japan)
by Yale University Press, Ltd., London. Distributed in Latin America
by Kaiman & Polon, Inc., New York City; in Australia and
New Zealand by Book & Film Services, Artarmon, N.S.W., Australia;
and in Japan by Harper & Row, Publishers, Tokyo Office.

Contents

Preface

In April 1971, a small group of social scientists from the United States, Europe, and Brazil came to Yale University to hold a workshop on contemporary Brazil. The decision to hold the workshop had been prompted by the realization that Brazil was passing through one of its most crucial periods since the birth of the Republic in 1889. Moreover, the authoritarian structure of the military regime that has been in power since 1964, combined as it was with one of the highest GNP growth rates in the world (11 percent in 1971), raised some extremely disturbing and yet fundamental questions about development, such as the relation between political authoritarianism and economic dynamism — questions that transcended the Brazilian case alone.

The regime that has developed since 1964 presents many analytic problems as well as social contradictions. Economically, the impressive growth rate since 1968 has been associated with regressive patterns of income distribution. As Brazil's President Médici himself acknowledged, "the economy may be going well but the people still fare poorly." Politically, in a nation that has prided itself on its unity and nonviolence, the system has been marked by repression and even torture, especially in the years 1969 and 1970. Yet even as political freedoms have been curtailed, many groups have accepted the military's claim that their policies are responsible for the economic boom and have granted the military a degree of support.

It was in order to unravel the significance of what was occurring in Brazil that the group of social scientists came together at Yale. Most of the group's members had been in informal contact with each other throughout the previous year, and all but one had carried out extensive field research in Brazil after the military came to power. The exception was Juan Linz, whose seminal theoretical work on authoritarian regimes made him a natural addition to our group.

This book is an outgrowth of the workshop. The authors have extensively revised their original papers to take into account the unusually fruitful exchanges of opinion and data at the workshop or, in some cases, to make more explicit the areas of continuing differences of interpretation. The articles do not attempt to provide a general overview of all aspects of contemporary Brazil. Rather they evaluate from different perspectives some of the major political and economic characteristics of the development process that has emerged since 1964. Precisely because events there appear to many to contain new economic and political components that might eventually be significant in other countries, there is throughout the volume a deliberate search for new conceptual frames of reference to help put the process in Brazil in a larger comparative perspective. Because of the important normative issues raised by the Brazilian style of development, there is also an attempt to clarify what values the regime promotes and what values it denies.

The volume is divided into three parts, which focus on the basic theoretical and political questions that one should ask about an authoritarian regime such as Brazil's. What are the conditions that contributed to the emergence of the authoritarian regime? What socioeconomic policies does it pursue? And what are the factors working for, and against, its institutionalization? Uniting all three parts are some fundamental themes and debates about the nature of the regime that deserve brief comment here.

The first debate concerns whether or not the current authoritarian regime in Brazil should be viewed as an extension of Brazil's previous authoritarian period, the Estado Nôvo (1937–45), or whether fundamentally new components are involved. The historian Thomas Skidmore performs the very useful task of comparing the two authoritarian regimes systematically. While he notes some policy differences, he also documents the fact that many of the authoritarian mechanisms and structures in use in the present regime were first elaborated during the Estado Nôvo. This argument is extended in the paper by political scientist Philippe Schmitter, who contends that in essence the present Brazilian regime is a "restoration" movement. His study of the sequence of development in follower countries and their patterns of interest representation suggests to him that Brazil's remodeled authoritarian rule may be representative of the "elective affinity between certain structural and behavioral attributes of delayed-dependent development and permanent authoritarian rule."

Fernando Henrique Cardoso and Alfred Stepan, though not denying that authoritarian structures have roots in the past, stress new transnational processes that have contributed to the emergence of the type of regime now found in Brazil. The Brazilian neo-Marxist theoretician Cardoso argues that the events since 1964 mark the emergence and solidification of a new process of "associated-dependent" development. According to Cardoso, the driving force of this process is the great growth of the multinational corporations that produce and market their products in the dependent economies. He maintains that this type of development, though socially exploitative, nonetheless contributes to sufficient economic dynamism in sectors of the dependent country to call for a theoretical reformulation of the impact of economic imperialism. He analyzes how the "associated-dependent" model has contributed to a new alliance between the antipopulist sectors of the military and the internationalized business sector that has an erosive effect on nationalism in dependent countries.

Alfred Stepan also draws attention to some new features of the Brazilian regime, notably the "new professionalism" of the military officers. He argues that since the 1950s, the Brazilian military has undergone a progressive professionalization that, in a context of growing concern about national development and internal security, has resulted in a military managerial ideology that goes far beyond the traditional institutional role of caudillo armies. Unlike the apolitical professionalism of officers in the armies of industrialized nations described by Huntington, where the main threat to security is external, the new professionalism of the Brazilian and the Peruvian military, Stepan contends, has contributed to the expansion of the military's role into all phases of society.

A second dialogue that runs throughout this volume concerns the relationship between repressive authoritarian rule and high economic growth rates. Many analysts are interested in determining whether the high growth rates in Brazil are dependent upon the coercive powers of the government, or are independent of coercion. Some observers argue, for instance, that specific policies, such as the export-expansion program or the tax-credit scheme for priority investments, are politically *extrinsic* to, and detachable from, the issue of a high level of coercion. Others, like Cardoso, stress that the marked wage compression which has led to a substantial decline in the real value of workers' take-home pay since 1964 in an *intrinsic* part of associated-dependent development and that this pattern of economic growth can only persist as long as repressive distribution patterns are maintained by military force.

It was partly in order to test these hypotheses that economists Samuel Morley and Gordon Smith developed an input-output model that "simulated the growth of Brazilian industry under different assumed changes in the distribution of income." They concluded that the simulations show that the impact of different income-distribution patterns is very slight and that growth could persist even if the military regime were to adopt a substantially more progressive income-distribution policy. This leads them to argue that, if one holds all inputs constant, the current Brazilian growth model is not dependent upon authoritarian power to repress worker demands. These and several other of their conclusions are controversial and challenging. Other analysts will want to examine the quality of their inputs and the nature of their assumptions very closely. Cardoso, for one, argues that the model is too static and that if repressive structures of the military were eliminated, investment rates would decline.

Economist Albert Fishlow attacks the relationship between authoritarian rule and economic growth from a different perspective. He concludes that several special circumstances surrounded the first years of economic growth of the military regime and that this makes it impossible to decide at the present time whether the boom will last and whether it is causally linked to military authoritarian rule. In any case, he argues that some of the most useful policies adopted by the military regime were not the result of technical decisions but rather the response to remaining elements of political pressure in the system.

A third theme of the volume concerns the future of the authoritarian regime. The attractiveness of military authoritarianism to many seems to rest on the military's ability to generate a coherent development policy and political stability. The fact is, however, that military governments are often as fragmented politically and as subject to military coups as civilian governments. Many of the classic problems of politics, especially the creation of a legitimacy formula and the establishment of rules of succession, apply to authoritarian regimes as well. These aspects of authoritarianism are raised in a number of the essays in this volume. Sociologist Juan Linz uses the Brazilian case to explore some of the subtypes of regimes within the authoritarian typology and to examine the conditions that facilitate or impede the institutionalization of authoritarian regimes. His comparative analysis leads him to the argument that in the post–World War II era, in countries such as Brazil with some history of commitment to the democratic process and some degree of previous social mobilization, permanent institutionalization of authoritarian regime will be difficult. His conclusion, which in some important respects differs from Schmitter's, is that in Brazil there is an authoritarian situation rather than an authoritarian regime.

In addition to the authors whose essays appear in this volume, several others participated in the discussions at the workshop and made valuable comments. These were Francine D. Blau, Ralph della Cava, Kenneth Erickson, Albert Hirschman, Luciano Martins, Janice Pearlman, Malori José Pompermeyer, H. Jon Rosen-

baum, Henry Steiner, David Trubek, Brady Tyson, and Richard
Weisskoff. Special recognition is due to Albert Hirschman and
Luciano Martins for chairing sessions of the conference and acting as formal discussants. Cândido Mendes was scheduled to participate but was unfortunately unable to attend at the last min-
ute; his advice was most useful in organizing the workshop and
is gratefully acknowledged. Bolivar Lamounier helped with translations from Portuguese into English.

I want to acknowledge the grants received from the Henry L.
Stimson Fund for Research in World Affairs and from the Council on Latin American Studies, both administered by Yale's Con-
cilium on International and Area Studies, which enabled me to
organize the workshop and to prepare this volume.

ALFRED STEPAN

PART I

ORIGINS OF THE AUTHORITARIAN REGIME

1 Politics and Economic Policy Making in Authoritarian Brazil, 1937–71

THOMAS E. SKIDMORE

THE ORIGINS OF THE REVOLUTION OF 1964

From 1945 to 1964 the Brazilian political system proved to be remarkably resilient. Many important economic decisions were taken despite the lack of strong parties or any well-established tradition of legislative support for activist government. Most observers of this period emphasized the absence of well-defined political institutions, parties, pressure groups, or even self-conscious social classes. Brazil was frequently seen as "different" — somehow saved from the crude clash of interest politics. One analyst saw this as the heyday of the autonomous technocrat.[1] Gilberto Freyre, the noted historian-essayist, attributed this happy condition to Brazilian national character, which in turn was the product of a unique Lusitanian patrimonial culture developed during the slave society of colonial Brazil.[2] More common were explanations based on such factors as personalism and regionalism. Another observer gave no explanation, satisfying herself merely with descriptions of Brazil's "institutionalized confusion."[3]

In historical perspective, the "democratic" era from 1945 to 1964 now appears as an interlude between authoritarian governments — between the Estado Nôvo (1937–45) and the "revolutionary" regimes of Castello Branco, Costa e Silva, and Garrastazú Médici. What was the historical process that led Brazil back into a nondemocratic system?[4] The authors of the "democratic" Con-

I am indebted to Tom Holloway for research assistance and to Felicity Skidmore, as usual. Very helpful comments were provided by Joseph Love, Keith Rosenn, Carlos Peláez, and John Wirth.

1. Nathaniel H. Leff, *Economic Policy-Making and Development in Brazil, 1947–1964* (New York: Wiley, 1968).

2. Gilberto Freyre, *New World in the Tropics: The Culture of Modern Brazil* (New York: Knopf, 1959).

3. Phyllis Peterson, "Brazil: Institutionalized Confusion," in *Political Systems of Latin America*, ed. Martin C. Needler (Princeton: Van Nostrand, 1964), pp. 463–510.

4. Greater detail on the background to the coup of 1964 may be found

3

stitution of 1946 were reacting to the centralized structure that they identified with the personal dictatorship of Vargas during the Estado Nôvo. From the time Vargas returned to the presidency in 1951, however, the pressures inherent in nation building and economic development were driving Brazil to reverse its postwar attempt at decentralization.

First, the thinking of the political elite became more polarized. This resulted in part from the world political context — first the cold war and then the phase of national liberation movements like those in Vietnam and Cuba. By early 1964 it appeared that Brazil would soon experience a confrontation between the armed revolutionaries of the Left and the anticommunist military officers. It turned out to be no contest. The leftist revolutionaries were few, disorganized, and poorly armed; meanwhile the military had mounted a major conspiracy whose leadership has controlled Brazil since Goulart's overthrow. Politically, it was the failure of the moderates, who lost far more than they dared guess in 1964.

This increased polarization was the result of the class or sectoral tensions inherent in the process of economic development. The propertied classes feared popular mobilization and were therefore receptive to the anticommunist rhetoric of extremists. In retrospect the "subversive" threat from the Left in the early 1960s looks pathetically minor. In the tense atmosphere of late 1963 and early 1964, however, it seemed grave enough to the privileged middle and upper sectors.[5] They feared an irreversible coup from the top leading to a socialist regime bent upon wholesale change in the social and economic structure. In short, the economic stakes of political brinkmanship, *as perceived by* the propertied classes, had risen very high by 1964.

There was a second cause. The economic crisis had grown acute since the end of the Kubitschek presidency.[6] By early 1964 Brazil was experiencing a negative per capita growth (−1.5 percent in 1963) and was on the verge of hyperinflation (the annual rate had exceeded 100 percent in the quarter) and default on international debts ($2 billion due before the end of 1965). The policy-making

in Thomas E. Skidmore, *Politics in Brazil, 1930–1964: An Experiment in Democracy* (New York: Oxford University Press, 1967). An important Brazilian interpretation of the same period is L. C. Bresser Pereira, *Desenvolvimento e crise no Brasil*, 2nd ed. (São Paulo: Zahar Editores, 1970).

5. Evidence of middle- and upper-sector fears may be found in Skidmore, *Politics in Brazil*, pp. 223–25, 253–55.

6. A useful survey of the varying explanations for the slowdown of the 1960s may be found in Werner Baer and Andrea Maneschi, "Import Substitution, Stagnation, and Structural Change: An Interpretation of the Brazilian Case," *Journal of the Developing Areas* 5, no. 2 (January 1971): 177–92.

chaos was so great and confidence so low that the crisis could only be met by a government armed with extraordinary powers. Both Right and Left were increasingly aware that the economic challenge was too great for any government that could have been elected in the deeply divided political atmosphere of early 1964. From this political deadlock the Right emerged victorious in the struggle to establish authoritarian rule.

CASTELLO BRANCO: THE PAINFUL POLITICS OF STABILIZATION, 1964–67

Although the breakdown of open politics had become virtually certain by early 1964, there was nothing inevitable about the exact nature of the new system that emerged.[7] It turned out to be a compromise between the two major groups who had made the "revolution" — the "hard-liners" (authoritarians) and the moderates. The latter included a military faction known as the Sorbonne group, of which General Castello Branco was a leader. During his presidency, however, Castello Branco was increasingly forced to adopt hard-line policies.[8] The extreme authoritarians were primarily officers, and the moderates were more evenly divided between officers and civilians. The hybrid nature of the new government, a mixture of old constitutional procedures and new arbitrary powers, was obvious from the beginning. This uneasy bal-

7. One of the most careful political analyses of the Castello Branco presidency can be found in James Rowe, "The 'Revolution' and the 'System': Notes on Brazilian Politics," American Universities Field Staff Reports, East Coast South America Series, vol. 12, nos. 3–5 (1966); and his "Brazil Stops the Clock: Part I: 'Democratic Formalism' before 1964 and in the Elections of 1966," Ibid., vol. 13, no. 1 (1967); and "Brazil Stops the Clock: Part II: The New Constitution and the New Model," Ibid., vol. 13, no. 2 (1967). For a useful chronicle of the 1964–67 period see José Wamberto, Castello Branco, Revolução e Democracia (Rio de Janeiro, 1970). The author was Castello Branco's press secretary. For a careful year-by-year analysis of the 1964–70 period, see Ronald M. Schneider, The Political System of Brazil: Emergence of a "Modernizing" Authoritarian Regime, 1964–1970 (New York: Columbia University Press, 1971). My essay makes no effort at a comprehensive analysis of economic policy making since 1964. A number of areas, including agriculture, education, housing, and social welfare, have been omitted. These topics are covered in two recent volumes on Brazil: H. Jon Rosenbaum & William G. Tyler, eds., Contemporary Brazil: Issues in Economic and Political Development (New York: Praeger, 1972) and Riordan Roett, ed., Brazil in the Sixties (Nashville, Tenn.: Vanderbilt University Press, 1972).

8. For an authoritative analysis of military politics between 1964 and 1968, see Alfred Stepan, The Military in Politics: Changing Patterns in Brazil (Princeton, N.J.: Princeton University Press, 1971), pp. 213–66.

ance was altered several times after 1964 — with the weight steadily
tipping toward authoritarianism.[9] The First Institutional Act (9
April 1964) had given the president arbitrary powers for 90 days.
Congress and the civil service were purged, several governors removed, and the military officer corps screened to force early retirement of officers who had been prominent Goulart supporters.
With its political flank apparently protected, the government
turned to the economic crisis. A willing team of technocrats was
waiting in the wings when the military conspirators ousted Goulart. They were led by Roberto Campos and Octávio Gouvéia de
Bulhões, key figures in the stabilization program that had been
jettisoned by President Kubitschek in 1959 when its political costs
became too painful.[10]

The Campos-Bulhões team moved in quickly and immediately
drew up a "Plan of Government Economic Action."[11] By mid-
1964 they had launched a flexible anti-inflation program that
Castello Branco had made his first priority.[12] Orthodox economic

9. Clear documentation of the shift can be found in the speeches of the
president: Humberto de Alencar Castello Branco, Discursos: 1964; Discursos:
1965; Discursos: 1966. All three volumes were published by the Secretaria da
Imprensa (n.d.).

10. One leading student of postwar Brazilian monetary history argues that
"it was in 1959 that Brazilian inflation really broke into a gallop, the proximate cause being the government's abandonment of a promising program
for monetary stabilization." Mário Henrique Simonsen, "Brazilian Inflation:
Postwar Experience and Outcome of the 1964 Reforms," in Economic Development Issues: Latin America, Committee for Economic Development,
Supplementary Paper no. 21 (New York, August 1967), p. 267.

11. Ministério de Planejamento e Coordenação Econômica, Programa de
ação econômica do govêrno, 1964–1966 (Rio de Janeiro: Documentos EPEA,
1964). Many of the ideas and personnel for economic policy making in the
Castello Branco period came from the Instituto de Pesquisas Estudos Sociais-
Guanabara (IPES-GB), a business-sponsored pressure group in Rio de Janeiro.
Campos had been closely associated with the group before taking office.
Norman Blume, "Pressure Groups and Decision-Making in Brazil," Studies
in Comparative International Development, vol. 3, no. 11 (1967–68). Blume
stresses the differences between the IPES groups in Rio and São Paulo. The
latter had virtually no influence in the government. IPES influence was also
confirmed by Stepan, The Military in Politics, pp. 186–87.

12. Campos, the author of the programs, has rejected the classic "shock
treatment" strategy so long recommended by the International Monetary
Fund. Instead, he favored a gradualistic policy that involved the systematic
step-by-step correction of the many inflationary distortions built into the
Brazilian economy. There is a rapidly growing literature on Brazilian anti-
inflation policies since 1964. Among the principal studies are: Alexandre
Kafka, "The Brazilian Stabilization Program, 1964–66," Journal of Political
Economy 75 (August 1967): 596–631; the chapters by Howard S. Ellis, Mário

measures were applied — an abrupt cut in the rate of growth of the money supply, slashes in public spending, a freeze on the federally decreed minimum wage. The result was a severe recession in the industrial heartland of São Paulo by late 1964. The compensatory measures hoped for in Campos's plan, such as an increased housing investment, took too long to initiate. Employment plummeted.

Critics on the left and center accused Campos of producing the recessionary traumas long thought to be typical of the stabilization policies endorsed by the International Monetary Fund (IMF) in Latin America. Criticisms were all the more violent because Campos's plan was purportedly gradualistic, and not the shock treatment long preached by the monetarists, especially those within the IMF.[13] The government acted quickly — deciding to

---

Henrique Simonsen, and Octávio de Gouvéia Bulhões, in *The Economy of Brazil*, ed. Howard S. Ellis (Berkeley and Los Angeles: University of California Press, 1969); and Samuel A. Morley, "Inflation and Stagnation in Brazil," *Economic Development and Cultural Change* 19, no. 2 (January 1971): 184–203. One of the most detailed and authoritative analyses is Mário Henrique Simonsen, *Inflação: Gradualismo x tratamento de choque* (Rio de Janeiro: APEC Editôra, 1970). These accounts are essentially favorable to the government's stabilization efforts, if often critical about details. There have been many hostile analyses, although only a few go into much technical detail. Censorship and increased political repression since 1968 virtually eliminated such publications. A typical left-wing criticism of government economic policy during the Castello Branco presidency was Cibilis da Rocha Viana, *Estratégia do desenvolvimento brasileiro: Uma política nacionalista para vencer a atual crise econômica* (Rio de Janeiro: Editôra Civilização Brasileira, 1967). A milder critique, which appeared in the press during the 1964–66 period, was published in book form: Antonio Dias Leite, *Caminhos do desenvolvimento* (Rio de Janeiro: Zahar Editores, 1966). Dias Leite was the best known of the "moderate" critics, and later became minister of mines in the Costa e Silva government.

13. As one who relished polemics, Campos did not shrink from replying to his critics. Speeches given while he was planning minister are included in Roberto de Oliveira Campos, *Política econômica e mitos políticos* (Rio de Janeiro: APEC Editôra, 1965). Articles published after he left office were collected in *Do outro lado da cêrca* (Rio de Janeiro: APEC Editôra, 1967); and *Ensaios contra a maré* (Rio de Janeiro: APEC Editôra, 1969). It was ironic that Campos himself should have first suggested the contrasting labels of "monetarist" and "structuralist" in describing anti-inflation policies. Roberto de Oliveira Campos, "Two Views on Inflation in Latin America," in *Latin American Issues: Essays and Comments*, ed. Albert O. Hirschman (New York: Twentieth Century Fund, 1961), pp. 69–79. The thinking of Bulhões, Castello Branco's finance minister who was overshadowed by Campos, is spelled out in Octávio Gouvéia de Bulhões, *Dois conceitos de lucro* (Rio de Janeiro: APEC Editôra, 1969).

relax their stabilization attempt, if only temporarily. Although the campaign to reduce the federal deficit continued, deliberate steps were taken to promote employment. In an attempt to stimulate industrial production, a schedule of tax reductions on consumer durables was announced in early 1965. The huge coffee surplus of 1964–65 was purchased at generous prices, thereby swelling the public deficit, which in turn was partially financed by the familiar inflationary method of increasing the stock of money. During 1965 the money supply increased 75 percent, more than double the target figure of 30 percent that had been established in Campos's 1964 plan. In part this inflationary expansion resulted from inadvertent errors (some technical and some due to lack of promptly available statistics). Yet it was also in part a deliberate attempt to soften the severe distortions caused by the first nine months of the deflationary squeeze — a Brazilian version of the "stop and go" stabilization cycle. This relaxation may also have been aimed at strengthening progovernment candidates in the gubernatorial elections scheduled for 11 states in October 1965. Industrial production did recover, but not even elaborate "legal" steps to disqualify the popular opposition candidates could stop prominent protégés of Kubitschek from winning the governorships of Minas Gerais and Guanabara. The victory of pro-Castello Branco (or at least neutral) candidates in all of the other gubernatorial races did not prevent the Castello Branco regime and the public from interpreting the victories of Negrão de Lima and Israel Pinheiro as evidence of widespread popular opposition. The hard-liners were infuriated; they felt the victories heralded the return of the "corrupt" and "irresponsible" politicians who had just led Brazil to the brink of a communist or caudillo-type takeover. The moderate supporters of the 1964 coup were worried because they had been unable by *their* political efforts to prevent the electional comeback of the pro-Kubitschek figures. The technocrats, led by Roberto Campos, were worried for a different reason. They could see their gradualistic stabilization program, if resumed, remaining a political albatross for the Castello Branco government in the presidential election scheduled for November 1966.

After bitter argument between moderates and extremists, a compromise was negotiated.[14] The two Kubitschek protégés would be permitted to take office, but only if the government were al-

14. The bitter arguments are described in Rowe, "The 'Revolution' and the 'System,' " pp. 24–26; and Stepan, *The Military in Politics*, pp. 254–57. Stepan based his analysis on extensive interviews with participants and observers.

lowed to issue a Second Institutional Act that sharply curtailed political competition. All existing political parties were abolished and the elections of 1966 were made indirect, with the president and vice-president to be chosen by the Congress. Congressmen and all other elected officeholders were once again made subject to immediate dismissal by the president, who also regained power to suspend any citizen's political rights for 10 years.

Instead of proposing any alternative to representative democracy, the Castello Branco government clung to its ad hoc political strategy. On the one hand, it continued the periodic purges by suspending the political rights of an ever-widening circle of public figures. Congress was purged again in 1966 when leaders of the official opposition party, Movimiento Democrático Brasiliero (MDB), called for a return to direct elections. At each stage the government justified such measures as necessary to defend the liberal ideal. The revolutionaries never faltered in their verbal commitment to democracy; to them, these were merely extraordinary short-term measures designed to make democracy more viable in the future.[15] On the other hand, it relied upon the old-line moderate-to-conservative civilian politicians, primarily from the former UDN — the antipopulist party par excellence that had failed to generate any wide popular appeal between 1946 and 1964. Meanwhile, economic policy making and the direction of the state administrative apparatus gravitated toward the technocrats, drawn from both civilian and military ranks.

Having gambled and lost in the electoral battle of 1965, the Castello Branco government returned to the tasks of stabilization. Now able to ignore the short-run political costs because the Second Institutional Act had restored extraordinary powers to the presidency for the remainder of Castello Branco's term (until March 1967), the Campos team pressed on with their strategy of 1964. The orthodox monetary constraints were applied, once again producing a severe industrial recession in 1966. Real wages declined, imports slumped, and business failures multiplied. But this time the government did succeed in reducing significantly the rate of inflation (as measured by the official cost-of-living figures). From 66 percent in 1965, it fell to 41 percent in 1966, and 31

15. Typical was the president's speech of 11 December 1965, in which he predicted that Brazil would "gradually and uninterruptedly resume the normal life of a democracy." Castello Branco, *Discursos: 1965*, pp. 289–91. The commitment continued even with President Médici, who said in October 1969 that he hoped "to leave democracy definitively established in our country at the end of my administration." Emílio Garrastazú Médici, *O jôgo da verdade* (n.p., 1970), p. 10.

percent in 1967, the year Costa e Silva succeeded Castello Branco.[16] Inflationary expectations were sharply lowered — thus accomplishing one of the most important and difficult tasks of stabilization. Furthermore, an appreciable part of the inflation in 1965 was "corrective," that is, it consisted of price increases in services (especially in the public sector) which had previously been subsidized. These increases represented the working out of the "repressed" inflation which was a nonrecurring adjustment, assuming that subsequent pricing policies accurately reflected costs (which they have). Finally, the federal deficit was sharply reduced, declining from the startlingly high level of 4.2 percent of GDP in 1963 to 1.1 percent of GDP in 1966. The first revolutionary government had achieved a large measure of the stabilization goals Campos had expected to accomplish — but it had taken three years instead of a year and a half.[17]

The Castello Branco government took great pride in the relative success of the stabilization program and the extensive reorganization of the public sector. The president and Planning Minister Campos had constantly called for a return to "rational" policies. They saw themselves as guiding Brazil back to a "realistic" understanding of her own potential and of the rate at which it could be developed.[18] The targets for their attack were the

16. My figures on economic data are taken from Albert Fishlow's chapter in this volume, and from the very useful overview of the economic record of the post-1964 revolutionary governments in Werner Baer and Isaac Kerstenetzky, "The Brazilian Economy in the Sixties," in *Brazil in the Sixties*, ed. Riordan Roett (Nashville, Tenn.: Vanderbilt University Press, 1972). For an "inflation rate" I have used the official cost of living index for Guanabara as given by Fishlow. This index shows a higher rate of increase for 1965, 1966, and 1967 than the price index cited in Fishlow. An up-to-date summary of the economic record of the post-1964 governments may be found in First National City Bank, *Brazil: An Economic Survey* (March 1971).

17. The figures on the budget deficit come from Albert Fishlow's chapter in this volume. Campos's plan of 1964 called for inflation to be reduced to 25 percent in 1965 and 10 percent in 1966. There was an implication that the "residual" rate might remain at 10 percent. In fact, the "residual" after 1966 proved to be about 20 percent. Ministério de Planejamento e Coordenação Econômica, *Programa de ação econômica*, p. 35.

18. See, for example, Campos's stern lectures to businessmen in late 1964 and early 1965. Campos, *Política econômica e mitos políticos*. One observer, in summing up the Castello Branco "model of development," noted that it emphasized the increased ties to the United States and the other capitalist nations and that it "expresses a lower level of expectations regarding primarily Brazilian solutions to certain key problems." Rowe, "Brazil Stops the Clock: Part II," p. 8.

populist politicians who had allegedly misled the country by promising more than the economy could produce, while incompetently managing government policy. Furthermore, it was alleged, these politicians had threatened the basis of the market economy — private property and foreign investment. Goulart and his government were the most immediate symbol of this "irresponsibility." Attacks on Goulart were a constant refrain in the Castello Branco government's claim to legitimacy.[19]

As the day of transition to the Costa e Silva presidency drew near, however, the incumbent government became worried that its hard-won efforts at stabilization might be sacrificed by a new source of populist opinion: the military. Costa e Silva was known to have contacts with some hard-line officers led by General Albuquerque Lima who were also outspoken economic nationalists. Campos and Castello Branco pressed hard to sell their case for "continuity" in economic policy, by which they meant continuing the policy of collaboration with foreign capital — public and private — and maintaining the fight against inflation.

They also hoped to ensure continuity in the political system. By 1966 the "legalists" of the Castello Branco government finally saw that they had no choice but to rewrite the constitution (the fourth since 1930), hoping thereby to bequeath to succeeding administrations a new institutionalized structure. They devised a system that retained elections (only indirect for governors and the president and vice-president) but gave the federal executive greatly expanded powers to control law making, administration, and dissent. The new constitution and the flood of executive decrees during Castello Branco's last months in office in early 1967 represented a final effort by the moderates to contain the new arbitrary power within constitutional limits. It was also aimed at boxing in the new president, whose possible populist or nationalist tendencies still worried the first revolutionary regime.[20]

19. See, for example, the president's speech of 22 December 1965. Castello Branco, *Discursos: 1965*, pp. 109–23.

20. The *castellista* worries over continuity are reported in *Visão*, 29 July 1966, p. 11; 12 August 1966, p. 11; 5 August 1966, pp. 22–26; 3 March 1967, p. 11. After mid-1966 there was constant speculation that Castello Branco might try to continue in power. *Visão*, 19 August 1966, p. 13. The Constitution of 1967 was later modified by the new series of institutional acts that began appearing in December 1968 and then by the constitutional amendment of October 1969. The text of the constitution, as amended through October 1969, with commentary, is given in Rosah Russomano, *Anatomia da constituição* (São Paulo: Editôra Revista dos Tribunais, 1970).

THE REVOLUTION SINCE 1968: ECONOMIC GROWTH
AND POLITICAL REPRESSION

There was little need to worry about a resurgence of inflation or economic nationalism under Costa e Silva. The nationalist officer group proved to be small, or at least lacking in any significant influence at the decision-making level of the military. Economic policy continued to be entrusted to civilian technicians. The central figure of the new economic team appointed by Costa e Silva in March 1967 was Finance Minister Delfim Neto, an economics professor from São Paulo.

Relatively successful at stabilization, the Castello Branco government had failed, however, on another economic front: the resumption of growth. The orthodox fiscal, monetary, and wage policies had served their purpose by 1967. Yet the Campos team appeared to lack a strategy that would guide Brazil back onto the path of growth. In part this appearance was deceptive. The relative success in controlling price increases was itself a prerequisite for renewed expansion. Inflationary distortions previously promoted by the government had to be removed. Most important, the government deficit was sharply reduced, primarily by increasing federal revenues. The extensive rationalization of the public sector, including better management of public corporations and the simplification of bureaucratic procedures in key areas such as export promotion, was indispensable. Increased efficiency in the private sector — now induced by the deflationary squeeze — was another prerequisite. Finally, the renegotiation of the large short-term foreign debt, the increase of capital inflows (private and public), and the promotion of exports all helped to strengthen Brazil's balance of payments, thus relieving external pressure on policy makers. By 1967 Brazil was ready to resume growth.

The fears of the Castello Branco government that its successor might scuttle stabilization and play for political popularity by loosening the fiscal and monetary brakes were unfounded. There were policy changes, but none that increased inflation. A new diagnosis of the inflationary process led to a new economic strategy.[21] In order to overcome what was now considered pri-

21. The new diagnosis was offered in May 1967 by a group of government economists, who contended that Brazil had experienced a "profound" change in the nature of the inflationary process. Since 1966, they argued, the process had become "cost-push," whereas the Campos policy had continued to suppress demand. The Castello Branco government was criticized for pursuing a monetary and fiscal policy that lacked any "great continuity" in 1964 and

marily a "cost-push" inflation, Delfim Neto eased credit to the hard-pressed private sector. The money supply was increased 43 percent in both 1967 and 1968. Increases in the minimum wage were now kept constant with increases in the cost of living, a move that halted the slide in real wages (as measured by the minimum wage). This more flexible use of credit and tax policy, begun under Costa e Silva (1967–69) and continued under Garrastazú Médici (1969–   ), helped restore demand, leading to an impressive resumption of growth in gross domestic product — 4.8 percent in 1967, 8.4 percent in 1968, 9.0 percent in 1969 and 9.5 percent in 1970. This expansion did not intensify inflation, which fell to 22 percent in 1968, remained at 22 percent in 1969, and declined to 21 percent in 1970. Both the Costa e Silva and Médici governments chose to tolerate a "residual" inflation rate of 20 percent, reasoning that any attempt to push inflation much lower in the short run would cripple much needed economic growth.[22]

Performance in the foreign sector was equally encouraging. The export promotion drive that began in 1964, coupled with the "crawling peg" system of mini-devaluations started in 1968, helped push Brazilian exports to the unprecedented total $2.7 billion in 1970 — twice the level of the early 1960s and 60 percent higher than for any year during the 1964–67 period. The balance of payments showed large surpluses for 1969 and 1970, contributing to a record level of $1.2 billion in foreign reserves. These surpluses

1965, and then adopting a "rather inflexible [monetary] policy" in 1966. Ministério do Planejamento e Coordenação Geral, *Diretrizes de govêrno: Programa estratégico de desenvolvimento* (n.p., 1967), pp. 145–62. An influential critique of Campos's failures (as well as accomplishments) in monetary policy was given in articles in the annual volumes published by APEC [Análise e Perspectiva Econômica]: *A economia Brasileira e suas perspectivas.* Mário Henrique Simonsen's summary assessment of the 1964–69 period is included in his *Inflação: Gradualismo x tratamento de choque,* chap. 2. A convincing analysis of the way in which credit policy had inadvertently promoted both inflation and stagnation between 1962 and 1967 is given in Morley, "Inflation and Stagnation in Brazil." Morley was in Brazil in 1966–68 and worked with the EPEA group of economists who authored the critical diagnosis cited above.

22. These data are taken from the table 3.1 in Albert Fishlow's chapter in this volume. The recent high levels of growth may have been attributable to the use of the large amount of underutilized capacity already available in the mid-1960s. If so, future growth will require a much higher rate of domestic savings to finance the investment necessary to produce additional capacity. The inadequacy of recent domestic savings rates is stressed in Albert Fishlow's chapter. The same criticism is raised in an unimpeachably capitalist source: the First National City Bank's *Brazil: An Economic Survey.*

could be attributed both to a dramatic increase in exports (sharply exceeding the rate of growth of imports during 1969 and 1970) and to increases in net capital inflows.[23] Did this economic success — first stabilization and then renewed growth — accompany a return to open politics? On the contrary. Just as the economy was entering a new dynamic phase the regime took a sharply authoritarian turn.

Costa e Silva's attempt to project a more "humane" image for the "revolution" had aroused hopes of a possible liberalization. The militant opposition — especially within the student movement — reappeared in the streets in 1968. Wildcat strikes occurred in São Paulo and Minas Gerais. Even though there could be few illusions about the possibility of undermining a government in which the military were so clearly prepared to use repression, the small increase in "public disorder" strengthened the hand of the hard-liners. In December 1968 they were presented with a dramatic opportunity when the Congress rejected an urgent presidential demand to lift the parliamentary immunity of Deputy Márcio Moreira Alves whom the military wished to prosecute for supposedly insulting the armed forces during a congressional speech. The congressional defeat of the presidential ultimatum created a political crisis that shook the Costa e Silva government. The military commanders had confidently expected the official government party, Aliança Renovadora Nacional (ARENA), which had emerged from the 1966 elections with a majority of 277 to 132 in the Chamber of Deputies, to produce a favorable majority. Instead, many ARENA deputies voted to protect their congressional colleague, a member of the MDB. The vote can be seen as a symbolic gesture of allegiance to constitutionalism by civilian moderates who had finally reached a breaking point in their submission to the protection of "military honor." It was also an act of defiance of the real power arbiters.

In military eyes the politicians had discredited themselves yet again. The government party could not even deliver a majority vote on an issue that the president had clearly defined as essential to national security. In the ensuing crisis the hard line again prevailed, just as it had in October 1965. Congress was closed indefinitely. Once again a new institutional act (the fifth) was issued, now giving the president virtually unlimited powers to protect national security. And, unlike earlier acts, this one carried no time limit. Hundreds more had their political rights suspended, federal universities were hit by a new wave of dismissals, and scores of political dissidents and intellectuals fled into exile. The principal victim was the Supreme Court, which had remained

23. First National City Bank, *Brazil: An Economic Survey*, pp. 35-41.

the last line of defense against authoritarianism. Three judges were purged, another (close to retirement age) was forcibly retired, and the president resigned in protest. The court's jurisdiction was further reduced by the Sixth Institutional Act (1 February 1969).

During 1969 a new pattern was set: a terrorist underground pitted against police and military authorities who did not hesitate to torture their suspects. The pattern continued through 1970 — kidnappings, bank robberies, assassinations, and terrorist attacks on military installations, answered by mass arrests and brutal mistreatment of prisoners, including numerous clergy. Brazil began to resemble Salazar's Portugal in its elaborate security precautions.

Veteran foreign observers were impressed with the controls which the police and military were able to impose in a country long known for bureaucratic inefficiency. The rigid enforcement of the requirement for personal-identity documents, the widespread monitoring of telephone and mail, the close checks on travelers by frequent searches of luggage — all indicated the government's determination and ability to suppress any organized opposition outside of the officially sanctioned boundaries, which were narrowing. In short, the Revolution of 1964 had left the moderates far behind; it now resembled the "emergency state" that militant anticommunist officers had urged since the early 1950s.

Significantly, however, it was only after the authoritarian turn of 1968 that the armed opposition succeeded in stepping up their activities. Previously, Brazil had been conspicuous for its lack of guerrilla movements. The urban terrorists, who became much bolder in 1969, were able to point to the repressive police apparatus as justification for their argument that violence was the only alternative to the economic, social, and political policies of the military-technocratic Revolution.

Thus 1968 was a turning point. The trend away from an open system of competitive politics accelerated. Castello Branco had succeeded in maintaining an uneasy compromise between moderates and hard-liners. Under Costa e Silva the advocates of repression clearly gained the upper hand. Their dominance was shown again in 1969, when Costa e Silva fell mortally ill and was succeeded (after the arbitrary disqualification of the civilian vicepresident, Pedro Aleixo) by General Garrastazú Médici, who continued the hard line of repression and censorship.[24]

24. An analysis of Médici's succession is given in Stepan, *The Military in Politics*, pp. 264–65.

Although repressive, the regime's use of political controls after 1968 stopped short of being as total as in most of postwar Eastern Europe, Castro's Cuba, or Salazar's Portugal. For millions of Brazilians, in fact, the years since 1968 have probably seemed little different from previous eras. The relatively low degree of previous political participation, even before Goulart's overthrow in 1964, meant that many (perhaps most) middle-sector Brazilians were not greatly disturbed at their loss of political options.

Nonetheless, at each successive stage the government found itself "forced" to suspend the political rights of an ever-growing circle of politicians and public figures, including many of no prominence before 1964. Post-1964 governments have slowly discovered that they are committed in theory to a democratic structure that fails in practice to give the results that the technocrats and the hard-liners want: rapid economic growth without overt political strife. The result by 1971 was a compliant façade of a Congress, shorn of any independent powers. The military extremists have not allowed any civilian politician to emerge who might serve as a rallying point for opposition. Thus the government is more authoritarian than at any point since 1964, and at the same time has left itself no "extrication option" — no shadow government of civilians to whom it might consider delivering power after a transition period.

THE ALLIANCE OF HARD-LINERS AND TECHNOCRATS

The extreme authoritarian military officers regard themselves as realistic.[25] They do not believe that their country has the ability over the short run to achieve economic growth under an open political system. As a militant minority, they are determined to prevent any access to power by the rival minority who made, they thought, near-fatal inroads before 1964 — the subversive Left.

25. Sources on the hard line are hard to come by. One of the best examples of their anticommunist thinking is Pedro Brasil [pseud.], *Livro branco sôbre a guerra revolucionário no Brasil* (Pôrto Alegre: O Globo, 1964), a pamphlet written in the format of a military staff paper and published just before the coup of 1964. Transcripts of the innumerable trials before military tribunals since 1964 would be an excellent source, although they are evidently unavailable to the public. Examples of the thinking behind such trials may be found in Inquérito Policial Militar 709, *O comunismo no Brasil*, 4 vols. (Rio de Janeiro: Biblioteca do Exército, 1966–67). For the flavor of hard-line rhetoric in the midst of the 1968 political crisis, see "Críticas sérias de jovens oficiais," *Visão*, 22 November 1968. This includes excerpts from the manifesto of officers from the Escola de Aperfeiçoamento de Oficiais.

They see Brazil as plagued by weak-willed politicians and disloyal intellectuals. Because the hard-liners have never emerged into the public arena to defend their ideas, their power can only be assessed by looking at the policies they have forced upon successive governments. And the tightening authoritarian rule is eloquent testimony to that power.

The principal reason for their failure to take a public stance can be found in the structure of the military. The essence of organization within any military officer corps is hierarchy and discipline. Yet this structure in Brazil allows room for an intricate process of participatory decision making.[26] The higher levels retain the final word, but they cannot diverge too far from the views of their junior officers. In each political crisis the officers have heatedly debated the proper government policy. Manifestos occasionally leak to the press, but the controversy is essentially private. The exact line-up of factions and arguments is known only to the higher-level participants and a few privileged outsiders (including some journalists who protect their sources by seldom giving details).

Thus the heart of decision making in Brazilian politics since 1964 — the formation of officer opinion — remains hidden from the public. In order to preserve discipline and the image of unity, the disagreements are submerged in the final policy adopted by the higher command. That policy may be subject to subsequent attack and revision, but only within the private channels of officer contact. With only rare exceptions the losers guard their silence. This maintenance of unity, at least in public, contrasts sharply with the frequent divisions that arose among the officers in the political-military crises between 1945 and 1964. When divided, as in 1961, the military found it impossible to intervene effectively. Since 1964 their power has made their need for unity much greater, lest they fall into the pattern of the Argentine military whose warring factions are unable to impose any consistent policy on the civilians.

Within this private opinion-making context, the more authoritarian officers have increasingly held the initiative. Castello Branco was clearly identified as a moderate; but Costa e Silva was known to have pushed for more arbitrary presidential power in 1964–65. Médici was unequivocally identified with the more repressive faction. At every turn the president has been dependent for his very power on the active support of the officer corps, which in turn has been dominated by the hard-liners.

26. Decision making within the Brazilian military is clearly explained in Stepan, *The Military in Politics*.

Because the military have wished to retain their image of unity, and also because the moderates have struggled to preserve remnants of liberal constitutionalism, the revolutionary government has often relegated the explanation of its authoritarian side to civilian apologists, such as Justice Ministers Gama e Silva, Carlos Medeiros, and Alfredo Buzaid.[27] The truly militant officers do not believe in the official commitment to the principle of liberal democracy, but they have so far lacked either the will or the intellectual self-confidence to emerge *on their own* and drop the pretense of civilian government. So, unlike their Peruvian counterparts, they have used stalking horses. A further explanation for this reticence to rule openly in the capacity of military leaders is an apparent agreement among the higher officers that no one caudillo should be allowed to establish himself as a personal dictator, Franco-style.

In this absence of any hard-line rationale, the government lawyers have had to continue revamping the old constitutional forms in order to "legalize" the growing powers of the executive. Although it has avoided repudiating the liberal ideal per se, the government has used constitutional amendments, institutional acts, and executive decrees to eliminate any independent role for the legislative or judicial branches. At the same time it has circumscribed (and often suspended) civil liberties and rights of political organization.

The tightening authoritarian system has made possible political "stability" — defined by the hard-line military as the absence of any serious opposition or criticism. These extremist officers have satisfied their intense desire to suppress the overt conflict and tension of an open system. They no longer have to tolerate Marxist rhetoric, student demonstrations, or widely debated political trade-offs among states, regions, or social groups. The simplistic ideological preoccupations of an antidemocratic cadre have spread far through the apparatus of government.

Yet the application of this extremist political philosophy can hardly be the exclusive function of the authoritarian system. On the contrary, for most middle-sector Brazilians it is probably not even the principal function. They do not share the extremist conception of national security, nor the polarization (torturers vs. terrorist-kidnappers) forced upon them. But they do quickly acknowledge the remarkable economic progress made since 1964

27. Medeiros, for example, rejected direct presidential elections for Brazil, explaining that they caused too much "agitation" and thus would make the country ungovernable. "Medeiros responsabiliza eleições directas pelas crises." *Jornal do Brasil,* 23 June 1968.

and appear to accept tacitly the authoritarian system because it has made possible a new continuity and coherence in economic policy making.

The result is a working alliance between extremists and technocrats. Each has his own reasons for wanting an authoritarian regime. Each needs the other. The hard-line military need the technocrats to make the economy work. The high growth rates in turn give pragmatic legitimacy to the authoritarian system — "it works." The technocrats and managers need the military in order to stay in power, or at least in order to have the power and authority to carry out their policies.

The partners in the alliance have found no single rationale for their authoritarianism. The technocrats and middle sectors do not share the political paranoia of the hard-liners and the latter do not really understand the economic strategies of the former. Brazil today appears to lack any explicit consensus on its goals and the means to achieve them.

Undoubtedly the technocrats have been less happy about this growing authoritarianism than the extremist military who had never entertained any illusions about the virtues of liberal democracy. Whatever qualms they may have felt about the unsavory illiberalism or arbitrary purges and constitutional sleight of hand demanded by intransigent colonels, however, the technocrats appreciated the extraordinary power base that they would enjoy if the military continued to grant them virtual carte blanche in economic policy making. In 1965–66 the uneasy alliance between the hard line and the technocrats was forged more strongly, and at every turning point in the succeeding five years (1965–71), the alliance has been strengthened further. De facto evidence of this mutual alliance can be found in the fact that the military extremists and their civilian allies have spared economics faculties in their periodic purges of Brazilian universities.

TECHNOCRATS AT WORK: REMOVING THE OLD CONSTRAINTS?

Once authoritarianism came, how much difference did it make for economic policy making? Did the authoritarian system make possible options that had been ruled out for a democratic, representative government of divided and sharply defined constitutional powers? There is much evidence that it did, especially during the Castello Branco presidency.

A prime example is stabilization policy. One theme of the history of Brazil's economic policy making from 1951 to 1964 is the repeated but largely unsuccessful attempt to control inflation.

There were incomplete attempts at stabilization in 1953–54, 1955–56, 1958–59, 1961, and 1963–64. Until 1961 the failures did not prevent a resumption of growth, although the inflationary distortions increased. By 1964 it was doubtful if any democratically elected president could carry out the stabilization program that was essential if Brazil was to resume growth within the capitalist system. It was either stabilization under an authoritarian government or social revolution under a government of the Left.

The coup of 1964 ruled out the latter. How did Campos and Bulhões achieve success (even if limited) where earlier attempts had failed? Essentially, they succeeded because they were given great latitude by a military government, which could ignore public opposition, especially after 1965. Time was necessary in order to break the public's well-established inflationary expectations. Normal politicians shrink from this economic therapy because of the popular opposition it arouses. Campos and Castello Branco could rely upon the arbitrary powers the hard-liners had forced on the revolutionary government. The Campos team needed at least two years; the backing and filling of 1964–65 added another year.

Most unpopular, not surprisingly, was the deliberate policy of letting wage increases lag behind increases in the cost of living. This reduction in real wages, which amounted to approximately 20 to 25 percent by 1967, was justified by a geometric explanation of the lag effect of lowering inflationary wage expectations, and was billed as temporary. But it is difficult to imagine how such a "corrective" wage policy could have been carried out by a government that had to face a test at the polls — even under the imperfectly democratic system of pre-1964 Brazil. Given the "political cover" of a military regime, the technocrats were able to carry out a stabilization policy that weighed most heavily on one social sector — the working class.[28]

The Campos-Bulhões policy also contradicted the interests of many domestic businessmen. Policy makers fully intended to force the private sector to slough off the inflation-induced habits of concentrating on inventories and credit policy, rather than quality and productivity. There was a reduction in the level of effective

28. Government wage policy was briefly outlined in Ministério de Planejamento e Coordenação Econômica, *Programa de ação econômica*, pp. 83–85. This geometry is explained in Simonsen, *Inflação*, pp. 26–28. For a highly original analysis of the relationship between inflation and the demand structure in Brazil see Nicholas Georgescu-Roegen, "Structural Inflation — Lock and Balanced Growth," *Economies et Sociétiés* 4, no. 3 (March 1970): 557–605.

protection[29] and an end to the frequent policy of providing publicly subsidized credit from the central banking system in times of liquidity crisis. As a result, Brazilian business went through several painful shake-out phases, during which foreign firms, especially American, were able to acquire Brazilian companies that could no longer find domestic sources of credit. Here again was a brand of "corrective" stabilization that few elected governments would even have aspired to for long.[30]

Management of public enterprises was another area in which stabilization policies inevitably resulted in political unpopularity. The Campos diagnosis correctly assumed that inflation had been fed by federal government deficits. Failure both to increase prices and to control expenditure had resulted in large deficits financed by monetary issues. The Castello Branco government moved quickly to end the huge deficits in the state-owned railroads, shipping industry, and oil industry. In every case it meant increasing the price of services — a step that directly increased the cost of living in the short run. But covering costs meant that long-deferred investment could be made in these public enterprises, thus increasing productivity and thereby lowering costs for the future. Furthermore, an important cause of federal deficit financing was eliminated. But it is doubtful if any elected regime could have withstood the storm of public protest over costlier bus fares and other public services.

29. Joel Bergsman, Brazil: Industrialization and Trade Policies (London: Oxford University Press, 1970), pp. 42–54.

30. This "denationalization" of Brazilian business was one of the most vigorously debated results of government policy. One of the best-known critics was Fernando Gasparian, whose articles and speeches are collected in Em defesa da economia nacional (Rio de Janeiro: Editôra Saga, 1966). The problem became serious enough to become the subject of a congressional inquiry (although there were few illusions in the purged Congress about the possibility of any "action"). The congressional commission's published report may be found in Rubem Medina, Desnacionalização: Crime contra o Brasil? (Rio de Janeiro: Editôra Saga, 1970). Celso Furtado appeared as an expert witness before the commission (returning only briefly to Brazil for the testimony). His testimony was later published in Celso Furtado, Um projeto para o Brasil (Rio de Janeiro: Editôra Saga, 1968). An English translation is included in his Obstacles to Development in Latin America (Garden City, N.Y.: Anchor Books, 1970). Furtado sees post-1964 Brazil as a prime example of what is essentially a new "structuralist" interpretation of the technologically imposed "dependence." The advantageous credit position enjoyed by foreign-owned firms is discussed also in Samuel A. Morley and Gordon W. Smith, "Import Substitution and Foreign Investment in Brazil," Oxford Economic Papers 23, no. 1 (March 1971): 134.

Another area of public finance that policy makers had previously found it virtually impossible to change was the income tax. Underdeveloped countries are notorious for the practical problems they present to the tax collector. Indirect taxes are supposedly the least difficult to collect. The ease of fraud makes income tax one of the hardest. The dictatorial powers of the military government have transformed the situation in Brazil, however. Individual income-tax payers increased from 470,000 in 1967 to over 4,000,000 in 1969.[31] Under an elected government these new tax payers could have been expected to lobby effectively to undermine such a dramatic change in tax policy.

The foreign sector is another area where policies that were adopted after 1964 would have been dangerous if not impossible for any elected government in the Brazil of the mid-1960s. On the eve of Goulart's ouster Brazil faced a crushing short-term international debt. It could be renegotiated only if the new government could satisfy her creditors that she was serious about domestic stabilization — something Goulart failed to accomplish. The Castello Branco government did more than that. It immediately moved to repudiate the economic nationalism that had grown steadily since the mid-1950s.

The first step was to repeal the profit-remittances law passed by the Congress in 1962. Although there was no referendum on policies toward foreign investment, politicians who held nationalist views had enjoyed growing success at the polls from 1960 on. The party of most of the economic nationalists, the PTB (Partido Trabalhista Brasileiro), grew steadily in size and became the largest single party in Congress in 1962. A profit-remittances bill introduced by President Quadros in 1961 was significantly rewritten and made more restrictive by nationalist congressmen. The bill was vigorously opposed by foreign investors and the United States embassy (the American ambassador lobbied extensively against the measure). Although it was adopted in 1962, the law did not go into effect until President Goulart issued the enabling decree in January 1964. Significantly, this law did not originate with the technocrats, who probably regarded it as an administrative nuisance if not an obstacle to obtaining needed capital.

Compliance with Castello Branco's request for repeal of the profit-remittances law was virtually assured by the government's prior purge of almost all the congressmen who had led the battle

31. Thomas G. Sanders, "Institutionalizing Brazil's Conservative Revolution," *American Universities Field Staff Reports, East Coast South America Series*, vol. 14, no. 5 (1970), p. 6.

for its original passage. No openly elected Congress in 1964 would have been likely to move with such alacrity.[32]

Rapprochement with foreign private investors was only one part of Campos's strategy toward the foreign sector. Yet it was important because the government hoped for a rapid increase in private foreign investment, which it was believed would bring badly needed technology as well as strengthen the balance of payments. Such investment might also help take up the slack resulting from the deflationary squeeze on Brazilian business-men.[33] Equally important, the Castello Branco government saw this rapprochement as offering proof to international agencies — IMF, World Bank, and Inter-American Development Bank (IADB) — and the United States government that Brazil was firmly committed to the "free world" economy.[34] This repudiation of "romantic nationalism" (as Campos had termed it in 1961) was an important counterpart to the government's commitment to stabilization.[35]

It is also apparent that the Castello Branco government used the ideology of the hard-liners to help sell its stabilization plan to the American government and public, who were then riding the tide of anticommunist interventionism into a land war in Asia. By portraying themselves as having saved the largest Latin American country from communism, the 1964 revolutionaries gained legitimacy with many sectors of opinion within the United States government and the international financial agencies. This crusading anticommunist policy and the welcome to foreign capital would not have been likely from an elected regime. Indeed, it was the populist opponents of such a policy whom the military had removed from the political arena in 1964.

32. A study of the profit-remittances controversy would make interesting reading. A bare outline is included in Skidmore, *Politics in Brazil.*

33. In fact, net foreign investment did not resume on a significant level until after 1967 — and even then it was primarily short-term. The majority of capital inflows attracted by the Castello Branco government were *public* loans or credits. First National City Bank, *Brazil: An Economic Survey,* pp. 35–41.

34. In a speech in July 1964, Castello Branco announced that the anti-inflationary policy would not be paid for with stagnation. Growth would come from, among other things, a "restoration of the inflow of foreign capital" and a "return to serious understandings with the international financial organizations, including the Alliance for Progress." Castello Branco, *Discursos: 1964,* p. 66.

35. Roberto de Oliveira Campos, *A moeda, O govêrno e o tempo* (Rio de Janeiro: APEC Editôra, 1964), p. 184.

Brazil was very successful in winning assistance from the international financial agencies and the United States government. From 1964 through 1968 (fiscal years) United States economic assistance averaged $312 million a year.[36] After 1968, however, the United States cut back its support by drastically reducing new program loans (none were authorized in fiscal 1969), in part to indicate its displeasure with Brazil's increasingly authoritarian domestic policy, and in part because the country's economic recovery rendered aid less urgent, especially in view of congressional cuts in USAID funding. In recent years the World Bank and IADB have found Brazil to be an exemplary debtor and have maintained a high level of lending.[37]

The early concessions to foreign capital were continued in the incentives given to foreign firms engaged in export trade. Here was another area considered crucial by the economic policy makers since 1964. Before 1964 Brazil had conspicuously failed to expand exports and had thus created a serious "import bottleneck." One might wonder whether any elected government could have undertaken such a vigorous export-promotion policy. Certainly the export incentives to foreign firms were bound to be unpopular, as was confirmed by the experience of the Castello Branco regime in the field of iron-ore mining. His government approved highly controversial concessions to the Hanna Corporation to exploit iron ore. This move touched a raw nerve among nationalists and military, and they protested vigorously to the military president. After considerable debate within the government the concession was balanced by a sharp increase in the government investment in the state-owned iron-ore monopoly — the Rio Doce Valley Corporation. Even an authoritarian government was not able to flout nationalist opinion completely.[38] Since his pro-foreign investment attitude had been one of the policies for which Campos had been most viciously attacked during the sta-

36. Agency for International Development, Bureau for Program and Policy Coordination, Office of Statistics and Reports, *U.S. Overseas Loans and Grants and Assistance from International Organizations: Obligations and Loan Authorizations, July 1, 1945–June 30, 1971* (Washington, D.C., 1972), p. 38.

37. The "basic identity of views" between the Castello Branco government and the international financial authorities and U.S. government is stressed in Teresa Hayter, *Aid as Imperialism* (London: Penguin Books, 1971), pp. 135–42.

38. The case is analyzed in Raymond F. Mikesell, "Iron Ore in Brazil: The Experience of the Hanna Mining Company," in Mikesell et al., *Foreign Investment in the Petroleum and Mineral Industries: Case Studies of Investor-Host Country Relations* (Baltimore: Johns Hopkins Press, 1971), pp. 345–64.

bilization crisis of 1958–59, one can well imagine the political storm if the political system had remained open in 1965–66.

The export-promotion policy of the new technocrats was unpopular in another respect. It contradicted the technical diagnosis of their "structuralist" colleagues who had long argued that Brazil had little hope of significantly expanding her exports. Here was an important split that had developed within the technocratic elite. Those most identified with the position of the Economic Commission for Latin America (ECLA) had apparently written off Brazil's export potential, in fact if not in theory. They had argued persuasively for commodity stabilization agreements and a general alteration in the rules of world trade. During the Goulart regime Brazil had led the Latin American fight for a basic revision in world trading regulations at the first United Nations Conference on Trade and Development in New Delhi in early 1964. This was a quixotic venture, as the Prebisch-led delegates soon learned. None of the developed nations, including the Soviet Union, was prepared to take seriously the developing nations' plea for trade concessions.

The Brazilian technocrats who achieved prominence in April 1964 correctly saw that Brazil *did* have the potential to increase her exports dramatically — not only raw materials, but also manufactures. They planned to exploit not only the enormous natural resources (iron ore, timber, and foodstuffs, for example) but also the finished goods in which Brazil had become a more efficient producer than the structuralist planners had realized. The subsequent success of the export drive proves that the technocrats led by Campos and Bulhões were correct in their diagnosis. One might reasonably doubt whether they could have sold such a policy to an elected government in 1964 — when the animus against the export sector was still great among politicians who remained under the influence of the ECLA thesis. The strength of the latter was reinforced in Brazil by the intuitive autarkic logic of the "exportable surplus" theory that had hobbled economic policy makers throughout the postwar era.[39]

39. The best overall source on the history of Brazilian commercial policy is Joel Bergsman, *Brazil: Industrialization and Trade Policies*. Nathaniel Leff has analyzed the "import bottleneck" extensively in two articles: "Export Stagnation and Autarkic Development," *Quarterly Journal of Economics* 81 (1967): 286–301 and "Import Constraints and Development: Causes of the Recent Decline of Brazilian Economic Growth," *Review of Economics and Statistics* 49 (1967): 494–501. The latter article provoked a critical commentary by Joel Bergsman and Samuel A. Morley in *Review of Economics and Statistics* 51 (1969): 101–02. Even if one accepts their qualification of the

Coffee policy was another area where policy makers were able to carry out economic measures whose unpopularity would have caused great political problems in the open system of 1945–64. The introduction of a "flexible" price policy in the coffee surplus purchase program[40] is an example of deliberate defiance of an economic group that had achieved significant political influence before 1964 but that got short shrift in the era of the "autonomous" technocrat, especially after 1966.

It should be clear, however, that the principal constraint removed by the authoritarian system was popular pressure. Popular mobilization, whether through elections, strikes, or street demonstrations, was sharply curtailed, sometimes by heavy-handed repression. Policy makers were able, for example, to assume that a deliberate policy of depressing real wages would not produce mass strikes, nor would concessions to foreign investment risk giving nationalist politicians bargaining power in a divided legislature, nor would full-cost pricing of government-produced gasoline provoke paralyzing bus boycotts in major cities. Policy makers have not *had* to worry about the income share going to the lower sectors of Brazilian society. The suppression of most

---

relative importance of the import component in the economic sectors that had apparently stagnated most during the economic slowdown of the early 1960s, it is nonetheless true that the successful export drive has given the government much more room for maneuver in policy making.

40. Coffee policy deserves further research — especially its political aspects. The best source to date is Edmar Lisboa Bacha, "An Econometric Model for the World Coffee Market: The Impact of Brazilian Price Policy" (Ph.D. diss., Yale University, 1968). A translation of chapter 1 appeared in *Dados*, no. 5 (1968), pp. 144–61. The failure of the production-control program up to 1968 is described in Kenneth D. Frederick, "Production Controls Under the International Coffee Agreements," *Journal of Inter-American Studies and World Affairs* 12, no. 2 (April 1970): 255–70; and Stahis Panagides, "Erradicação do café e diversificação da agricultura brasileira," *Revista Brasileira de Economia*, vol. 23, no. 1 (January–March 1969). Source material may be found in *Instrumentos da Política Cafeeira*, 2 vols. (Rio de Janeiro: Escola Interamericana de Administração Pública, 1967), published under the sponsorship of the Fundação Getúlio Vargas and the Banco Interamericano de Desenvolvimento. Only after 1967 did the market incentives (if the "market" is defined to include government purchase of surpluses!) turn against investment in coffee for many farmers, as Frederick explains. Leff's claim that coffee growers were powerless in gaining government support before 1964 is therefore unsupported by the evidence — especially the enormous surplus purchases of the early 1960s. Leff, *Economic Policy-Making and Development*, esp. pp. 19–33. The Castello Branco government continued the heavy surplus purchase policy in 1965 and 1966, thereby undermining the anti-inflation program.

rural organizations after 1964 removed any effective popular pressure from the countryside.[41] The manipulation of urban labor unions has eliminated any independent source of organized pressure from the urban poor.

Given this relative freedom from pressures that might be brought by (or on behalf of) the marginalized masses, policy makers have been free to pursue an economic policy based on the market-oriented high-consumption society of the industrializing Center-South region. Policies have been chosen to stimulate the mixed capitalist economy geared to the consumer demand of the middle and upper sectors. The rapid expansion of the São Paulo automobile industry symbolized the success of this policy. In short, the hard-line military have made it possible for technocrats to manage a consumption-oriented economy whose benefits the middle and upper sectors can enjoy with little apparent fear of disruption from the marginal population.

Has pressure from the middle and upper sectors been a constraint? The middle sectors were undoubtedly angered by the stabilization program in 1964–65 and helped contribute to the two electoral victories against the government in 1965. But since 1967 the middle and upper sectors have had few grounds for complaint. They are the primary beneficiaries of the technocrats' policy-making success. The income taxes they must now pay are probably more than offset by their increased prosperity.[42] And investors in areas disfavored by government have been able to find ample areas for alternative investment. Furthermore, they are able to bring their influence to bear in direct ways that do not require open politics. Private interests such as business firms and professional associations can take their case directly to the government agencies responsible for implementing policy.[43]

41. The suppression of the rural movements is described briefly in Clodomir Moraes, "Peasant Leagues in Brazil," in *Agrarian Problems and Peasant Movements in Latin America,* ed. Rodolfo Stavenhagen (Garden City, N.Y.: Doubleday, 1970), pp. 453–501.

42. The regressive nature of the total tax burden is explained in Philippe Schmitter's chapter in this volume. A pioneering attempt to analyze the tax burden for 1962–63 may be found in Gian S. Sahota, "The Distribution of Tax Burden Among Different Education Classes in Brazil," *Economic Development and Cultural Change* 19, no. 3 (April 1971): 438–60. For an analysis of the changes in income distribution between 1960 and 1970 see Albert Fishlow, "Brazilian Size Distribution of Income," *American Economic Review,* 62 (1972): 391–402.

43. On the system of interest representation see Philippe C. Schmitter, *Interest Conflict and Political Change in Brazil* (Stanford: Stanford University Press, 1971).

In sum, the military governments have enjoyed more "freedom" in policy making because they have repressed certain social sectors, such as labor and the rural masses, whose economic shares have correspondingly fallen. Other sectors, such as the officer corps and foreign investors, who were well placed to pressure the government, have gained. Unlike the anti-Peronist Argentine military of the 1960s, Brazil's military government has had the will and the ability to impose a socially regressive policy over an extended period.

AVOIDING POLITICAL CRISES: THE USE OF "AUTOMATIC" DEVICES IN ECONOMIC POLICY MAKING

A further explanation for the consistency of policy making since 1964 lies in the use of "automatic" devices — usually established by executive decree. This use of the decree power is an excellent example of the turn back to the arbitrary power exercised by the president during the Estado Nôvo (1937–45).

To illustrate the value of policy making by decree one need only consider how often political crises arose in Brazil between 1946 and 1964 as a result of congressional votes on increases in salaries for civil servants and military officers. The stabilization crises of 1953–54, 1958–59, and 1962–64 all involved bitter debates in the Congress over these wage decisions. Tension was all the greater because the minister of labor had discretionary authority to set the general minimum wage but not to set military and civil-service salaries. Since 1964 the power to set these latter salaries has also been assumed by the executive.

To take another example, the profit-remittance law of 1962 had to be passed by the Congress, while the foreign exchange regulations, such as SUMOC (Superintendência da Moeda e Crédito) Instruction #70 (1953) or #113 (1955) were simply set by executive action. Credit policy could be determined on discretionary authority but the structure of secondary education was a matter for detailed congressional legislation. Thus the existence of an open and active Congress between 1946 and 1964 offered an arena in which political constraints became obvious. The very fact that the government which came to power in 1964 found it necessary to purge the Congress repeatedly and eventually to close it despite these purges shows that these authoritarian leaders feared "interference" in policy making. Many of the constitutional revisions carried out by the new government involved direct attacks upon congressional authority over economic policy. The Constitution of 1967 deprived Congress of the power to initiate money bills and prohibited it from increasing any appropriations requested by the president.

Taking advantage of their greatly broadened executive powers, the military governments have adopted a number of automatic devices that minimize the degree of apparent choice in economic policy making. "Monetary correction" is the most obvious example. The system of automatic adjustments is geared to a supposedly objective index — the cost of living as certified by the National Economic Council. Making virtually all government contracts — both for sale and purchase — subject to monetary correction removes the need to decide, for example, whether to make inflationary adjustments for one set of government workers and not another. Thus the individual cases of discretionary policy making are reduced — easing the pressure on the policy makers and providing fewer occasions for public protest.

There may be controversy about pay differentials, frequency of monetary correction, methods of computing the indices, and the system of monetary correction itself. Yet the apparent success of the general scheme suggests that it reduces the range of overt conflict, and one would expect it to spread to other countries, perhaps even to some in the developed world.

It has another attraction — it helps to maintain the government's income in real terms. By applying monetary correction to tax liabilities, for example, the government no longer finds itself collecting tax bills in greatly depreciated currency. Since chronic government deficits have fed inflation and thereby caused further political problems, this correction of tax receipts has undoubtedly reduced another pressure on the policy makers since 1964.[44]

A second automatic device is the use of frequent small exchange-rate devaluations since 1967. Previously the government had waited much longer between devaluations of the cruzeiro. Usually there were one or two devaluations of the official rate per year. The result was a rise in tension surrounding each devaluation decision. Speculation was encouraged and a black market inevitably developed — and was quite openly tolerated in the major cities. Because the devaluation inevitably raised the cost of living (as a result of the import component in such key consumption items as bread and bus transportation), governments dreaded the consequences of making foreign-exchange policy. With frequent small devaluations similar to the "crawling peg," Brazil is able to avoid the shock of infrequent large changes in official rates. Here again, the government has reduced the overt occasions for public controversy over economic policy, although, of course, the overall policy can still be criticized.

Tax incentives are another automatic instrument liberally used

44. Keith S. Rosenn, "Adaptations of the Brazilian Income Tax to Inflation," *Stanford Law Review* 21, no. 1 (November 1968): 58–105.

by post-1964 governments. The forgiveness of taxes can be a powerful weapon for directing economic activity, as amply demonstrated by developed countries. Depreciation write-offs, for example, have been an important stimulant to capital investment in most industrial economies since the war. Developing countries usually find tax incentives difficult to use, however, because taxes are so inefficiently collected in the first place. Military governments in Brazil since 1964 have greatly tightened the tax collection procedures and thus made tax incentives a much more effective policy instrument.

Tax write-offs have been used to stimulate private investment in the Northeast and to encourage public participation in the stock market. Even before 1964, the government had established a 50 percent tax write-off for corporations that invested in the Northeast. This measure led to a surge of investment in the new industrial parks around Bahia and Recife. The ultimate effect on the local economies has been questioned by many critics because the investment has been in capital-intensive techniques.[45] Nonetheless, this tax incentive was an automatic device for channeling investment toward one region of the country. It did not involve allocating public funds for the investment — a decision that would have involved far more political conflict, even under the authoritarian regimes since 1964.

The second example of a tax write-off is the 12 percent deduction in the personal income tax bill allowed for investment in stock shares. Brazil, like other developing economies, has until recently lacked a well-developed capital market. This disorganization has impeded private investment. In order to stimulate the expansion of what had been a tiny market for publicly traded shares, the government established a special concession. The result was dramatic. The stock market has burgeoned beyond anyone's expectations, leading to enormous capital gains, many untaxed. It has also facilitated access to credit for established firms that earlier could have found no such public source.[46]

45. Cid Eduardo Porto, "SUDENE: Uma Semente Posta em Questão," *Cadernos Brasileiros* 12, no. 2 (March–April 1970): 13–18; A. O. Hirschman, "Industrial Development in the Brazilian Northeast and the Tax Credit Scheme of Article 34/18," *Journal of Development Studies* 5, no. 1 (1968): 5–28. For a former United States government official's pessimistic view of the failure to promote employment in the Northeast, see Harold T. Jorgenson, "Impending Disaster in Northeast Brazil," *Inter-American Economic Affairs* 22, no. 1 (summer 1968): 3–22.

46. Details on the tax incentives for participation in the capital market are given in the carefully documented study by David Trubek, "Law, Plan-

Again, this tax incentive was a substitute for the direct allocation of public funds, or the indirect allocation through such devices as government subsidized loans through the banking system. All three of these examples — monetary correction, frequent small devaluations, and tax write-offs — represent an attempt to use the price mechanism to channel private resources. Underlying all three is the assumption that the use of public investment and expenditure is not the only way to direct economic development. Thus all three are automatic devices that also fit the neoliberal emphasis on the market mechanism — to which post-1964 governments have been publicly committed.

The political effect of the use of these devices is to disaggregate potentially large policy crises into a series of much smaller automatic decisions that are far less likely to arouse large-scale public concern. Adapting to a succession of relatively small increments that follow a well-established schedule of adjustments is undoubtedly easier psychologically than having to face large and unpredictable monetary changes. Thus the authoritarian regime has used the arbitrary powers of a "strong" government to help reduce the occasions for the crystallization of opposition.

INSTITUTIONAL CONTINUITY: THE CORPORATIST ADMINISTRATIVE STATE

Given the fact that an antipopulist authoritarian political base offered technocratic policy makers room for maneuver they had lacked before 1964, how much new administrative machinery did they need to create? Relatively little. The technocrats were able to assume control of the institutional structure bequeathed by Getúlio Vargas's Estado Nôvo (1937–45) and expanded during the postwar era.

In emphasizing the authoritarian turn in politics since 1964 one must not underestimate the degree of institutional continuity during the last three decades. Earlier interpretations, including my own, were misleading on this point, as Philippe Schmitter correctly observes in his contribution to this volume. The recent years of authoritarian rule in Brazil offer powerful evidence of

ning and the Development of the Brazilian Capital Market," *Bulletin of the Institute of Finance, New York University Graduate School of Business Administration,* nos. 72–73 (April 1971); Thomas G. Sanders, "Making Money: From Animal Game to Stock Market," American Universities Field Staff Reports, East Coast South America Series, vol. 14, no. 4 (1970); and Antonín Basch and Milic Kybal, *Capital Markets in Latin America* (New York: Praeger, 1970), pp. 111–21.

the importance of this institutional continuity. It now appears increasingly apparent that the essence of government in Brazil since the war has been the administrative state that Vargas and his lieutenants had created before his overthrow in 1945.[47]

The presidency has been the most important single institution in this structure. From the moment Vargas assumed the position of provisional president in November 1930, the federal executive has remained the focus of policy making. Between 1930 and 1934, when a new constitution was approved, the president had governed by use of executive decree. The checks were few. But after the coup of 1937 the president assumed unlimited powers. From his office flowed the decrees that reorganized employer-employee relations, laid the pattern for state enterprises, reconstituted most of the cultural institutions, and formulated monetary policy. Because the presidential system gave the president such extensive power of appointment, the rapid expansion of the public sector meant that any president would have vast power to influence public policy, should he gain carte blanche to replace incumbent officials.

The next most important feature of the administrative structure of the Estado Nôvo was the network of state corporations and regulatory agencies. The public enterprises included railroads, shipping, and steel (oil, electric power, and synthetic rubber were added after 1945). Coffee, tea, pine, sugar, and others were subject to the supervision of federal agencies. When one adds to this list the heavy state investments in road building, education, and public construction, the importance of the publicly controlled or directed sector of the economy becomes obvious.

One of the least understood features of the administrative state inherited by the 1964 revolutionaries was the network of compulsory representative organizations. These were the corporatist creations of a government that wished to preempt any form of voluntary organization that might arise and thereby constitute an independent political force. Most important of these corporatist bodies were the labor unions.[48]

47. There is no single survey of this structure. Perhaps the best approximation is Alberto Venâncio Filho, *A intervenção do estado no domínio econômico: O direito público econômico no Brasil* (Rio de Janeiro: Fundação Getúlio Vargas, 1968). Important for its explanation and analysis of the corporatist representation system is Schmitter, *Interest Conflict and Political Change in Brazil.*

48. One of the clearest accounts of the creation of this system of labor organization is José Albertino Rodrigues, *Sindicato e desenvolvimento no*

Vargas and his aides — both technocrats such as Oliveira Viana[49] and politicians such as Lindolfo Collor — succeeded, during the provisional government of 1930–34, in taking over the old union structure, which had been rent by quarrels among anarchists, socialists, communists, and Catholic organizers. In its place they created a systematic network of compulsory syndicates under the close control of the Ministry of Labor. The system was institutionalized in the Labor Code (Consolidação das Leis do Trabalho) in 1943. This complex body of law remained in force thereafter, governing the systems of labor tribunals and syndicates.[50] There are six essential features that explain its effectiveness. First, workers in the designated industries must pay compulsory dues (*impôsto sindical*), which are deducted from the worker's March paycheck and sent directly by the employer to the Bank of Brazil. Actual membership, however, comes only upon payment of another fee, set by the individual union. Second, the Ministry of Labor retains control over the dues collected from the syndicate members, because it has the power to approve budgets and release funds to the officials, according to a formula setting relative shares for different levels of the union bureaucracy. Third, only one syndicate can be recognized in each industry. Any jurisdictional disputes are resolved unilaterally by the Ministry of Labor. Fourth, the minister of labor has the legal authority to validate the elections of syndicate officials. Fifth, the ministry enjoys the legal right to "intervene" whenever it considers the interests of the workers to have been violated by the elected officials. Finally, the right to strike (forbidden under the 1943 Labor Code) is either precluded (as for many public employees) or made subject to revocation by the labor courts.

One must add that this union structure has covered only the urban sector, except for the brief flurries of rural organizing in 1954 and the earlier 1960s. But it was the urban sector where a preemptive government-controlled system was most essential. Rural Brazil was so dominated by the patrimonial social structure

---

Brasil (São Paulo: Difusão Européia do Livro, 1968). See also Kenneth Erickson, "Labor in the Political Process in Brazil: Corporatism in a Modernizing Nation" (Ph.D. diss., Columbia University, 1970).

49. For an example of this influential thinker's writings on social policy between 1932 and 1940, see Oliveira Viana, *Direito do trabalho e democracia social: O Problema da incorporação do trabalhador no estado* (Rio de Janeiro: José Olympio, 1951).

50. Subsequent decrees have been simply added onto the original legislation. For a recent edition, see Adriano Campanhole, *Consolidação das leis do trabalho*, 27th ed. (São Paulo: Editôra Atlas, 1970).

that the government had little reason to fear any popular challenge from that sector.

Another of the institutions involving compulsory coverage was the social security system.[51] Brazil was a pioneer among developing countries in its early commitment to extensive social security coverage. During the 1930s the coverage increased rapidly, reaching 1.8 million employees in 1938. In that year more than 5 million beneficiaries were eligible, including dependents. This was an impressive total for a country whose entire population was only 41 million in 1940, with 68 percent of the active population still engaged in agriculture, and coverage of agricultural workers was virtually nonexistent.[52]

The network of social security coverage was not an original creation of the Estado Nôvo. In fact, the first national insurance institutes had been established in 1933–34. But they continued to grow during the dictatorship, and although not corporatist in origin they do incorporate one feature common to the corporatism — compulsory coverage. The system spread by the creation of new "institutes" or "funds" (caixas). First came the maritime workers (1933), then the commercial employees, coffee-warehouse workers, stevedores, and bank workers (all in 1934). The list grew rapidly, with the creation of many smaller funds and institutes.[53] Since 1964 the government has made vigorous efforts to rationalize this network into a single system. All the funds and institutes had the basic purpose of providing pensions. The additional social services varied widely. Most frequent was health care. Often included also were subsidized housing, subsidized food shops, job retraining, and recreational facilities. The comprehensiveness only becomes obvious when one realizes how many different workers have been affected. Compulsory coverage of commercial employees, for example, extends to shop clerks, beauticians, gas station attendants, and journalists.

This means that virtually the entire urban sector (with the conspicuous exception of domestic servants!) has been incorporated into a welfare system more comprehensive than that of many

51. I have taken much of this information from an unpublished paper by Chalmers S. Brumbaugh: "A History of Social Security Legislation in Brazil, 1923–1966."

52. Pedro Pinchas Geiger, Evolução da rêde urbana brasileira (Rio de Janeiro: Centro Brasileiro de Pesquisas Educacionais, 1963), p. 19.

53. This description in no way represents an attempt at a comprehensive survey of the social security system. I have merely taken some highlights from an informational handbook published by the Ministério das Relações Exteriores: Brasil: 1960 (Rio de Janeiro, 1960).

developed economies. Thus the most politically conscious sector
is integrated into a state-controlled network of social services that
helps to buffer the periodic declines in real wages and salaries.
If a significant proportion of the real income comes in services
(medical care, recreational facilities), then the frequent variations
in cash income become more tolerable. Despite the fact that the
services are often substandard, the real benefits are nonetheless
significant in a society of low wage levels and high underemployment and disguised unemployment.

In sum, the social security system is so comprehensive in coverage and satisfactorily adequate in benefits that it undercuts
what might otherwise be a source of urban discontent. Most
important, it is done through compulsory organization under
state management. As in the case of the labor syndicates, there
is no private, voluntary organization that has been able to build
up a loyal membership on the basis of material gains achieved
by the effects of group militance and strong leadership. In practical terms, this has meant that governments have not had to deal
with any significant centers of organized opposition among the
urban workers. The early development of a corporatist union and
social security system prevented the growth of any following for
the kind of independent workers' organizations that emerged in
Argentina and Chile.

What happened to this administrative structure during the so-
called democratic era of 1946–64 when the country was reopened
to political competition? The repressive apparatus of the Estado
Nôvo was largely dismantled, as Brazil returned to the path of
liberal representative democracy. By reinstituting elective offices,
Brazil invited the rapidly expanding politically conscious public
to pass judgment on policies and policy makers. Basic social and
economic questions could be publicly debated. And there were
legislators to be elected at the city, state, and federal level, as well
as mayors, governors, and a president and a vice-president. These
officials, in turn, presided over an administrative apparatus largely
created during the Estado Nôvo. Obviously there were additions
and changes during the postwar period of rapid industrialization.
Yet the basic structure continued to be the corporatist framework
laid out during the Estado Nôvo.

Between 1946 and 1964 the power of the presidency naturally
became the focus for conflicting political pressures. The president,
the Congress, and the bureaucracy were forced to reconcile an-
tagonists of different states, regions, classes, parties, and interest
groups. Similar pressures arose on municipal and state levels of
policy making. The result was usually an accommodation of in-

terests, by which certain areas of economic policy became highly
sensitive to political pressure. Examples were credit policy, wage
policy, and foreign-investment policy. In all three cases the executive enjoyed a vast range of discretionary authority. Yet no step
could be taken without an eye to the probable political consequences. Policies were often adopted or discarded on the basis
of how they were regarded by important sectors of opinion.

As shown earlier, although the administrative structure remained largely intact, the politics of its management changed
sharply. The political constraints created by mobilized group
pressures could significantly affect economic policy making.
Equally important, the possession of political influence became a
major factor in the staffing of the administrative state. The merit
system, so carefully introduced during the Estado Nôvo, was
scuttled in favor of patronage based on party affiliations. The
politicians, long in the wilderness against Vargas's dictatorship,
were anxious to recapture and distribute the fruits of power. Employment in the administrative state headed the list.[54]

Since 1964, and especially since 1967, the military governments
have suppressed the democratic overlay of the postwar era. The
hard line has made the elimination of "corruption" and "petty
politics" a principal goal, although many observers see little
change in the frequency of corruption. Translated into practical
terms, this has meant a suppression of the networks of competitive political brokerage. The independent sources of influence
have been progressively eliminated in favor of a technocrat-domi-
nated system that creates a minimum of institutionalized opposition. The military governments have thus returned to the Estado
Nôvo model of low mobilization. Public policy is made by an
elite whose power rests on the arbitrary power of military hard-
liners. Public debate is thereby reduced to a level of technical
discussion — virtually ruling out dispute over basic goals.

Reliance on the administrative state of Vargas can be seen also
in the great concentration of power in the presidency since 1964.
The revolutionary governments have steadily moved back toward
the absolute executive powers assumed by Vargas during the
Estado Nôvo. The push has come both from hard-liners and
technocrats, each group of which has its own reasons for wishing
to reduce outside checks on presidential power — whether from
legislatures, courts, or elsewhere.

54. One of the few contributions of the "democratic" era was the undermining of professional standards in the civil service, which is carefully described in Lawrence S. Graham, *Civil Service Reform in Brazil* (Austin: University of Texas Press, 1968), chap. 9.

The use of labor unions is another area where the Vargas legacy has proved useful to the revolutionaries. Every government since 1945 has found this true. Elected politicians of both Right and Left have discovered the enormous powers to be an invaluable instrument for controlling and directing the labor movement. Whether it was a case of purging the Communists (Dutra in 1947), attempting to mobilize a popular base (Vargas in 1953–54 and Goulart in 1961–64), imposing a declining real wage during stabilization (Castello Branco in 1964–67), or breaking strikes (Costa e Silva in 1967–68), the corporatist labor system has been used effectively by all regimes.

As Philippe Schmitter notes in his chapter, the military governments have set about purging the Vargas institutional legacy of the pluralistic accretions gathered between 1945 and 1964. They sought to use the techniques of one Vargas era (the Estado Nôvo of 1937–45) against those of another Vargas era (the populist presidency of 1951–54). It is a mark of Getúlio's historical impact that the 1964 revolutionaries should have found him to be both their enemy and their benefactor.

Authoritarianism: A New Departure in Brazilian History?

Although Getúlio is virtually never mentioned, his corporatist structure has served the revolutionaries well. This is hardly surprising, since the revolutionaries of 1964 came to power in a manner that showed many similarities to the origins of the Estado Nôvo (1937–45). Both owed their existence to a coup against an elected government threatened from both right and left.

In each case the coup climaxed a sharp increase in political violence. Dissident groups had begun arming. In the 1930s the ferment could be traced back to the lieutenants' rebellions of the early 1920s, which divided the national political oligarchy and made possible the revolution of 1930. The legitimacy of a new constitutional structure had been carefully rebuilt by 1934, only to be undermined by highly organized paramilitary movements of the communist-led National Liberation Alliance and the fascist-style Integralists (Integralistas).[55] Repression increased immediately after the communist attempt at a coup in November 1935.[56]

55. The best account of this period is Robert M. Levine, *The Vargas Regime: The Critical Years, 1934–38* (New York: Columbia University Press, 1970).

56. Details may be found in my "Failure in Brazil: From Popular Front to Armed Revolt," *Journal of Contemporary History* 5, no. 3 (July 1970): 137–58.

That armed revolt, centered in the army commands in Natal, Recife, and Rio de Janeiro, offered the pretext for congressional approval of a state of emergency, thereby suspending constitutional guarantees. Soon thereafter the Congress also acquiesced in the president's request to deprive four left-wing deputies of their parliamentary immunity. Between November 1935 and October 1937, the Congress compliantly renewed the state of emergency. Open political competition had been largely suppressed by the time Vargas and the army staged their coup of 19 November 1937. It was the culmination of a growing authoritarianism guided by the president himself.

In 1964 the coup was staged by a civilian-military conspiracy that overthrew the legal president. The years between 1964 and the new authoritarian turn of December 1968 could be compared to the 1935–37 period, which saw a continuous renewal of the state of siege. The First Institutional Act (9 April 1964) had its parallel in the state of siege passed by Congress in November 1935, although the former had to be decreed by the military command after the congressional leaders refused to guide a comparable measure through Congress. The Fifth Institutional Act (13 December 1968), in turn, gave the president powers almost comparable to those contained in the constitution decreed by Vargas on the evening of his 1937 coup. In 1968 President Médici gained vast powers to suspend civil liberties in defense of national security. As had been the case in 1937, all legislatures were closed. In 1968, however, they were only "recessed," whereas in 1937 they had been abolished. These presidential powers were institutionalized in the 1969 constitutional amendment, which further approximated the Vargas constitution of 1937.

The similarities of their origins naturally led to similarities in the goals and actions of the Estado Nôvo and the post-1964 governments.[57] Such similarities are most obvious in the social and

57. There are few studies of the Estado Nôvo. A recent survey is Lourdes Sola, "O golpe de 37 e o Estado Nóvo," in Carlos Guilherme Mota et al., *Brasil em perspectiva* (São Paulo: Difusão Européia do Livro, 1968), pp. 285–315. Further references may be found in Skidmore, *Politics in Brazil*, pp. 341–49. Vargas's speeches from this period are collected in Getúlio Vargas, *A nova política do Brasil*, 11 vols. (Rio de Janeiro: José Olympio Editôra, 1938–47). The presidential speeches of the 1964–66 period may be found in Humberto de Alencar Castello Branco, *Discursos: 1964*; *Discursos: 1965* and *Discursos: 1966*. For the Costa e Silva presidency there is Arthur da Costa e Silva, *Pronunciamentos do candidato* (n.p., n.d.); Costa e Silva, *Mensagem ao congresso nacional* (Brasília: Imprensa Nacional, 1968); Costa e Silva, *Pronunciamentos do presidente* (Brasília), published quarterly by the Departamento de Imprensa Nacional. For the following period, see Emilio Garrastazú Médici, *O jôgo da verdade*.

ideological characters of the regimes, which are briefly summarized below.

Anticommunist. In both periods the government justified itself primarily in preventive terms: power was seized in order to pre-empt an allegedly impending move by the Left. In both cases the declared enemy was the Brazilian Communist party (Partido Comunista Brasileiro) with its ties to the world conspiracy, although both in 1937 and 1964 the PCB was only one among many forces on the left. After both the coups the governments moved quickly to justify their rule in ideological terms, declaring their commitment to the defense of Christian civilization. Both thus assumed a mantle of moral righteousness that was used to generate support among the middle and upper classes.

Defense of class interests. Both regimes began as reactionary governments in the basic sense — in *reaction* to a growing popular mobilization. Both clamped a lid on popular participation, although the Estado Nôvo was quicker and more complete in its repression than the post-1964 regimes.[58] In both cases labor organizations were quickly neutralized by arrests of leaders and confiscation of records, although Vargas later went on to institutionalize a new labor-union system. The beneficiaries in both cases were the military and the propertied classes. The military gained control of high official positions and were able to commandeer higher salaries and budgets. The propertied classes were able to relax from any fears that mass organizations like labor unions or popular militia might seize their property.

Repression. Both regimes resorted to suspension of civil liberties and assumed arbitrary powers of arrest, imprisonment, and censorship. In both cases the repression was justified under "emergency" powers made necessary by an immediate threat to national security. Torture of political prisoners was used in both eras. By instilling fear among their critics and potential opponents, both regimes were able to maintain a high degree of social control with a relatively low investment in police personnel.

There were similarities also in the economic and administrative spheres:

Expansion of the public sector. In both periods the economic impact of the public sector increased. In the case of the Estado Nôvo, Brazil faced a world depression that meant a virtual absence of foreign private capital and a shortage of foreign markets. Furthermore, the Estado Nôvo was a conscious imitation of some

58. Long-term trends in participation are examined in Joseph L. Love, "Political Participation in Brazil, 1881–1969," *Luso-Brazilian Review* 7, no. 2 (December 1970): 3–24.

continental fascist models (Italy and Portugal especially) that at‑
tributed a dynamic economic role to the state.

In 1964, however, the government declared that it wanted to
resuscitate and support the private sector. It was avowedly pro
private enterprise and antistatist, in contrast to the Estado Nôvo.
Nonetheless, the percentage share of the public sector in the Bra‑
zilian economy continued to climb in the first two years of sta‑
bilization. Although public-sector savings have greatly exceeded
public investment since 1967, the total tax burden has risen from
18 percent of GDP in 1963 to approximately 30 percent in 1970,
one of the highest in the world.[59] This fact is perhaps proof that
any activist government in Brazil will find it very hard to avoid
increasing the public sector role if it maintains a strong commit‑
ment to growth.

Government centralization. Both periods saw a sharp swing
back toward more centralized government. The constitutions of
1891 (somewhat modified in the Constitution of 1934) and 1946
had decentralized. The new documents of 1937 and 1967 (as
modified by the institutional acts) produced by the authoritarian
regimes strengthened federal power at the expense of the states
and *municípios.*

Any attempt to establish chronological parallels between the
1930s and the 1960s also highlights the differences. The coup of
1937 was more definitive than any single step since 1964. The
institutional acts issued after 1964 were used primarily as "tem‑
porary" devices. Even the more authoritarian turn of December
1968 was not definitive, although the Fifth Institutional Act
lacked an expiration date. Legislatures were not abolished, only
recessed. Political parties (only two officially sanctioned parties
were legal) were not abolished, only purged. This difference helps
to explain why the post-1964 governments have been more un‑
stable than the Estado Nôvo. There were other significant differ‑
ences:

Nationalist vs. cosmopolitan. The Estado Nôvo began on a note
of economic nationalism aroused by the world economic depres‑
sion. Vargas suspended all foreign-debt payments within a month
after the coup of 1937, and his government continued to apply
the restrictions on foreign participation in the economy laid out

59. First National City Bank, *Brazil: An Economic Survey*, p. 32. Bulhões
lamented his inability to reduce the role of the public sector. *Visão*, 2 Sep‑
tember 1966. The Médici government also pledged itself to reduce "the
participation of the government in the national product to the lowest pos‑
sible level, both in expenditure and in the tax burden." Presidência da
República, *Metas e bases para a ação do govérno* (n.p., 1970), p. 10.

in the Constitution of 1934 and reiterated in the new Constitution of 1937. Of course, there were virtually no new foreign private commitments to Brazil because of the depression. Yet the rhetoric of *defending* Brazil's interests against foreign economic powers — especially the capitalist regimes of the United States and Britain — continued. The post-1964 governments, on the other hand, reacted strongly against the economic nationalism that had increased in the 1950s and early 1960s. Special concessions were made to foreign private investors, who were regarded as an indispensable part of Brazil's future. The military regimes spent much time renouncing the nationalist rhetoric of the populist era that preceded them.

Statist vs. free enterprise. The Estado Nôvo drew its statist rationale from the fascist models of Portugal, Italy, and Poland, as well as from the New Deal interventionism of the United States. The state was elevated to the role of a powerful director of all major economic and social activities — through the corporatist structure of government-controlled councils, labor unions, and cultural institutions. After 1964, however, the initiative was supposed to be returned to the private sector. In theory, at least, the revolutionaries of 1964 were repudiating the policies that had allegedly stifled private business, both foreign and domestic. Interestingly enough, however, none of the major state corporations was dismantled. Instead, they were reorganized, thereby increasing both their production and productivity.[60] The result was a pro-free-enterprise government that helped make the state sector — largely begun during the Estado Nôvo — more effective, while at the same time creating conditions in which efficient private business could prosper.

Corporatist vs. individualist. In its political theory the Estado Nôvo differed greatly from the announced theories of post-1964 governments. The former espoused a systematic philosophy of corporatism, in which every social and economic sector was to find its place within the government-directed network of councils and syndicates. Parts of this structure remained mere paper creations. Yet Vargas and his government went remarkably far

60. One of the ablest defenders of the Campos policies during the Castello Branco era never tired of baiting leftists over the fact that it was a supposedly right-wing government that was rescuing the state sector of the economy: Gilberto Paim, "Realidade econômica," in Mário Pedrosa et al., *Introdução à realidade brasileira* (Rio de Janeiro, Editôra Cadernos Brasileiros 1968), pp. 35–71. Paim published widely in the Rio press in 1967–68. See, for example, his "Aliança com a modernização," *Jornal do Brasil,* 7 July 1968. Paim also wrote the preface to Campos, *Do outro lado de cêrca.*

toward incorporating every major social group into a state-directed structure. One exception was obvious: rural workers, who were too insignificant a political force in the 1930s to warrant actual inclusion in the corporatist structure, although the Labor Code provided for rural syndicates. After 1964, on the other hand, the government claimed to be restoring personal freedom (except for those who threatened national security — a category that grew by leaps and bounds). According to their rhetoric, at least, the revolutionaries wanted to eliminate the restrictions on the market process that the corporatist cartels had supposedly created. In fact, however, they readily utilized the corporatist structure and their increasingly repressive police tactics contradicted their professed allegiance to the liberal value of individual freedom.

The differences between the two authoritarian eras could perhaps best be explained by reference to the contrasting world situations in which they existed. The Estado Nôvo reflected the rightist authoritarian trends throughout the Western world. As events in Europe demonstrated, nationalism was compatible with a repressive, anti-Bolshevik domestic policy. Nationalism in Brazil was a logical parallel to the nationalism of Mussolini in Italy, Hitler in Germany, and Salazar in Portugal.

Yet Vargas had one great advantage over the military governments of post-1964. He was able to direct the creation of many of the basic institutions of a modern society. Some — such as social security — had been given preliminary form in the 1920s and early 1930s. It was only under the Estado Nôvo, however, that the corporatist structure was so clearly imposed in the form of the administrative state that has persisted since 1945. In one sphere after another Vargas preempted independent organizations by setting up state-sponsored associations or institutes. Labor and management have already been analyzed. Intellectuals were reached through the National Book Institute (Instituto Nacional do Livro), as well as the government-subsidized National Union of Students (União Nacional dos Estudantes). Within the corporatist structure, Vargas's regime reached out to co-opt leaders in as many sectors as possible. Since many of these groups had long been ignored by government, Vargas was able to gain credit for giving them state support (usually financial subsidies) and at the same time create a network of sectoral leaders whose political loyalty would be a natural consequence of the co-optive governmental strategy.

This corporatist institution building was made easier by the fact that Vargas had led the overthrow of the regime of which he had been the (indirectly) elected president. He did not have to establish his legitimacy *de novo,* although he had to produce a rationale for his new dictatorial powers. The revolutionaries of 1964, on the other hand, had overthrown the incumbent government and had to establish their authority by replacing thousands of elected politicians and high administrators. Much of their energy was spent in attempting to prove how dangerous the Goulart government had been. In order to govern, however, they relied upon Vargas's administrative state, just as had their predecessors. Because they were using essentially an inherited structure, they forfeited any opportunity to gain credit for pioneering a new, uniquely "Brazilian" solution to national problems.

Authoritarian government is nothing new in Brazil. In its political origins, its social basis, its ideological content, and its repressive police, the military governments — especially since 1968 — have resembled the Estado Nôvo. The greatest difference lay in the more favorable international economic scene of the late 1960s. This may be the best explanation for the less nationalistic economic policy of the post-1964 regimes.

THE FAILURE TO INSTITUTIONALIZE

If the hard-line military have held the initiative throughout this era, and if they have been so determined to restrict political conflict to conform to their own conception of the tolerable limits of dissent, why have they kept up the pretense of an eventual return to liberal democracy? Why have they failed to promote the creation of a totally new political system, perhaps along the lines of the Partido Revolucionario Institucional (PRI) in Mexico? [61] In short, why have they failed to remove the ambiguities as Vargas did in 1937? By creating a one-party system, for example, the government could resolve social conflicts outside the public eye more effectively than by using the emasculated legislatures of recent years.[62] To abolish parties and legislatures altogether, as the military government has done in Peru, would probably create a stronger government position.

Yet neither course has been taken. Why? Some high members of Castello Branco's government *did* consider establishing a one-

61. It should be clear that I share only the first half of Sanders' statement that "the revolution may be conservative but it is now institutionalized." Sanders, "Institutionalizing Brazil's Conservative Revolution," p. 17.

62. An interesting attempt to study one-party regimes comparatively includes introductory and concluding chapters analyzing the many different conditions under which such regimes have emerged: Samuel P. Huntington and Clement H. Moore, eds., *Authoritarian Politics in Modern Society: The Dynamics of Established One-Party Systems* (New York: Basic Books, 1970).

party system on the Mexican model. It was discussed but apparently rejected. After the crisis surrounding the gubernatorial elections of 1965, the government abolished all existing parties and reorganized them into two officially recognized parties — the only ones henceforth considered legal — Aliança Renovadora Nacional (ARENA) and Movimento Democrático Brasileiro (MDB). But there has been no serious attempt to go beyond this artificial bi-party structure.

One explanation may lie in the persistent but ill-founded belief that the malfunctioning of the representative system is only temporary — that if just one *more* set of corrupt or subversive or irresponsible politicians can be purged then all will go well in the political system. This attitude — which seems naive in retrospect — prevailed strongly during the Castello Branco era. At first his government actually believed that they would be able to hold the presidential elections on schedule in 1966. That expectation was rudely shattered by the political crisis generated by the gubernatorial elections of 1965 and the realization that the economic stabilization program could not possibly be far enough completed by 1966 to allow the government to win a true test of opinion at the polls.

Another explanation for the attitude of the civilian revolutionaries may be their attitude toward Vargas and what he symbolized for them. For the former UDN leaders who were prominent in the Castello Branco government, such as Juracy Magalhães, Milton Campos, Eduardo Gomes, Juarez Távora, and Luiz Vianna Filho, the coup of 1964 offered a chance at federal power that they had seldom been able to win against the populist politicians. Now they might be able to reverse history and undo the damage done by their arch opponent, Getúlio. Yet which Vargas were they attempting to reverse? Was it the democratically elected politician of 1951–54 or the dictator of the Estado Nôvo? Their doctrinaire antipopulism did not allow them to distinguish. One might suspect that their memories of the Estado Nôvo inhibited them from considering how to create a new structure for the Revolution of 1964. In short, many civilian moderates feared Getúlio's political ghost too much to emulate his authoritarian institution-building efforts of the Estado Nôvo.

Such naiveté can be attributed to the moderate military and civilians, but not to the hard-liners. The latter have never had many illusions about the viability of representative democracy in Brazil over the short run or even the medium run — at least ten years. Yet they have avoided publicly repudiating the Brazilian political elite's faith in the liberal idea.

Ironically, it may be that the military extremists have lacked confidence in their own ability to proclaim and direct a straightforwardly authoritarian regime because they fear the disapproval of international opinion. Influenced in a major way by their contacts with the American military, they wish to maintain a close alliance with the United States. They prize American support not only for its military and economic significance, but also for its symbolic importance. They see America as the bastion of anticommunism, an ideology that furnishes the justification for their unrelenting hold on the levers of power in Brazil. America's enormous investment in Vietnam has been proof to them of her commitment to the battle against subversion they wage at home.

At the same time, however, America preaches the doctrine of liberal democracy. Thus the dependence of these authoritarian officers on America has reinforced their contradictory position in domestic politics. On the one hand, they demand emergency powers to fight the counterinsurgency war that United States foreign policy would seem to promote. On the other hand, they seek the approval of United States public opinion, which prefers democratic government and guaranteed civil liberties.[63] The technocrats may also have shied away from embracing authoritarianism more openly because they fear the impact on world opinion. Educated in the ideals of political liberalism, they admire the technical and economic advancement achieved by the United States and the European democracies. Most would apparently prefer to believe that Brazil need not opt for a long-term authoritarian solution.

How long can this alliance of hard-liners and technocrats last? Will 1945 repeat itself? Will the oft-spoken commitment to liberal democracy finally come back to haunt the revolutionaries? The answer will undoubtedly depend on two variables: the world context and the economic record. It is worth remembering that Vargas's Estado Nôvo ran aground when the defeat of the Axis doomed fascist governments all over Europe — except the Iberian

63. On the eve of the gubernatorial elections of October 1965 Castello Branco noted that it was Brazil's commitment to civil liberties and democratic procedures that explained "the growing respect of other free peoples and the continuous influx of foreign resources," Castello Branco, *Discursos: 1965*, p. 285. A month later this commitment was seriously compromised by the Second Institutional Act.

peninsula. The coup of 1964 coincided with a swing toward
"pragmatism" in United States policy toward Latin America.
The anticommunist, private enterprise theme was resuscitated
after its lull during the Kennedy presidency. That emphasis has
continued in United States Latin American policy, and the
Rockefeller Report (1969) can be seen as a basic document in
that policy. Should that policy change, the Brazilian authoritarian regime might find the international atmosphere much
less supportive.

The second variable is the regime's economic success. Failure
to maintain the growth rate would alienate much of middle-
sector support because the middle sector has never accepted the
hard-line justification for authoritarianism. With continued expansion in the world economy there is no a priori reason why
an intelligently managed Brazilian economy cannot continue to
grow rapidly. Yet continuous economic success is a rare commodity in history — especially in Latin America. It would only
be prudent to assume that sometime the growth rate will falter,
especially if the domestic savings rate proves inadequate. If so,
the contradictions in the present Brazilian political model will
become more evident. It is only then that the cost of the failure to
institutionalize the Revolution of 1964 will become clearly evident.

Seen in historical perspective the growing authoritarianism
since 1964 seems the product both of chance and long-term factors. The deep antagonism of the conservative military toward
the populist politicians had erupted frequently since the war —
against Vargas in 1954, Kubitschek in 1955, Quadros in 1961,
and finally Goulart in 1961 and 1964. It had been gaining its
own momentum, akin to the Argentine military's hostility to
Perón. This "antipolitical" drive of the hard-liners, however,
might not have prevailed if the unpopularity of stabilization had
not driven the moderates back into a reliance on arbitrary rule
in 1965. In order to achieve his short-run economic goal Castello
Branco undercut his own commitment to liberal constitutionalism.

But having gained this victory in 1965, the hard-liners felt more
dominant. Their hand was further strengthened by the lack of
any effective government party that might have had sufficient
power or experience to co-opt the opposition. Despite growing
prosperity, the stage was set for the further turn to authoritarianism in 1968. When the armed opposition increased in 1969,
it served the hard-liners as continuing justification for arbitrary rule.

2 The New Professionalism of Internal Warfare and Military Role Expansion

ALFRED STEPAN

Since 1964 the Brazilian military establishment has steadily assumed control over a widening area of the country's social and political life. Indeed, there exists the possibility that what we are witnessing in Brazil is the creation of a new political and economic model of authoritarian development. Other contributors to this volume examine the internal workings, policy outputs, and institutionalization possibilities of this model. My focus is on how changing military ideology contributed to the events leading up to the military coup of 1964 and the emergence of the military-bureaucratic and authoritarian-developmentalist components of the model.

In this chapter I argue that what happened in Brazil was, to a significant extent, part of the wider military phenomenon of what I call the "new professionalism of internal security and national development." In analyzing how the ideology of new professionalism arose and how it contributed to the expansion of the military's role in politics, I also endeavor to identify some of the institutional and political variables that are peculiar to Brazil and that help account for some of the special characteristics of the military regime.

Conflicting Paradigms: New Professionalism vs. Old Professionalism

In the 1960s, the political roles of the Brazilian and Peruvian military establishments underwent a great expansion. Yet, as measured by a number of indicators, these military establishments are probably the two most professional in Latin America.[1] They have relatively universalistic procedures for the recruitment and promotion of officers, highly structured military schooling programs that prepare officers for passage to the next stage

1. See Alfred Stepan, *The Military in Politics: Changing Patterns in Brazil* (Princeton: Princeton University Press, 1971), chap. 3; and Luigi Einaudi, *The Peruvian Military: A Summary Political Analysis* (Santa Monica: RAND Corporation, RM-6048-RC, May 1969).

of their careers, highly articulated and well-disseminated military doctrines and well-programmed military-unit training cycles, all coordinated by extensive general staff systems. If there is one central concept of modern civil-military relations, it is the concept of "professionalism." According to this concept, as the professionalism of a military establishment increases along the lines indicated above, the military tends to become less political in its activities. In the case of Brazil, however, professional standards coexisted with increasing politicization in the years leading up to 1964. Thus, either Brazil must be considered a deviant case, or one must suggest an alternative framework that is capable of incorporating Brazil, Peru (where a similar process of professionalization and politicization has been at work), and, I suspect, a number of other countries, such as Indonesia, as the predictable outcome of the new paradigm.

It is the argument of this chapter that the highly bureaucratized, highly schooled, and yet highly politicized armies of Brazil and Peru are best viewed not as lapses from the paradigm of the "old" professionalism, but as one of the logical consequences of the "new" professionalism. To clarify the theoretical and empirical aspects of this assertion, I briefly consider first the components of the old professionalism. Though many aspects of the argument are widely reproduced by writers who have not studied his work, the classic formulation of the argument about military professionalism and its relation to the political activity of the military is Samuel Huntington's. As quoted or paraphrased from his own writings,[2] his argument is as follows:

1. *On the nature of modern warfare and the requisite skills.* Modern warfare demands a highly specialized military; the military cannot master the new skills needed to carry out their tasks while at the same time "remaining competent in many other fields" as well. [*The Soldier,* p. 32.]

2. *On the impact of pursuit of professionalism.* As a result of this specialization, "the vocation of officership absorbs all their energies and furnishes them with all their occupational satisfactions. Officership, in short, is an exclusive role, incompatible with any other significant social or political roles." ["Civilian Control," p. 381.]

3. *On the relationship between political and military spheres.*

2. Samuel P. Huntington, *The Soldier and the State: The Theory and Politics of Civil-Military Relations* (New York: Vintage Books, 1964); idem, "Civilian Control of the Military: A Theoretical Statement," in *Political Behavior: A Reader in Theory and Research,* ed. H. Eulau, S. Eldersveld, and M. Janowitz (New York: Free Press, 1956).

The functional specialization needed for external defense means that "it became impossible to be an expert in the management of violence for external defense and at the same time to be skilled in either politics and statecraft or the use of force for the maintenance of internal order. The functions of the officer became distinct from those of the politician and policeman." [*The Soldier*, p. 32.]

4. *On the scope of military concern.* "At the broadest level of the relation of the military order to society, the military function is presumed to be a highly specialized one. . . . A clear distinction in role and function exists between military and civilian leaders." ["Civilian Control," pp. 380–81.]

5. *On the impact of professionalism on military attitudes to politics.* "Civilian control is thus achieved not because the military groups share in the social values and political ideologies of society, but because they are indifferent to such values and ideologies." ["Civilian Control," p. 381.]

6. *On the impact of professionalism on civil-military relations.* "The one prime essential for any system of civilian control is the minimizing of military power. Objective civilian control achieves this reduction by professionalizing the military" and by "confining it to a restricted sphere and rendering it politically sterile and neutral on all issues outside that sphere." [*The Soldier*, p. 84; "Civilian Control," p. 381.]

This argument runs through a large part of American military writing and appears frequently in congressional discussions of the rationale for United States military assistance policies to developing countries. The argument that assistance policies should be given in order to professionalize the military has been rationalized on the grounds that in doing so the United States could help convert traditional, politicized armies into modern, apolitical ones. However, as the extensive quotations from Huntington illustrate, the professionalization thesis was rooted in the assumption that armies develop their professional skills for conventional warfare against foreign armies. In his later writing Huntington has stated that if the focus shifts from interstate conflict to domestic war it will encourage a different pattern of civil-military relations than that expounded in the passages quoted above.[3] Since many later writers have failed to note this qualification, the concept of military professionalism is

3. See in particular his "Patterns of Violence in World Politics," in *Changing Patterns of Military Politics,* ed. Samuel P. Huntington (New York: Free Press, 1962), pp. 19–22.

still widely misunderstood, and it is useful to formulate explicitly the differences between the old professionalism of external warfare and the new professionalism of internal security and national development.

In reality, by the late 1950s and early 1960s, the success of revolutionary warfare techniques against conventional armies in China, Indochina, Algeria, and Cuba led the conventional armies in both the developed and underdeveloped world to turn more attention to devising military and political strategies to combat or prevent domestic revolutionary warfare. In fact, by 1961, the United States military assistance programs to Latin America were largely devoted to exporting doctrines concerned with the military's role in counterinsurgency, civic action and nation building.[4] In Latin America the process by which the military came to define its mission primarily in terms of dealing with threats to internal security was accelerated by the defeat and destruction of the conventional army in Cuba by Castro's guerrilla force. In Brazil and Peru, where the military was highly institutionalized, the perception of the threat to the internal security of the nation and the security of the military itself led to a focusing of energies on the "professionalization" of their approach to internal security. The military institutions began to study such questions as the social and political conditions facilitating the growth of revolutionary protest and to develop doctrines and training techniques to prevent or crush insurgent movements. As a result, these highly professionalized armies became much more concerned with political problems.

Thus there was a dual process at work. Because of their preoccupation with subversion and internal security, many military establishments in Latin America attempted to undertake institutional professionalization and development and were given extensive United States military assistance in doing so. Yet, given the changed political climate, the formulators of United States military assistance programs and the chiefs of many Latin American military establishments now believed that professional

4. This shift has been well documented. For an overview and a guide to the United States government programs and publications see W. F. Barber and C. N. Ronning, eds., *Internal Security and Military Power: Counterinsurgency and Civic Action in Latin America* (Columbus: Ohio State University Press, 1966). See also M. Francis, "Military Aid to Latin America in the United States Congress," *Journal of Inter-American Studies* 6 (July 1964): 389–401. A strong criticism of this policy from the Latin American perspective is John Saxe-Fernández, *Proyecciones hemisféricas de la pax Americana* (Lima: IEP ediciones y CAMPODÓNICOediciones, 1971).

military expertise was required in a broader range of fields. Instead of increasing functional specialization, the military began to train their officers to acquire expertise in internal security matters that were defined as embracing all aspects of social, economic, and political life. Instead of the gap between the military and political spheres widening, the new professionalism led to a belief that there was a fundamental interrelationship between the two spheres, with the military playing a key role in interpreting and dealing with domestic political problems owing to its greater technical and professional skills in handling internal security issues.[5] The scope of military concern for, and study of, politics became unrestricted, so that the "new professional" military man was highly politicized.

The new professionalism of internal security and national development almost inevitably led to some degree of military role expansion. However, variables stemming from the larger political system in addition to those associated with the military subsystem affect the degree of this role expansion. The weaker the civilian government's own legitimacy and ability to supervise a "peaceful" process of development, the greater the tendency will be for the new professionals to assume control of the government to impose their own view of development on the state.

The old professionalism of external security and the new professionalism of internal security and national development share many external characteristics, especially those of highly developed military schooling systems and elaborate military doctrines. However, the *content* and *consequences* of the two forms of professionalism are quite distinct, as is shown schematically in table 2.1. It is useful to distinguish the two types of military professionalism for reasons of policy as well as theory.

5. A thorough and brilliant analysis of some psychological and political implications of this type of military ideology of total counterrevolutionary warfare (especially in the context of a weak political system) is Raoul Girardet's discussion of the French army. See his "Problèmes idéologiques et moraux," and "Essai d'interprétation," in *La Crise militaire française, 1945–1962: Aspects sociologiques et idéologiques*, ed. Raoul Girardet (Paris: Librairie Armand Colin, 1964), pp. 151–229.

In the early 1960s the Indonesian army's Staff and Command School formulated a development and security doctrine that was later implemented in large part when the military assumed power in 1965. For the doctrine and an insightful analysis see Guy J. Pauker, *The Indonesian Doctrine of Territorial Warfare and Territorial Management* (Santa Monica: RAND Corporation, RM-3312-PR, November 1963).

Table 2.1
Contrasting Paradigms:
The Old Professionalism of External Defense
The New Professionalism of Internal Security and National Development

	Old Professionalism	New Professionalism
Function of military	External security	Internal security
Civilian attitudes toward government	Civilians accept legitimacy of government	Segments of society challenge government legitimacy
Military skills required	Highly specialized skills incompatible with political skills	Highly interrelated political and military skills
Scope of military professional action	Restricted	Unrestricted
Impact of professional socialization	Renders the military politically neutral	Politicizes the military
Impact on civil-military relations	Contributes to an apolitical military and civilian control	Contributes to military-political managerialism and role expansion

Since 1961, United States military policy toward Latin America has been to encourage the Latin American militaries to assume as their primary role counterinsurgency programs, civic-action and nation-building tasks. This policy has often been defended in the name of helping to create a professional army, and by implication, an apolitical force in the nation. However, in terms of the schema presented in the table, technical and professional specialization of the military in conjunction with doctrines and ideologies of internal security will tend to lead toward military role expansion and "managerialism" in the political sphere.[6]

It also seems useful to point out for reasons of politics as well as theory that the new professionalism is not only a phenomenon of the developing countries. Some of the key ingredients of the new professionalism were observed in France in the 1950s and played a major role in the civil-military crises there in 1958 and 1961. Even in the United States, the military's development of the new professionalism in the fields of counterinsurg-

6. I develop this argument at greater length in my congressional testimony; see U.S. Congress, House of Representatives, *Hearings before the Subcommittee on National Security Policy and Scientific Developments of the Committee on Foreign Affairs on Military Assistance Training*, 91st Cong., 2nd sess., October 6, 7, 8, December 8, 15, 1970, pp. 105–11, 117–29 passim.

ency and civic action has resulted in the development of skills that, though originally developed for export to the developing countries such as Brazil in the early 1960s, were by the late 1960s increasingly called upon within this country. Huntington's view of the old professionalism, where the military was functionally specific and unconcerned with domestic political events, is now less meaningful for this country. The United States Army has increasingly been used to quell riots and given the function of maintaining internal order. Once given this function, the internal logic of the new professionalism comes into play, and the military sets about in a "professional" way to train to perform this function. In the late 1960s, many units such as the crack 82nd Airborne Division spent an increasing amount of their time training how to occupy American cities in case of domestic riots. The next "new professional" question for the United States military was to inquire into the nature of the enemy. This involved the military in a surveillance and intelligence-gathering role within the United States.[7]

New Professionalism in the Brazilian Political Crisis

The processes leading toward the development of the new professionalism were evident in Brazil before 1964. In Brazil, many of the external standards of the old professionalism had greatly increased before this date. The military schooling system was highly evolved. To be eligible for promotion to the rank of general an army line officer was required to graduate from the Military Academy (Academia Militar das Agulhas Negras, AMAN), the Junior Officer's School (Escola de Aperfeiçoamento de Oficiais, EsAO), and the three-year General Staff School (Escola de Comando e Estado Maior do Exército, ECEME), whose written entrance examination is passed by less than a quarter of the applicants. In terms of rank structure, the rank distribution was roughly similar to that of the United States. According to Janowitz, 21.7 percent of officers in the United States Army were colonels or generals in 1950. In 1964, the figure for Brazil was only 14.9 percent.[8]

At the same time, new military institutions were developing in Brazil that were to become centers of the new professionalism. Of prime importance was the Superior War College (Escola Superior de Guerra, ESG) which was formally established by presi-

7. For a more detailed discussion of these themes, see Bruce Russett and Alfred Stepan, eds., *Military Force and American Society* (New York: Harper & Row, Torchbook, 1973).

8. For documentation see Stepan, *The Military in Politics*, chap. 3.

dential decree under Dutra in 1949. At the time of its founding,
the United States played a key role through a military advisory
mission that stayed in Brazil from 1948 to 1960. By 1963, the
ESG decreed its mission as that of preparing "civilians and the
military to perform executive and advisory functions especially
in those organs responsible for the formulation, development,
planning, and execution of the policies of national security." [9]
That the new professionalism of national security as developed
at the ESG was very different in conception from that of the
old professionalism, which in theory confines military activity
to a more restricted sphere, is clear from an examination of the
seven academic divisions of the college. These were (1) political
affairs, (2) psychological-social affairs, (3) economic affairs, (4)
military affairs, (5) logistical and mobilization affairs, (6) intelligence and counterintelligence, and (7) doctrine and coordination.[10]

One interesting aspect of the new professionalism was its relation with civilians. In the 1950s in Brazil, the participation of
civilians became a key aspect of the college's program. Precisely
because the military viewed the situation in Brazil as going beyond questions handled by the old professionalism, and because
the ESG was to be concerned with all phases of development and
national security, it was felt the Brazilian military needed to socialize civilians from such fields as education, industry, com-
munications, and banking into the correct national security perspective. By 1966, in fact, the ESG had graduated men from many
of the key sectors of the political and economic power structure
in Brazil: by this date, 599 graduates were military officers, 224
were from private industry and commerce, 200 from the major
government ministries, 97 from decentralized government agencies, 39 from the federal Congress, 23 were federal or state judges,
and 107 were various professionals, such as professors, economists, writers, medical doctors, and Catholic clergy.[11]

By the late 1950s and early 1960s, the ESG had developed its key
ideological tenet: the close interrelationship between national

9. Decreto No. 53,080, December 4, 1963.
10. Ibid.
11. For a short official history of the ESG see the heavily documented
essay by General Augusto Fragoso, written while he was commandant of the
school, "A Escola Superior de Guerra (Origen — Finalidade — Evolução),"
*Segurança & Desenvolvimento: Revista da Associação dos Diplomados da
Escola Superior de Guerra,* ano 18, no. 132 (1969), pp. 7–40. The figures on
occupations of graduates were provided by the ESG and reprinted in Glauco
Carneiro, "A guerra de 'Sorbonne,'" *O Cruzeiro,* June 24, 1967, p. 20.

security and national development. The doctrines taught at the college emphasized that modern warfare, either conventional or revolutionary, involved the unity, will, and productive capacity of the entire nation.

The low-mobilization, high-control policies of the military governments since 1964 had their intellectual roots in the ESG's doctrine that an effective policy of national security demands a strong government that can rationally maximize the outputs of the economy and effectively contain manifestations of disunity in the country. The new professionalism contributed to an all-embracing attitude of military managerialism in regard to Brazil's political system. The ideas and suggestions aired at the ESG at least five years before the coup of 1964 ranged from redrawing state boundaries (to eliminate old political forces and restructure the federation along "natural" economic boundaries) to the enforcement of a two-party system.[12] The language in the 1956 ESG lecture quoted below foreshadowed the tone, substance, and rationale of later military government attempts to impose a hierarchical, semicorporatist unity on the Brazilian political system.

> We live in a climate of world-wide war that will decide the destiny of Western civilization.
> A decentralized system is fundamentally weak in periods of war, which demand a centralized and hierarchic structure. As total war absorbs all people, institutions, wealth, and human and national resources for the attainment of the objectives, it seems certain that centralization and concentration will increase the efficiency and ability of the political and national power.[13]

Though the ESG always concerned itself to some extent with conventional warfare, it became the center of ideological thought concerning counterrevolutionary strategy in Brazil. In early 1959 the chief ideologue of the school, Colonel Golbery, argued that

12. See, for example, Christovão L. Barros Falcão, Capitão-de-mar-e-guerra, *Mobilização no campo econômico*, Curso de Mobilização Nacional, Escola Superior de Guerra, C-03-59; and David Carneiro, *Organização política do Brasil*, Escola Superior de Guerra, Departmento de Estudos, C-47-59. These and all subsequent ESG documents that I cite I found either in the archive of Castello Branco located in the library of ECEME or in the Biblioteca Nacional. Most ESG documents are still classified by the Brazilian government.

13. Ildefonso Mascarenhas da Silva, *O poder nacional e seus tipos de estructura*, Escola Superior de Guerra, C-20-56, pp. 32–34.

indirect attack from within was a much more real threat to Latin
America than direct attack from without:

> What is certain is that the greater probability today is
> limited warfare, localized conflict, and above all indirect
> Communist aggression, which capitalizes on local discon-
> tents, the frustrations of misery and hunger, and just na-
> tionalist anxieties. . . . Latin America now faces threats
> more real than at any other time, threats which could result
> in insurrection, outbursts attempting (though not openly)
> to implant . . . a government favorable to the Communist
> ideology and constituting a grave and urgent danger to the
> unity and security of the Americas and the Western
> world.[14]

It was this perception of threat, in conjunction with the ESG's
underlying preference for "ordered politics," that led to their
advocacy of the primacy of the politics of national security (implicitly directed by the military) over competitive politics. Golbery contended that in times of severe crises,

> the area of politics is permeated . . . by adverse pressures,
> creating a form of universalization of the factors of security,
> enlarging the area of the politics of national security to a
> point where it almost absorbs all the national activities.[15]

It was from this perspective of the relation between internal
security and national development that the ESG set about studying all problems viewed as relating to the security issue. Its civil-
military, national security elites studied inflation, agrarian reform, banking reform, voting systems, transportation, and education, as well as guerrilla warfare and conventional warfare.
In many of these studies, some of the fundamental aspects
of Brazilian social and economic organization were depicted as
needing change if Brazil were to maintain its internal security.

Initially, these critiques of Brazilian society by military intellectuals seemed academic, and the influence of the ESG's doctrine
was not pervasive within the military in the mid-1950s. But by

14. Golbery do Couto e Silva, *Geopolítica do Brasil* (Rio de Janeiro: José
Olympio, 1967), pp. 198–99 (from a chapter originally written in 1959). This
book is based on ESG lectures. The developments in the Cuban revolution
in late 1960 and 1961 intensified the ESG fear of the "communist threat."

15. Golbery do Couto e Silva, *Planejamento estratégico* (Rio de Janeiro:
Biblioteca do Exército Editôra, 1955), pp. 38–39. Most of this book had its
origin in lectures originally given at the ESG. The book is one of the major
sources for the ideology of the ESG.

the early 1960s, as the military perceived a deepening crisis in Brazil, the ESG's emphasis on the need for a total development strategy to combat internal subversion found an increasingly receptive audience in the military. Through the military's highly structured and well-developed publication and education systems, the ideology of internal warfare was widely disseminated throughout the officer corps. The ECEME, one of the major institutions of the old professionalism, became a central vehicle for socializing an entire generation of military officers in the internal-warfare doctrines. The training program is three years long, and entrance is highly competitive. Unless an army line officer is graduated from the ECEME he is ineligible for promotion to general, for appointment to the teaching staff of any military school, or to the general staff of any senior command. Thus the ECEME is the central recruitment and socialization institution of the senior army officer corps of the Brazilian army.

An examination of the curriculum of the ECEME shows that, like the ESG, it increasingly became devoted to the doctrines of the new professionalism, with its emphasis on the expanded political, economic, and social roles of a modern army in times of internal-security threats. In the 1956 curriculum, for instance, there were no class hours scheduled on counterguerrilla warfare, internal security, or communism. By 1966, however, the curriculum contained 222 hours on internal security, 129 on irregular warfare, and only 24 hours on the "old" professional military topic of territorial warfare.[16] Through military publications, such as the newsletter *Boletim de Informações,* sent from the Estado Maior to key troop commanders, the content of the new professionalism was systematically disseminated to all army units.[17]

In their studies of the Brazilian political system the new professionals had, since the early 1960s, moved toward the position that (1) numerous aspects of the economic and political structures had to be altered if Brazil were to have internal security and rational economic growth and (2) the civilian politicians were either unable or unwilling to make these changes. By early

16. Based upon my examination of the curriculum of ECEME on file at their library.

17. Ministério da Guerra, Estado Maior do Exército, *Boletim de Informações.* Copies of this are on open file at the Biblioteca do Exército in Rio de Janeiro. Before October 1961 the format was that of a very straightforward review of professional topics and routine surveys of international news. From October 1961 on, the format changed to one much closer to the framework and terminology of the ESG and, most significantly, began to deal with the question of the threat to internal security presented by communism.

1964, through the prism of internal-warfare doctrines of the new professionalism, a substantial part of the Brazilian military establishment perceived the rising strike levels, the inflation rate of over 75 percent, the declining economy, the demands of the Left for a constituent assembly, and the growing indiscipline of the enlisted men as signs that Brazil was entering a stage of subversive warfare.

Moreover, the new professionals had come to believe that, in comparison to the civilian politicians, they now had constructed the correct doctrines of national security and development, possessed the trained cadres to implement these doctrines, and had the institutional force to impose their solution to the crisis in Brazil. Thus, after overthrowing the civilian president in 1964, the Brazilian military did not return power to new civilian groups, as they had in 1930, 1945, 1954, and 1955, but assumed political power themselves for the first time in the century.

Since 1964, the military has frequently been internally divided over specific policies and the problems of succession. Nevertheless, one must not lose sight of the important point that many of the doctrines of internal warfare, formulated originally at the ESG and later institutionalized in the ESG-influenced government of Castello Branco, permeated almost all major military groups in Brazil and were accepted as a basic new fact of political and military life. The central idea developed at the ESG was that development and security issues are inseparable. Even when differences over policies developed between the Castello Branco government and the Costa e Silva government, almost all military officers agreed that since labor, fiscal, educational, and other problems were intrinsic to the security of the nation, it was legitimate and necessary for military men to concern themselves with these areas. From this basic premise came the steady broadening of military jurisdiction over Brazilian life after the military assumed power in 1964, despite the fact that an important faction of the military had hoped to eventually allow the inauguration of liberal political forms.

Even within the military government itself, security matters have been given special prominence. A new agency, the National Information Service (Serviço Nacional de Informações, SNI), combining the functions of the FBI and CIA in the United States, has been created, and its director has been granted cabinet rank. In 1968 and 1969, national security laws were passed that have greatly increased the role of SNI and other intelligence units. Since 1969, every ministry has had an SNI representative, responsible for ensuring that all policy decisions of the ministry give full consideration to national security issues. Thus the new professionalism of internal warfare and national development contributed to the expansion of the military's role in Brazil that led ultimately to the military's assumption of power in 1964, and afterward to a widening of military control over those aspects of Brazilian life perceived in any way as threatening to the executors of the national security state — that is, the military.

NEW PROFESSIONALISM IN PERU

The argument that the internal logic of the new professionalism tends to contribute to an extension of the role of the military in politics receives support from a study of the only other country in Latin America to have developed fully an ideology relating internal security to national development and to have institutionalized that ideology within the military. This country is Peru.[18] The grouping of Peru with Brazil may at first seem incongruous because the policies of their military governments have been very different. However, the two countries are strikingly similar when analyzed from the perspective of the central part played by their respective war colleges in the process of military role expansion. In both countries the staffs and students at the war colleges attempted to systematically diagnose their nation's security-development situation. In the end both colleges had forged a doctrine that implicitly "legitimated" long-term military supervision of the development process. Furthermore, in both military establishments there was the belief that the war colleges and general staff schools had trained the cadres capable of administering this military-directed process. Both, in short, are examples of the new professionalism.

In Peru, as in Brazil, reasonably developed standards for the professional officer's education, promotion, and training exist. In Peru, educational performance is central to any officer's advancement. Eighty percent of all division generals on active

18. Argentina, which I would rank highest after Brazil and Peru among the countries of Latin America on a rough scale of new professionalism, experienced a military coup in 1966. Analysts specifically pointed to the evolution of a military ideology concerned with internal security and national development as an important factor in the inauguration of the authoritarian military regime. This would be in keeping with the thesis of the present chapter. See Guillermo A. O'Donnell, "Modernización y golpes militares: Teoría, comparaciones e el caso Argentino," (Buenos Aires: Instituto Torcuato Di Tella, Documento de Trabajo, September 1972).

duty between 1940 and 1965, for instance, had graduated in the
top quarter of their military academy class.[19] A comparable
figure for generals in the United States Army in Morris Janowitz's
1950 sample was 36.4 percent.[20]

In 1950, the Peruvian military established its own superior
war college, called the Center for Higher Military Studies (Centro
de Altos Estudios Militares, CAEM). By the late 1950s, CAEM
had largely turned its energies to analyzing the nexus between
internal security and national development. As in Brazil, the
military's assessment of the development process led the Peruvian military officers into political diagnosis, but in the case
of Peru their orientation was markedly more nationalistic and
antioligarchical in tone. Five years before the Peruvian military
assumed power, a CAEM document stated:

> So long as Peru does not have programmatic and well or-
> ganized political parties, the country will continue to be un-
> governable . . . The sad and desperate truth is that in Peru,
> the real powers are not the Executive, the Legislature, the
> Judiciary, or the Electorate, but the latifundists, the ex-
> porters, the bankers, and the American [United States] in-
> vestors.[21]

19. Luigi Einaudi, *The Peruvian Military*, p. 7. The analysis of Peru owes
much to my discussions with Einaudi. We coauthored the monograph *Latin
American Institutional Development: Changing Military Perspectives in Peru
and Brazil* (Santa Monica: RAND Corporation, R-586-DOS, April 1971), in
which Einaudi is primarily responsible for Peru and I am primarily responsible for Brazil.

In 1972, while on a SSRC-ACLS grant I carried out research in Peru and
visited CAEM. Although the discussion in this chapter reflects some of the
results of this research, extensive analysis and documentation of the material must await a later publication. One particularly relevant finding is
based on my study with Jorge Rodríguez of the University of York, England.
Of the 404 articles to appear in the *Revista de la Escuela Superior de Guerra*
(Peru) from 1954 to 1967, the percentage of articles whose content met our
criteria of "new professionalism" increased from virtually zero in 1954–55
to well over 50 percent by 1964.

20. Morris Janowitz, *The Professional Soldier: A Social and Political Por-
trait* (New York: Free Press, 1960), pp. 134–35.

21. CAEM, *El estado y la política general* (1963), pp. 89, 92, cited in
Einaudi and Stepan, *Latin American Institutional Development*. Víctor
Villanueva, in his important book, *El CAEM y la revolución de la fuerza
armada* (Lima: IEP ediciones y CAMPODÓNICOediciones, 1972), pp. 85–
88, notes that while this document was initially released with the approval
of the director of CAEM, it was withdrawn due to pressure. Villanueva
argues that this document is considerably more nationalistic and concerned

CAEM studies in the late 1950s and early 1960s diagnosed a number of problems of Peruvian society. Against a background of growing social tensions and political paralysis, the organization of peasants by Hugo Blanco and later the guerrilla outbreak of 1965–66 served to broaden the consensus within the military that direct action was necessary. Though the military defeated the guerrillas in six months, they intensified their investigations of the causes of insurgency. They concluded that rural conditions in Peru were so archaic and unjust that, unless there was a profound change in the rural structure of the country, more guerrilla outbreaks could be expected. The military concluded from their studies that Peru was in a state of "latent insurgency," which could only be corrected, in their view, by a "general policy of economic and social development." [22] In Einaudi's words, "elimination of the latent state of subversion became the primary objective of military action." [23]

The military's analysis of the factors contributing to latent insurgency included elite intransigence, fiscal and technical inefficiencies, and a wide variety of administrative weaknesses traceable to the weakness of the government and the underlying contradictions of the social structure.[24] As in Brazil, the military educational system in Peru had produced a whole cadre of officers

---

with structural change than most CAEM studies in this period. Nonetheless for purposes of our comparison the document reveals a set of concerns very different from those found at the ESG in Brazil.

22. See Peru, Ministerio de Guerra, *Las guerrillas en el Perú y su represión* (Lima, 1966), p. 80. Articles in this vein had been appearing in Peruvian military journals even before the guerrilla movement of 1965–66. See in particular Lieutenant Colonel Enrique Gallegos Venero, "Problemas de la guerra contrarrevolucionaria," *Revista de la Escuela Superior de Guerra,* año 11, no. 2 (1964), pp. 97–106.

23. In Einaudi and Stepan, *Latin American Institutional Development.* A civilian social scientist who has been on the faculty at CAEM since 1959 told the author that from 1959 to 1962 CAEM experienced a phase of radicalization aimed at bureaucratic and organizational reform in Peru and that many of these policies were implemented by the 1962–63 military government. From 1964 to 1968 CAEM underwent a new phase of radicalization, but this time the studies explored and advocated much deeper social and structural changes because of the realization that organizational changes alone had been insufficient to resolve Peru's security and development crisis. Interview with Jorge Bravo Bresani, Lima, June 22, 1972.

24. See Brigadier General E. P. Edgardo Mercado Jarrín, "La política y estrategia militar en la guerra contrasubversiva en la América Latina," *Revista Militar del Perú* (Chorrillos), November–December 1967, pp. 4–33. In many ways this article is a classic example of new professionalism.

with a highly articulated ideology of internal security and national development, and with a new confidence as to the utility of their technocratic and managerial education. These officers feared that the country could evolve into a dangerous state of insecurity if fundamental changes in thè polity and economy were not brought about. Like the Brazilian military officers schooled at the ESG, the Peruvian officers trained at CAEM came to the conclusion that civilian governments were incapable of bringing about these changes, and that their own CAEM training in the new professionalism gave them the trained cadres and correct ideology for the task of restructuring the country. This attitude strongly influenced the military's decision to assume and retain political control of the country.

Significantly, in Einaudi's interviews with key Peruvian generals, implicit reference was made to the impact the new professional training has had on military confidence to rule. A former minister of war commented that in the past the military felt culturally inferior and that "when a general met an ambassador, he turned red in the face and trembled." But a leading general in the current regime argued that whereas past military attempts to induce change, such as the regime of Colonel Sánchez Cerro, were doomed to failure because military men were not adequately trained in matters of national development, the present military officers possessed the correct training to be successful. He commented: "Sánchez Cerro was alone. I am but one of forty. And behind us comes a generation of still better trained officers ready to carry on should we falter." [25]

Brazil and Peru: Their Contrasting Policies

Peru is relevant for our analysis of Brazil not only because it is an example of the new professionalism, but also because it illustrates that the new professionalism contributes more to the military's general attitude to political action than to specific policies. In the two countries, the new professional military men have chosen quite different paths. Why has this occurred, and what are the chances that the military in Brazil might take a Peruvian turn?

This is not the place for an extensive comparative analysis of the two regimes, but some of the factors contributing to the different policies of the two military regimes should be stated. First was the impact of World War II. During the war, Brazil sent a combat division, the Fôrça Expedicionária Brasileira (FEB), to fight in Italy as allies of the United States. My extensive interviews with many of the key leaders of the 1964 military government in Brazil indicate that some of the distinctive characteristics of the Castello Branco government — its pro-Americanism, its favorable attitude toward foreign capital, its distaste for "excessive" nationalism — had their roots in this experience. The ally relationship also prepared the way for close personal and institutional ties between the United States and the Brazilian military establishment.[26] In this area, Peru has no comparable experience.

A second area of divergence between the two countries involves their superior war colleges. The Brazilian war college was established and largely dominated by veterans of World War II, who saw the college as the place to "institutionalize the learning experience of World War II." When officers training at the ESG were sent abroad, they were normally sent to United States military schools, and this experience reinforced the security emphasis, which had found a place in United States schools. Some of the officers associated with CAEM, however, had direct contacts with French-Catholic reformist priest Lebret or attended United Nations civilian-directed schools in Chile. These experiences reinforced CAEM's emphasis on development and helped cast the school's concern for development in a nationalistic light. At the Brazilian ESG many of those attending the courses were private businessmen, and undoubtedly this contributed to the ESG's bias in favor of capitalism and efficiency. The private civilian industrial sector has never been as heavily represented at CAEM.

A third factor influencing the direction and content of the military regimes in Brazil and Peru is the size of the private industrial sector. The much larger and more powerful private industrial sector in Brazil conditioned military attitudes by inhibiting the adoption of the Peruvian approach, because the private sector is considered so large, dynamic, and advanced that the military doubts its own ability to run the industrial sector efficiently. Industrialists are therefore viewed as allies in the low-mobilization, high-coercion development model in Brazil. In Peru, on the other hand, the industrial sector is smaller and less dynamic. It appears that in the less developed economy, the scope for military Nasserism is greater and the working-class groups far more amenable to the military nationalist-statist approach.

26. For a more detailed discussion and documentation, see Stepan, *The Military in Politics*, pp. 239–44.

A final factor to be considered in this chapter is the way in which the nexus between security and development issues was viewed by military officers at the time they seized power. In 1964, military officers in Brazil were primarily concerned with what they viewed as the immediate security threat. In Peru, on the other hand, the defeat of the guerrillas in 1966 gave military officers time to focus almost exclusively on the long-term development aspects of security. The initial acts of the Brazilian military regime after 1964 were consequently largely concerned with repression, which by 1968 had become institutionalized coercion. In Peru, the military government has been largely concerned with nationalism and development and this has meant that significant internal opposition from the Left is absent.

Even this cursory analysis of some of the different historical, institutional, and economic legacies in the two countries helps clarify why the "Peruvian wing" within the Brazilian military has not been able to assume control in Brazil and why it is unlikely to do so in the future. What in fact is the future of the new professionalism in Brazil?

One factor that must be taken into consideration is that in a number of ways the Brazilian military in the 1950s and 1960s was for the first time moving toward becoming a professional *caste*. In the period 1941–43, for instance, sons of military families represented 21.3 percent of all cadets admitted to the military academy. This figure had increased to 34.9 percent by 1962–66. More startling is the fact that, as the military professionalized its educational system, it expanded its military high schools in order to ensure the entry into the military school system of a sufficient number of attractive officer candidates. In 1939, 61.6 percent of all cadets at the military academy had attended civilian high schools. By 1963–66, only 7.6 percent of all cadets had attended civilian high schools. Thus, probably about 90 percent of the present army officers in Brazil entered the military educational system when they were about twelve years old.[27]

Once the military assumed power, the movement toward professional homogeneity was accelerated. About 20 percent of the field grade officers have now been purged from the military for ideological deviation. Possession of the "correct" revolutionary mentality is now indispensable for promotion or assignment to a key command. The purging of a significant group of senior of-

27. The data on social origins and educational background of cadets at the Academia Militar das Agulhas Negras were obtained at the academy by the author.

ficers, together with the purging of politicians, has created an "Argentine" extrication dilemma. The military fears leaving office because of the threat posed by the return to power of previously purged officers and politicians. Institutional factors such as these must be borne in mind in any assessment of the possibility of military rule ending in Brazil.

On the other hand, despite the new professionals' agreement on the inseparability of internal security and national development, the contrast between Peru and Brazil has helped point out that the ideology itself leaves unspecified most concrete policy decisions. Nor can the particular ideological unity of the military help resolve succession crises. In fact, the nine years of Brazilian military rule have gravely injured military unity. The military experienced major internal crises in October 1965, November 1968, and September 1969. "Defense of the military institution" was one of the keys to the new professionals' entry into national politics. If, however, internal disunity increases over policy or succession problems, "defense of the institution" may well be one of the keys to extrication, via a caretaker junta. The military leaders are attempting to institutionalize the system so that levels of coercion and dissent diminish and support rises. The Mexican model of institutionalization is often mentioned by the military. However, the absence of a revolutionary myth in Brazil and the much more advanced state of both the economy and, more importantly, social groups would seem to rule out this possibility.

PART II

THE POLITICAL ECONOMY
OF AUTHORITARIAN BRAZIL

3   Some Reflections on Post-1964 Brazilian Economic Policy

ALBERT FISHLOW

The Brazilian "miracle" now bids to take a position of honor among the legendary accomplishments of economic policy. Real rates of growth between 1968 and 1971 averaged above 9 percent annually, and inflation has apparently stabilized at a rate close to 20 percent. These results are a far cry from the decline in output per capita experienced in 1963 and the price rises of 25 percent in the first quarter of 1964 alone. Nor are prospects for the immediate future any less bright.

These economic accomplishments have come to be viewed not only as the direct consequence of the Revolution of 1964 and the structural reforms instituted thereafter, but increasingly as evidence of the incompatibility of democratic political institutions and rapid economic development in Brazil and elsewhere. This interpretation has been given special force by the accelerating prosperity since the Fifth Institutional Act of December 1968 further centralized decision-making powers. That act was soon rationalized by policy makers in a response to the requirements of economic development. The director of the Brazilian AID mission implicitly concurred in February 1969:

> In terms of general economic policies, I would say if anything there has been a net improvement; the Finance Minister can now do by decree things that before had to go through Congress; they have been passing out decrees left and right, and most of them are to the good.[1]

Subsequent events seem only to have confirmed that this early favorable prognosis was remarkably accurate.

This chapter examines more critically the economic changes

I wish to acknowledge the helpful comments of Samuel Morley, George Akerlof, and Pedro Malan, without implicating them, and the indispensable research assistance of Astra Meesook.

1. Testimony of William Ellis in U.S., Congress, House of Representatives, Subcommittee on Inter-American Affairs of the Committee on Foreign Affairs, 91st Cong.; 1st sess., 25, 26 February 1969, pp. 580–81.

wrought by the Revolution. In particular, I suggest that the stabilization model upon which the government embarked in 1964 was conditioned by inadequate analysis of the economy as well as characterized by inconsistencies in implementation. Paradoxically, the ultimate success of the model can at least partially be credited to the residuum of the political process that contributed to a change in economic policies in 1967. Moreover, the cost of the stabilization program was borne by those least able to afford it: the poor. To call such a program fully successful is a semantic confusion at the least.

Second, this chapter considers the sources and character of the recent prosperity. I argue that the return to higher rates of growth in more recent years is based in part upon lagged cyclical adjustment to previous import-substitution oriented industrial development. As such, the present expansion cannot be simply extrapolated, nor its potential imbalances ignored, despite the important strides in economic-policy execution since 1964.

The present Brazilian model is frankly capitalistic, relying upon the private sector and foreign investment. Yet the increased effectiveness of the market, particularly the capital market, owes much to governmental intervention in the form of tax incentives and other policies. The essentially *political* decisions concerning the volume of savings and investment, the structure of income distribution, and the extent of federal government centralization cannot be ignored. The political framework favorable to short-term resolution of these questions may not be equally felicitous with regard to the long term. Nor may the developmental consequences keep pace with the impressive rate of advance of gross domestic product.

STABILIZATION OF INFLATION

The Revolution of 1964 marked a renewed and considerably more propitious opportunity for Brazilian adherents to economic orthodoxy to sell their wares. Three times before — during the brief incumbency of Eugênio Gudin in the Ministry of Finance from September 1954 to April 1955, through the program of monetary stabilization introduced in the last part of 1958, and in the first months of Quadros' presidency in 1961 — efforts to restrain inflation by restricting demand had failed to secure firm and continued executive backing. In the first instance, the inevitable protests against the credit squeeze led to Gudin's resignation after only six months in office and thereafter to easier money. The second episode ended with the resignation of Finance Minister Lucas Lopes in August 1959 following Kubitschek's decision to break off negotiations with the IMF. In the last case, Quadros's wavering support of his minister of finance, Clemente Mariani, led ultimately to greater-than-planned issues of currency by August 1961, immediately prior to the former's dramatic resignation.[2]

By contrast, the deterioration of economic conditions in 1964 was so prominent that Castello Branco gave virtual carte blanche to Roberto Campos and Octavio Bulhões, the economic ministers of the new government. Their first priority, rightly, was stabilization. Their analysis of the inflationary process was not novel; it traced back directly to Gudin's first efforts a decade earlier.

> The Brazilian inflationary process has resulted from the inconsistency of distributive policy, concentrated in two principal points:
> (a) in governmental expenditure superior to the purchasing power withdrawn from the private sector in the form of taxes or public borrowing;
> (b) in the incompatibility between the propensity to consume, resulting from wage policy, and the propensity to invest, associated with the policy of expansion of credit to firms.[3]

Resolution of such excess-demand inflation required corresponding reduction of federal deficits, control over credit expansion to the private sector, and limitation of wages. Table 3.1 sets out the record of manipulation of these instruments, and the results achieved.

What stands out is the rapidity with which the government successfully operated upon these chosen instruments. By 1966, the size of the cash deficit relative to gross domestic product had been reduced to almost one-fourth its 1963 percentage. The money supply in that same year grew only 15 percent in nominal terms, and bank credit to the private sector had been similarly, if not so drastically, curtailed. Minimum wages after 1964 had increased at a rate distinctly inferior to the rising price level, especially as measured by the cost of living. The results of the policies appear still more impressive. By 1966, inflation had been curbed to less than half the 1963 rate, and the growth of real product had tripled.

2. For a discussion of these episodes, see Thomas E. Skidmore, *Politics in Brazil, 1930–1964* (New York: Oxford University Press, 1967).

3. Ministério do Planejamento e Coordenação Econômica, *Programa de acão econômica do govêrno, 1964–1966* (Rio de Janeiro, 1964) p. 28.

Table 3.1. Instruments and Objectives of Stabilization Policy

Annual percentage change of

Year	Union cash deficit (% GDP)	Money supply[a]	Bank credit to private sector[a]	Mini- mum wage	Cost of living[a]	Implicit GDP price index	GDP
1963	4.2	64.0	54.9	56.8	80.2	78.0	1.5
1964	3.2	85.9	80.3	91.7	86.6	87.8	2.9
1965	1.6	75.4	54.9	54.0	45.5	55.4	2.7
1966	1.1	15.0	35.8	30.6	41.2	38.8	5.1
1967	1.7	42.6	57.2	25.3	24.1	27.1	4.8
1968	1.2	43.0	62.7	21.6	24.5	27.8	9.3
1969	0.6	32.4	40.1	19.2	24.3	22.3	9.0
1970	0.4	26.7	38.1	20.0	20.9	19.8	9.5
1971	0.3	31.3	44.7	20.5	18.1	20.4	11.3

Source: *Conjuntura Econômica; Boletim do Banco Central do Brasil; Anuário Estatístico; Análise e Perspectiva Econômica.*
[a] December to December.

Yet this numerical chronicle conceals as much as it reveals. Upon the change of government in March 1967 there was little sign of the flourishing economy with inflationary expectations definitively extirpated that table 3.1 seems to imply. Rather, industrial output had been in frank decline throughout the latter part of 1966, and continued to falter in early 1967. The federal cash position was likewise in serious imbalance in the first three months of 1967: expenditures exceed by 52 percent their planned magnitudes, and private liquidity was raised to high levels by government borrowing from the Central Bank. The principal achievement of the previous two years of stabilization was a continuing deceleration in price inflation from a quarterly rate of 12 percent in the first quarter of 1966 to 8 percent in the initial 3 months of 1967.[4] Yet premonitions of a renewed surge of inflation were not lacking.

In response to these unsettled conditions, the new government embarked on an almost full reversal of earlier policies. The deficit was increased; the supply of money and, in particular, credit to the private sector was expanded more rapidly; minimum wage adjustments were scaled more closely to subsequent cost-of-living increases. Corresponding to this change in policy the economy

4. For these data see current issues of *Conjuntura Econômica* and *Boletim do Banco Central do Brasil.*

experienced sustained recovery accompanied by modestly reduced rates of inflation.

The new government, albeit a successor military government, thus demonstrated the same skepticism toward orthodox policies that had been observable earlier under civil regimes. The limited political process of electoral presidential succession had served to catalyze economic discontent and dissatisfaction and to motivate changed economic policies. Different therapy this time produced favorable results, however. Whatever merit the diagnosis of excess demand had in 1964, by 1967 it was incomplete at best.

To understand fully the post-1967 heterodoxy, one must first appreciate the thrust of the orthodox model as applied between 1964 and 1967. The orthodox model had three dimensions. One was the simple and straightforward Keynes-like excess-demand sequence quoted above. In it, money demand is viewed simply as the sum of consumption, investment, and governmental expenditure. In turn, consumption is dependent positively upon wage receipts and negatively upon taxes. Investment is a positive function of loans to the private sector, and it is negatively affected by taxes. The price level, then, is determined by the relationship of such money demand to given real capacity. If money demand grows at the same rate as real supply, prices remain stable. Inflation can result only from greater demand and can therefore be effectively controlled by operating on the factors influencing demand. Increased taxes, reduced real wages, and fewer loans to the private sector are the indicated policies.

Such a formulation excludes the special role of the money supply in generating inflation. That omission was rectified by the government plan's targets for monetary expansion: "The rates of expansion of the money supply will be fixed for each one of these years [1964, 1965, and 1966], rates which ought to maintain a reasonable correlation with price increases." [5] The rationale for such a policy is the quantity theory of money. Money holdings are proportional to money income. If the money supply is increased, recipients of the money will spend it until income has risen to compensate. Since real capacity is again given, such increased expenditure means only higher prices, not greater real income. The money supply in turn is crucially dependent upon the size of the government deficit. These borrowings from the Central Bank are in turn multiplied in a mechanical way by the commercial banking system.

Still a third mechanism for price determination is implicit in

5. *Programa de acão*, p. 34.

the wage policy adopted by the government. Statements other than those of the stabilization plan itself confirm the importance of wage policy to decision makers. Wages influence not only consumption demand, but also costs of production. If prices adjust to compensate nonwage income proportionally, then the rate of inflation will be exactly equal to the rate of nominal salary increase. Excessive wage increases thus produce inevitable price increases. As Campos explained for the Brazilian case,

> The first sin of past laborism was the obsessive preoccupation with massively high salaries. These were far beyond the productivity and growth increment possible from production. The natural result of this illusion was acceleration of the inflationary process.[6]

These three models reflect alternative, but not mutually exclusive, orthodox views of the inflationary process. As they stand, they obviously lead to overdetermination of the price level: we have three different rules — and policies — to deal with inflation. Such inconsistency can be resolved by joining the various dimensions in a single larger model and by allowing for various interactions between the money supply, the rate of interest, and money demand. With only slightly less validity, to the degree the most essential variables are captured in the partial models, the alternatives can be used to set minimum and maximum limits to price changes. In the absence of firm knowledge of parameters, and because of lags in the effects of policies, hardly more can be expected.

It is therefore not the conceptual inconsistency of the three models that is disturbing, but rather their empirical inadequacy. The excess-demand interpretation had much to offer as an explanation of the accelerating process of inflation in the early 1960s while deficits soared out of control. Yet the analysis of the role of the private sector in that experience is clearly defective. Real minimum wages had increased less than productivity change from 1959 through early 1964. Real bank loans to the private sector had also shown steady decline. Since inflation accelerated nevertheless, neither merits the importance the stabilization plan attached to them as causal elements.

The simple monetary formulation is equally questionable. In the first instance, the supply of money in Brazil is subject to more complicated influences than the cash deficit. Other im-

6. Quoted in Octavio Ianni, *Crisis in Brazil* (New York: Columbia University Press, 1970), p. 189.

portant determinants of the volume of high-powered money include loans of the Bank of Brazil to the private sector, the balance of coffee transactions, and the accumulation of foreign exchange reserves. These emissions are then multiplied by the banking system by a factor whose size is determined by official reserve requirements, voluntary reserves, and the public's demand for cash. While the deficit is the single factor best correlated with monetary expansion, the other influences are vitally important in individual instances. For example, the Lucas Lopes stabilization program failed in large part because of coffee policy, not because of the size of the federal deficit. The acquisition of coffee stocks in the second half of 1959 far in excess of the receipts of the coffee export tax led to greater monetary expansion than did the deficit.

This money supply mechanism was not unknown to the policy makers. Indeed, it is explicitly set out as a chapter of the stabilization plan itself. But in application and in focus, the cash deficit became the principal target of economic policy. As a result, in 1965 — although the federal deficit was substantially curtailed and bonds financed part of it — coffee purchases and the acquisition of foreign reserves led to excess monetary expansion.

A second deficiency of the simple monetary approach, also equally applicable to the other models, is the assumption of instantaneous price adjustment. No one, of course, believed naively in a world without lags. The stabilization program itself was avowedly gradualist precisely because it does take time to adjust expenditure, production, and asset decisions to new circumstances. Meanwhile, real output would no longer be a given and equal to full capacity. A substantial reduction in the rate of increase of the money supply, or of government expenditure, or zero nominal wage increases woud lead to intolerable output and employment consequences as the adjustment process occurred. Yet, urged on by AID and the international lending agencies, the government in the end paid too little attention to the inherent resistance of the Brazilian price level to aggregate economic policies. In 1966, Campos held firm and pursued restrictive policies in all dimensions. Prices nonetheless rose at more than twice the rate of monetary expansion, even as real industrial output went into serious decline.

Castello Branco's economic technicians interpreted this result to mean that inflationary expectations had not yet been adequately reversed. Prices continued to rise because entrepreneurs were not convinced that inflation would no longer be a way of life. The remedy was unpleasant, but inevitable: exposure to the "deception of the market." [7] Faced with diminishing demand as the government continued its restraint, expectations would definitively alter and price stabilization could become a reality. The cost in real output was unfortunate but likely to be modest. In any event, it would be outweighed by the longer-term benefits.

This brings us to the central question: were prices recalcitrant merely owing to the prior bout of accelerating inflation, or did the inflexibilities emerge more fundamentally from the structure of the Brazilian economy itself? In particular, did continuing price increases partially reflect rising costs of inputs created by the process of inflation control itself? If this were so — and the stabilization plan paid scant attention to the possibility — the output and employment consequences of orthodox monetary and fiscal policy might be severe indeed, and still without guarantee of ultimate success.

I shall argue that there were in fact powerful forces operating in the Brazilian economy leading to price inflation even in the absence of excess aggregate demand. Most importantly, the manufacturing sector was structured in a far from perfectly competitive fashion. This circumstance was in part the result of technological economies of scale over the range of relevant output that limited the number of firms — particularly in the new import substitutive sectors. In part it was the implicit concession of monopoly privileges to attract resources to those areas.

The presence of market power in turn permitted pricing determination by cost mark-up rules in the short run. It also provided a setting for discrete and lagged adjustment price responses to price (and cost) decisions in other sectors. Finally, as noted above, average costs tended to decline over a not inconsiderable range.

This combination meant that declining money demand did not set in motion the strong pressures upon price which would be anticipated in a competitive setting.[8] That sequence is one of price adjustments, including those of factor inputs, followed by output modifications. In fact the Brazilian experience was one of price maintenance, accumulation of inventories, and increased demand for credit that tended to elevate interest rates, and hence costs. This helps to explain why, despite sharply lower real wages — the only market where flexibility was enforced — there

7. The phrase is that of Mario Henrique Simonsen, *Inflação: Gradualismo e tratamento de choque* (Rio de Janeiro: APEC Editôra, 1970).

8. For a more detailed and more technical discussion of the implications of the alternative models, see appendix.

was no unequivocal signal from the cost side favoring price restraint.

This process should be differentiated from the Philips Curve analysis now familiar in the United States and Western Europe. There the culprit is the demand for real wages on the part of labor. To achieve price stability producers must be converted to more modest price expectations and thereby resistance to extravagant wage demands. Lesser demand and credit restrictions lead to reduced output and revised expectations. They also create unemployment and cause wage demands to be moderated. More modest settlements provide a lapse in inflationary pressures. Note the role of employee responses in the sequence. For Brazil, by contrast, the emphasis is solely upon *employer* reactions — for stabilization immediately enforced lower absolute real wages. While the patterns of reduced production and employment are similar and an element of price expectations remains central, the inherent asymmetry of the Brazilian case is exactly why conventional policies were so likely both to yield unsatisfactory results and to burden workers disproportionately.

It is useful now to restate these propositions in more specific form. First, the concentration of Brazilian industrial production can easily be established. For certain products like refrigerators, washing machines, electric motors, agricultural implements, and scales, the share of the three largest firms typically was above 80 percent.[9] This monopoly power seems to be characteristic of capital goods and consumer durables more generally. But even in such traditional consumer-oriented industries as tobacco, beverages, and foodstuffs, the participation of large firms was, and is, substantial. For these three, little more than 1 percent of the firms account for between a third and two-thirds of output. Only in textiles, clothing, leather, wood, and furniture does the structure approximate competitive requirements more closely; and this conclusion might be tempered for some newer product lines.[10]

Pricing behavior for manufactures in response to reduction in demand corresponds to what might be anticipated from such a structure. Price and quantity changes by sector in the periods 1955–58 and 1962–66 are correlated negatively in each, the co-

9. "The Growth and Decline of Import Substitution in Brazil," *Economic Bulletin for Latin America* 9 (March 1964): 54.

10. These sectoral concentration statistics are obtained from the value of production classified by size of firm reported in IBGE, *Produção Industrial, 1966.*

efficients being −.44 and −.21, respectively.[11] That is, those industries growing most rapidly raised prices least. Were capacity
constraints and excess demand the clear villains, a positive relationship would have been anticipated. This same negative
correlation is found on the basis of independent data on industrial growth in the state of São Paulo for the first two quarters
of the years 1965/1966 and 1967/1968.[12] Rapid growth presumably implied lower real unit costs, and hence less inflation. This
result can be related to the important role of import substitution
in the industrial development of the 1950s. The more prevalent
are new products and processes, the more potential economies of
scale can offset the pressures of demand. Conversely, lesser rates
of increase are more likely to be translated into excess capacity
at *higher* relative prices than into price restraint.

For the first half of 1967, relative to the comparable period
of 1966, there does exist a positive relationship between output
and price changes. This period is precisely one of substantial
decline of industrial production; 14 of the 16 observations of
real product growth are negative. Orthodoxy can apparently
ultimately prevail, but only at the expense of serious reductions
in economic activity. As capacity utilization declines (if it goes
low enough), price mark-ups and thereby inflation can evidently
be restrained, economies of scale notwithstanding. The trade-off
defined by the price-output equation in 1966–67 is highly un-
favorable, however. Attainment of an average rate of increase of
manufacturing prices of 20 percent implies an average reduction
of industrial output of close to 40 percent. This short-run reaction function obviously exaggerates the insensitivity of prices
to demand. Continuing excess capacity would undoubtedly have
produced greater price moderation, but still not without substantial intervening losses.

Our results thus far relate to industrial pricing behavior. Formation of prices in the agricultural and service sectors has not
been examined. Yet there is reason to believe that divergences

11. These rank correlation coefficients are calculated from price and quan-
tity data presented in Samuel A. Morley, "Inflation and Stagnation in Brazil,"
Economic Development and Cultural Change 19 (January 1971): 190, 192.
The value of −.44 is significant at the 5 percent level, that of −.21 is not.
What is relevant, however, is not merely the level of statistical significance
but the recurrence of the phenomenon in different samples and time periods.

12. Estimated using from the indices of real industrial sales in São Paulo,
calculated from nominal values deflated by the price index. The coefficients
of rank correlation are −.45 and −.41 respectively, the first significant, the
second almost.

from competitive flexibility also abound there. A simple correlation of excess agricultural supply and changes in relative food prices from 1947 to 1968, while it shows the anticipated negative sign, is not statistically significant. Equally to the point, the effect is weak. An increase of 1 percent in the growth of supply for domestic consumption causes its relative final price to consumers to decline by only .3 percent. The effect on wholesale prices is twice as great.[13] The wedge of inefficient and noncompetitive distribution facilities explains the difference.

Even for services, price flexibility does not characterize an inflationary environment. Habit substitutes for market power during the short run. A pronounced discontinuity of service prices is evidenced in the monthly index numbers from the late 1950s through 1964. At the beginning of every year many prices would be automatically rescaled. This upward tendency was strengthened by the linking of rents and charges for public services to other indices like minimum wages themselves. This last effect, along with the obvious opportunity for increasing prices it signaled to industrialists, made wage readjustments the occasion for inflationary acceleration in all sectors quite apart from cost pressures. After 1964, without such rationalization, other signals and excuses nevertheless could be found.

This evidence is highly suggestive of deeply rooted and pervasive price inflexibility. To the degree that supply conditions in Brazil in 1966 were elastic at a price largely influenced by mark-up over unit cost, the continuing battle against inflation as prosecuted was not only futile, but even counterproductive. Important features of the stabilization program to regulate demand were increased indirect taxes and higher real interest rates. To the extent that both were passed along in the form of higher prices, the efforts at stabilization were partially cancelled. Once the exaggerations of excess demand generated by undisciplined governmental expenditures had disappeared, further aggregative polices could provoke only slackening growth. More-

13. The two regressions are of the form:

$$\frac{P_{A_t}/P_{T_t}}{P_{A_{t-1}}/P_{T_{t-1}}} = a + b\left[\frac{\Delta O_t}{O_{t-1}} - .6\frac{\Delta(Y/P)_t}{Y/P_{t-1}} - \frac{\Delta P_t}{P_{t-1}}\right]$$

P_A and P_T are the agricultural and total price indexes respectively; O_t is agricultural production for domestic consumption; Y/P, income per capita; and P population. The assumed elasticity of demand is .6. For the food component of the cost of living index, and of the wholesale price index respectively, the numerical results are as follows:

$y_1 = 1.00 - .0037X$, $R^2 = .09$; and $y_2 = 1.00 - .0075X$, $R^2 = .14$.

over, the commitment to free previously regulated prices in the public sector, in housing, and in imported inputs actually conflicted with stabilization. Not only did "corrective inflation" cause a once-and-for-all change in prices (previously repressed) but contrary to orthodox expectations these changes were in turn amplified, extended, and made continuing by pricing policies in other sectors — all without producing the desired supply responses in the short run.

The decision to proceed with such adjustments for their allocative effects testifies to the true priorities of the government. It was committed to the establishment of a functioning free market system in Brazil, perhaps even more than to the struggle against inflation. This larger objective helps to explain the apparent inconsistency of the government's policy of extensive monetary correction which necessarily reinforced inflationary forces. Even during the Castello Branco period, the principal aim was not stabilization; it was making market capitalism work. In the long run these goals were viewed as mutually compatible, indeed as indispensably linked; in the short run they might conflict — to the consistent disadvantage of stabilization.

Indeed, in the battle against inflation, which was slower and less successful than planned, the government persisted in orthodox policies — although their inefficiencies were painfully apparent by 1966 — partly in order to change the system. The perceived task was to alter the market behavior and mentality that brought about perverse results, rather than to try to achieve stabilization by accommodation. Orthodoxy was the chosen instrument to impose the discipline of a declining market upon those who persisted in their traditional ways. It was not an easy challenge, but to confront it successfully meant a great deal, as Campos fully appreciated:

> It is not easy to change habits or attitudes. Even less so when those habits and attitudes come from people profiting from inflation. . . . The great challenge that the government and the entrepreneurial and salaried classes have to confront is . . . that of re-creating conditions in order that free initiative may hold an economic and a social meaning in our country.[14]

In early 1967, the issue was still in doubt. To some extent, errors in the execution of orthodox policies were to blame. In

14. From a speech by Campos in April 1965 before the Clube Nacional, as quoted in Ianni, *Crisis in Brazil*, p. 174.

both 1964 and 1965 the money supply increased substantially, despite a public posture to the contrary. Prices correspondingly rose but without producing favorable perspectives in the real sector. Excessive preoccupation with the Treasury cash deficit, and too little with other factors causing monetary expansion contributed to this setback. In part, too, it was a deliberate stratagem in 1965 to counter the spreading industrial depression. Then in 1966 there was a reflexive and overstringent curbing of monetary growth. With prices inflexible, this precipitated the inevitable recession. A policy of continuing and gradual restriction would have offered a better test of the applicability of orthodoxy to the Brazilian experience, as well as a clearer verdict upon its ability to yield the definitive victory sought by Campos.

One can only speculate; for the economic policies of the new Costa e Silva government were based upon other principles. Of this there can be little doubt in intention and execution. The Economist Intelligence Unit's *Quarterly Review of Brazil* for April 1967 immediately and correctly characterized the different thinking of the new government's economic strategist, Antonio Delfim Neto: "Sr. Delfim said that in the past few months its [inflation's] character had changed, from demand-inflation to cost-inflation. . . . The fact that Sr. Delfim Neto has publicly stated that an inflation rate of 15 percent would be tolerated . . . is a radical departure from the previous administration's declared aim of defeating the inflation altogether" (pp. 6–7). Cost inflation was dealt with as a reality. Aggregate policies were relaxed. A larger deficit and greatly increased credit to the private sector led to considerable growth in the money supply. Quarterly data unequivocally confirm the timing of the change in policy from April on. The total quantity of money increased more from the end of March until the end of June than it had in the entire previous year; the same was true of private loans. Rather than respond by restraint to the large first-quarter deficit occasioned by the payment of obligations deferred by the previous government to the new year, that short-fall was virtually equaled in the second three months because of continued outlays.

But inflation did not accelerate; real output did instead. The increased money supply was absorbed into depleted balances, not only because of reductions in the nominal rate of interest, but also because of revised expectations of growth. Instead of extirpating the cancer of inflation, even fuller recognition of its continuation was conceded by extending monetary correction to the exchange rate itself. The phenomenon of administered prices, and the potential for their control, was explicitly conceded by the creation of a Price Control Council in the Finance Ministry. Henceforth, prices in the private sector would receive continuing scrutiny. By contrast, Campos's famous Portaria No. 71 offered market incentives in return for price restraint. These could, and apparently did, work but only in the short run. In sum, the new government was implicitly committing itself to a world in which prices were inflexible downward, and also upward except for strong demand pressures. In such a world inflationary expectations could be countered by growth better than restraint.

Heterodoxy produced results. From 1967 on, inflation stabilized at about the 20 percent level, and output grew rapidly. Yet these results did not herald the definitive solution to which Campos had committed himself. Of that he left no doubt in his critical comments on post-1967 government policy even after it had proven successful.[15] Such opposition is a measure of the ideological, rather than the technical, content of economic policies in Brazil after 1964. For despite all the attention focused upon the new, rational technocrats presumably independently formulating economic policy, their decisions inevitably have had an important political overlay.

Indeed, the very transition from economic orthodoxy to heterodoxy was a direct consequence of the limited political process of presidential succession in 1967. Three aspects were important. First, choice of a successor simultaneously posed the question within the military of the desirability of continued economic restraint. Second, the election, albeit indirect and predetermined, was accompanied by a presidential campaign in conscious imitation of the Mexican style. It inevitably invited internal pressure groups to offer their views upon economic policies. Seminars to guide the new president in economic affairs were offered, and choices and options could be seriously debated. And third, the previous economic ministers themselves could be replaced without discrediting their policies. The ministerial rigidity consciously adhered to by the military government could be legitimately breached. Change and continuity could be reconciled. The enforced political recess of the Revolution was not therefore the magic formula for guaranteeing the success of stabilization. Rather, the limited opening afforded by the political process in 1967 is a highly significant part of the tale.

The substitution of orthodoxy by heterodoxy was one conse-

15. See his reprinted collection of newspaper essays from *O Globo* in 1967 and 1968, published as *Ensaios contra maré* (Rio de Janeiro: APEC Editôra, 1969), esp. pp. 309–18, 361–68, and 379–98.

quence of presidential succession. Another was a diminution of external pressures and a greater mobilization of internal opinion. It is no secret that Campos's policies, if not the details of their execution, received the enthusiastic support of AID and the international lending agencies. The enthusiasm was more than passive. Brazil, during the 1964–67 period, ranked behind only India, Pakistan, and South Vietnam in net official aid receipts. AID program loans ranked as the prime contributor.[16] Because they were general in character, designed to finance the foreign exchange requirements of the government's policies, and because they were disbursed only after quarterly reviews, these loans necessarily involved close association between American and Brazilian policy makers. Furthermore, because advances from the International Monetary Fund were involved, the program loan negotiations and reviews went beyond American participation. The foreign influence was fully on the side of orthodoxy.

In effect, by closing down the internal political process and giving virtual carte blanche to Campos and Bulhões, the military government had also opted for magnifying the external influence upon domestic economic policy. It is difficult to evaluate how significant external pressures were in shaping decisions. They were probably greater than most Brazilian officials would like to admit, while considerably less than the foreigners believed. Even if foreign counsel had been fully correct in its evaluation, such an imbalance between internal and external access to policy makers probably could not have long persisted. In fact, the outsiders' advice largely proved wrong. Program agreements did not stimulate development. The accumulation of foreign exchange obtained under program agreements went not to finance required imports but to debt repayment: the slower rates of growth had diminished considerably the demand for foreign intermediate and capital goods. In effect, the program loans contributed to debt realignment rather than served as a cushion against the internal disruptions of stabilization. Nor was significant foreign investment forthcoming to stimulate again the introduction of new products and processes. The problem increasingly was one of inadequate demand, not insufficient resources. Yet in 1967 and early 1968 foreign influence was almost unanimously aligned against the experimental departure from the orthodoxy of the Castello Branco years. Disbursement of the

16. See Carlos Díaz-Alejandro. "Some Aspects of the Brazilian Experience with Foreign Aid," in *Trade, Balance of Payments, and Growth*, ed. J. N. Bhagwati et al. (Amsterdam: North Holland Publishing Company, 1971), pp. 443–72.

program loans was considerably delayed for the first time, and prolonged negotiations were required to satisfy AID officials that the new policies continued the previous emphasis upon stabilization.[17]

With increased confidence in their own abilities after successfully reinitiating growth, the new economic policy makers after 1967 never again were to be as close to, or dependent upon, foreign influences. There is a certain irony in this sequence. The American presence in Brazil after 1964 was committed to restoration of constitutional processes and electoral participation. Yet simultaneously it preached the wisdom of an orthodox economic stabilization program whose greatest probability of success lay in continuing political restrictiveness. When the economy had turned around, American influence in the political sphere was diminished by its own prior inconsistency and inflexibility in the economic.

This analysis of stabilization policy suggests that the widely accepted role of military support and the political hiatus after 1964 in curbing Brazilian inflation must be qualified. There is no doubt that a chaotic situation requiring strong executive measures existed in 1963 and early 1964. Even the best of stabilization policies would have exerted depressive effects upon the real sector. It does seem, however, that the restrictive efforts through 1967 were on occasion mismanaged and, more fundamentally, misdirected. Fiscal policy bore the brunt of reducing aggregate demand, while the role of monetary control was more erratic. Even after it became clear that such instruments were not sufficient, faith in their efficacy remained undiminished — as if it were preferable to accept slower rates of economic activity and stagnant real income to *create* the type of economy and society in which such policies could work rather than to stabilize at minimum cost.

One instrument that was particularly abused in this fashion was wage policy, which, as the next section indicates, has had important implications for the distribution of income and has imposed an inordinate cost to stabilization efforts.

WAGE POLICY AND INCOME DISTRIBUTION

Upon taking power in April 1964, the options open to the government in the determination of wage policy were limited

17. See U.S., Senate Subcommittee on Western Hemisphere Affairs of the Senate Foreign Relations Committee, *United States Policies and Programs in Brazil*, 92nd Cong., 1st sess., p. 188.

indeed. There was immediate pressure for salary increases from civil servants. Minimum wages in the private sector had already been doubled in February under the Goulart regime. Government employees could hardly be expected to fare less well in the immediate aftermath of the transition. Military salaries were adjusted more than proportionately (120 percent) right away and civil employees received an increase of 100 percent in June. Only thereafter did the Castello Branco government formulate its policy of wage restraints applicable to the minimum wage and the public sector; in 1965 salary determination in the private sector was included as well. The basic principle of the policy was substitution of the previous peak-to-peak adjustments for inflation by interval calculations. Instead of an increase in nominal wages designed to recover the instantaneous peak real income achieved at the time of the previous adjustment, the new wage would reconstitute for the next year the *average* real wage of the previous two years. Since inflation had been accelerating, and had eroded the real wage in the early 1960s, the average was smaller than the peak.[18] The formula thus provided for lesser nominal wage increases designed to reduce cost pressures upon prices and thereby prove self-fulfilling.

Implementation of the policy also required an estimate of prospective inflation for the next 12 months, for which the nominal wage increase would compensate. This so-called inflationary residual was consistently, and deliberately, underestimated. Real wages therefore were systematically reduced between 1964 and 1967, 20 percent in the case of the minimum wage, and somewhat less for industrial wages. Despite the theoretical niceties of the formulation, the policy as practiced be-

18. An algebraic and graphic formulation may help. Let W_t be the nominal wage set at time t and continuing until $t+1$, and P a continuously variable price level. Then to compensate for inflation between t and $t+1$, the peak-to-peak adjustment implies a wage of W_{t+1}/P_{t+1}, and therefore a nominal wage increase equal to the rate of price increase:

$$W_{t+1}/W_t = P_{t+1}/P_t.$$

The interval calculation substitutes

$$\frac{\sum_{i=-24}^{0} W/P_i}{24}$$

as the target real wage, where W and P_t are monthly values over the previous two years. Since W_t/P_t at the moment of adjustment necessarily exceeds

came one of maximum wage containment.[19] As a consequence, the average real minimum wage received in 1967, despite such additional current fringes as the thirteenth monthly salary, family allowances, as well as improved future claims on pension funds, was at least 5 percent *smaller* than its 1955 level. Even though the income per capita was more than a third as great in 1967, twelve years of economic growth had come to naught for the unskilled wage earners of Brazil.

The economic basis for proceeding so forcefully against wages was fragile at best. To be sure, there were many advocates in the government camp who claimed that wages were an autonomous factor in the acceleration of inflation in the late 1950s and early 1960s. Such a prominent advocate of orthodoxy as Gudin wrote in 1961 (and continued to preach thereafter):

> This means that in the case of the Brazilian inflation, i.e., of the wage-price spiral in Brazil, it was not the increase in prices that determined the readjustment of salaries, but principally, *the elevation of real wages that pushed prices up*.[20]

Conclusions like this were based upon the evidence that the real minimum wage had increased somewhat more than per capita

$$\frac{\overline{\Sigma W_i P_i}}{24}$$ — because W_t was fixed and P_t was increasing — the required nominal wages increase was correspondingly diminished. In graphic terms, the alternative wage targets may be represented as follows:

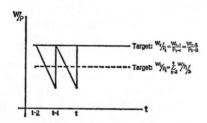

19. The minimum-wage data are presented in table 3.1. For industrial wages see Peter Gregory, "Evolution of Industrial Wages and Wage Policy in Brazil, 1959–1967," unpublished AID report, September 1968. Deflated by an *industrial* price index, real wages fell less; still in 1968 they were below their 1964 level.

20. Eugênio Gudin, *Análise de problemas brasileiros, 1958–1964* (Rio de Janeiro: Agir, 1965), p. 490. Italics in the original.

income between 1952 and October 1961. As illustrated in table 3.2, however, the discrepancy is modest. Furthermore, two other factors considerably dilute the force of the argument. Productivity in the urban sector, to which the minimum wage pertained, undoubtedly had increased more rapidly than in the economy as a whole. Thus the divergence was not necessarily a source of increased costs. This is the case even if full account is taken of the increased surcharges borne by employers as calculated in table 3.2. More significantly, the evolution of wage increases dur-

Table 3.2. Minimum Wages and Per Capita Income, 1952–64
(1952 = 100)

		Real minimum wages[a]	Real minimum wage costs[b]	Per capita income
January	1952	110		
	1952	100	100	100
	1953	88	87	100
July	1954	143		
	1954	106	99	106
	1955	116	116	110
August	1956	150		
	1956	118	118	111
	1957	131	129	116
	1958	114	112	121
January	1959	159		
	1959	131	123	124
October	1960	149		
	1960	114	119	133
October	1961	151		
	1961	132	120	141
	1962	112	110	144
January	1963	138		
	1963	105	101	142
February	1964	132		
	1964	103	111	142

SOURCE: Real minimum wages adapted from Peter Gregory, "Evolution of Industrial Wages and Wage Policy in Brazil, 1959–1967," unpublished AID report, September 1968, table 5; real minimum costs adapted from Edmar Bacha et al., *Encargos trabilhistas e absorção de mão-de-obra*, Relatório de Pesquisa no. 12 (Rio de Janeiro: IPEA/INPES, 1972), table 3.7.
[a] Nominal minimum wage in Guanabara deflated by cost-of-living index.
[b] Nominal minimum wage in Guanabara incremented by all employer payments, whether to employee or not, and deflated by industrial price index.

ing the 1950s reveals that the large nominal increases of 1954 and 1956 had not been substantially eroded by inflation. Through 1957, a real distributional shift in favor of wages had been effected, as the increased share of wages in urban income testifies. Thereafter the 1952 base loses significance unless we presume an implausibly long lag in adjustments by employers.

The relevant question is what nominal wage policy in 1956 would have been consistent with limited inflation and continued real wage gains. To answer it we must take calendar 1955 as the base, after the July 1954 wage increase had been reflected in price adjustments. Supposing the objective to be an annual rate of inflation of 15 percent over the next 30 months—representing mild deceleration of current trends—the solution is a minimum wage in current terms of NCr$3.60 per month.[21] The actual level decreed in August 1956 was NCr$3.80, some 6 percent greater than the optimal figure. Thus wage policy *was* compatible with monetary and fiscal policies designed to check gathering of inflationary momentum. And in fact through 1957 and for much of 1958, price increases were kept in check, inflation abated somewhat, and real minimum wages averaged modestly above their 1955 level.

By the same standard, the identical percentage nominal increase granted in January 1959 comes within an equivalently narrow range of a wage compatible with an inflation of 15 percent. The consequences this time were not the same. The announcement of the increase coincided with implementation of the Lucas Lopes stabilization program, and the signal provided to entrepreneurs immediately to adjust their prices with impunity complicated matters considerably. Critics of the governmental wage decision pointed to the 10 percent increase in prices in February as evidence of its excessiveness. Yet the principal contributor to the rise was foodstuffs, the component least affected on the cost side. At that time greater restraint was probably

21. The calculation presumes a constant income share for labor and a constant share of labor costs in total costs. Then prices and wages rise by a differential whose size depends upon the productivity increase in that period. Thus for an inflation of 15 percent annually, wages could increase at 17.5 percent *after* their 1955 annual level had been regained. To recapture that level in August 1956 implied an increase in nominal wages of 20 percent. Since nominal wages were to be fixed once and for all, while the objective was an *average* real salary over the next 30 months the calculation of the nominal wage increase reduces to:

$$\frac{1.2 + 1.2(1.175)^{2.5}}{2} = 1.5$$

called for, but more for its psychological than for its real effect. To a considerable degree because of the fiscal and monetary consequences of the abnormal acquisition of coffee stocks, the government ultimately could not hold the line.

As inflation accelerated in 1959 and 1960, reducing real wages considerably, pressures for earlier readjustment of the nominal minimum wage increased, and one was conceded after only 21 months. Thereafter, although larger percentage nominal readjustments were granted and their period of applicability shortened, the real minimum wage never again reached its January 1959 level. It fell progressively behind in the dizzying swirl of inflation.

Industrial wages followed a pattern somewhat at variance with that of the minimum wage. They lagged well behind productivity change in the period from 1955 to 1959, and thereafter showed some tendency to catch up. In particular, the 1963 data reflect an increase of average wages in *real* terms of 13 percent over 1962. Increasing militancy of labor unions, which elicited considerable and overt governmental sympathy, explain the results of the early 1960s. The autonomous inflationary impact created is hard to gauge because of the earlier lag. Nor must the results in manufactures, representing a small proportion of the labor force, be extrapolated to the many service activities where the minimum wage had greater impact.

This analysis suggests that the wholehearted commitment of the new government to the need to put an end to virulence of wage inflation had a dubious scientific basis. Gudin himself, writing later less polemically and more contemplatively, is inclined to agree:

> The main cause [of inflation] was the excess of federal expenditures over receipts. . . . It may also be said of wages that they rose with the increases in the cost of living *resulting* from federal deficits. Except for the 1954 wage push (forced by Goulart under the Vargas administration) discrepancies in the adjustment of minimum wages were not important.[22]

This is not, however, to defend the minimum wage policy as practiced. Largely because of the discreteness of the adjustments and and the uncertainty of their duration, increased wages were

22. Eugênio Gudin, "The Chief Characteristics of the Postwar Economic Development of Brazil," in *The Economy of Brazil*, ed. Howard S. Ellis (Berkeley: University of California Press, 1969), p. 17. Italics mine.

passed along more than proportionally by employers in the early 1960s. Instead of defending the standard of living of the unskilled as inflation accelerated, the increases in nominal salaries failed utterly to keep pace. One must therefore distinguish the advantage entrepreneurs took of the wage increases to defend and extend their income share from a causal influence of an excessive wage share upon the price level.

Nonetheless, to tie the preceding inflation to exorbitant wage demands and to act upon such a conviction had considerable ideological attraction. The great fear in March 1964 was of an imminent populist uprising: "The prospect of a union dictatorship rises above the national community, contributing to the aggravation of inflation from which the Brazilian people have suffered so." [23] The government could be in the position of pursuing a politically attractive policy antagonistic to urban workers that was wholly justified on technical grounds.

The consequences of such a program are not difficult to guess. Table 3.3 measures the recorded change in real monthly income between 1960 and 1970 for three distinct groups: urban and rural workers and entrepreneurs. The data derive from two comparable population samples, one from the census, the other from the Pesquisa Nacional por Amostra de Domicílios, and they have been arrayed for identical quarters to avoid seasonal biases.

For our purposes, two basic conclusions emerge. The first is the clear disparity between August 1960 and third quarter 1969 in the paths of earnings of entrepreneurs and the wages of employees in the nonagricultural sector. While the latter increase for all Brazil by 20 percent, the former are larger by a half. Nonagricultural wages are first available in 1969. Yet because wages increased more rapidly in 1968 and thereafter, we may infer that the comparison, if available, would have been worse in 1968, and even more so in 1967. This conclusion is borne out by the behavior of incomes of all employees — available for 1968 — after the 1960 total is adjusted to reflect the later sectoral mix. Between 1960 and 1968 wages are essentially constant. A potentially more accurate picture, because the data are more homogeneous, is possible by restricting comparisons to the industrial states of Guanabara, Rio de Janeiro, and São Paulo. Here we find equally dramatic evidence of redistribution between the two urban classes. In the case of the former states, nonagri-

23. From a confidential document delivered to the President by General Pery Constant Bevilacqua, Chief of Staff, on 31 March 1964. Quoted in Ianni, *Crisis in Brazil*, p. 138.

Table 3.3. Mean Monthly Incomes: 1960, 1968-70
(1960 NCr$)

	1960 August	1968 3rd qtr.	1969 1st qtr.	1969 3rd qtr.	1970 1st qtr.
Brazil[a]					
Agricultural employees	2.6	—[b]	2.4	2.4	2.5
Nonagricultural employees	8.0	—	9.6	9.9	10.5
All employees	6.6				
	(7.3)[c]	8.1	8.6	8.9	9.4
Nonagricultural employers and self-employed[d]	14.0	19.5	20.6	22.5	19.5
Guanabara and Rio de Janeiro					
Agricultural employees	3.0	—	3.1	3.0	3.3
Nonagricultural employees	11.0	—	11.8	11.6	12.1
All employees	10.1				
	(10.7)[c]	10.9	11.6	11.3	11.8
Nonagricultural employers and self-employed[d]	18.3	22.6	29.0	27.1	24.5
São Paulo					
Agricultural employees	3.4	—	3.4	3.6	3.8
Nonagricultural employees	9.3	—	11.2	11.8	12.7
All employees	8.0				
	(8.9)[c]	9.7	10.4	11.3	11.9
Nonagricultural employers and self-employed[d]	20.2	28.0	29.9	34.4	31.2
Northeast					
Agricultural employees	2.0	—	1.9	1.9	1.9
Nonagricultural employees	4.8	—	7.3	7.4	7.6
All employees	3.6				
	(3.9)[c]	5.7	5.7	5.7	5.9
Nonagricultural employers and self-employed[d]	6.6	10.2	11.6	13.0	10.0

[a] Excludes the North and Central-West regions.

[b] Dash indicates data not available.

[c] Total calculated on basis of 1969 third quarter agricultural and nonagricultural weights.

[d] Excluding fishing and extractive industries and personal services.

SOURCES AND METHOD: The data presented in table 3.3 come from two sources, the Demographic Census of 1960 and the Pesquisa Nacional por Amostra de Domicílios (PNAD) for 1968-70. The 1960 information is taken from a sample of about 11,000 families, while the PNAD sample contains 4,641 households.

In using the information for comparative purposes there are three problems: comparability of the population subsets in 1960 and later; comparability of income in real terms; and assignment of comparable mean incomes to the open-ended income groups. To verify that the subgroups as defined in the PNAD

Table 3.3 (*Continued*)

and replicated from the 1960 sample were comparable, the proportions of the labor force in each category were calculated for the two dates. The results are shown below for the three-region total:

	1960 Census	*1968 PNAD*
Employees		
Agriculture	13.5	10.7
Nonagriculture	33.7	42.2
Employers		
Nonagriculture	11.9	13.4

The proportions are of appropriate orders of magnitude; the principal difference is an expected increase in the relative number of employees in the nonagricultural sector.

To deal with inflation, all PNAD nominal income ranges were converted to 1960 cruzeiros by use of a cost-of-living index. Use of this measure, rather than the wholesale price index, say, seems more appropriate to the task of determining welfare changes over the interval. The cost-of-living index rose somewhat more rapidly than the wholesale price index because of increases in rents and public services; these effects of the stabilization program should be included. The index is that for Guanabara and readily available in the *Conjuntura Econômica*. Note that the choice of index is irrelevent for comparisons among groups and only modestly affects changes over time.

To calculate the mean of the upper-ended income classes from the PNAD surveys a method consistent with that used in 1960 was adopted. The logarithmic linear relationship between cumulated population with incomes greater than x, and income was calculated using the last two classes. From this coefficient, b, the exponent of a Pareto income distribution, the mean of the open-ended class is calculated as $\frac{b}{b-1}$ times the lower limit of the class. The last two classes alone were used for the calculation since the hypothesis of a single Pareto distribution over the entire income range was rejected for 1960. Rather the slope at the upper end is much steeper, and use of the coefficient for the entire income range would overstate the mean. Graphical analysis confirmed this same regularity in the PNAD data. In the distribution of employees in 1968, the open-ended class begins at income levels substantially lower than those for other years, and correspondingly incorporates a larger proportion of the population. A different method was therefore required. Specifically, it was assumed that the upper-income class was distributed like that in the first quarter of 1969 for which more detailed data are available.

Finally, because nonagricultural employees reported monthly rather than annual incomes, the estimated salary was increased by a factor of 13/12. This allows for the additional thirteenth monthly salary that was required after December 1962, and which likely does not appear in the money wages reported. Other direct fringes are paid on a monthly basis and should be reflected in the incomes. Increases in indirect fringes paid by employers to pension funds are

Table 3.3 (*Continued*)

excluded because a large part of them compensate for other benefits of job security previously enjoyed.

The concept of income used in the PNAD sample and maintained for 1960 is money income received. Real income, particularly in the agricultural sector where population for self-consumption is significant, is greater than money receipts, and distributed somewhat more equally as well. Such adjustments have in fact been made in studying the 1960 income distribution, and are necessary to any satisfactory comparison of sectoral divergences. For comparisons over a short interval, as here, involving homogeneous population subgroups, the monetary magnitudes are an acceptable substitute.

cultural employees exhibit modest growth while there is an evident gain for employers and self-employed. In São Paulo, the divergence between rates of increase of 20 and 48 percent correspond to national averages. In sum, the ratio of profits to average rates and salaries in the urban sector rose noticeably between 1960 and 1968; thereafter, while improving, it did not regain its 1960 value.

It is reasonably certain from the annual movements both of the average industrial wage and the minimum wage that the largest part of the gap would have opened between 1964 and 1967 as a consequence of stabilization policies. This is true despite the earlier corrosive effect of inflation upon real minimum wages. Unpublished distributional data underlying the national accounts reinforce this impression. The share of labor income in the urban sector (despite inclusion of some imputed entrepreneurial earnings) declines by more than two percentage points between 1965 and 1966, a larger change than in any of the preceding five years when it had been a stable 59 to 60 percent.[24] Unfortunately data for more recent years are unavailable. Such a decline in share further denies, as do the statistics of industrial employment, compensation for lower real wages in the form of correspondingly increased employment opportunities.

One further observation is relevant with regard to the internal distribution of wages and salaries. From other independent data, we know that, among industrial employees, workers (as opposed to salaried administrative personnel) experienced larger declines in real wages between 1962–63 and 1967, and smaller gains in 1968 and 1969. Even among production workers, there has been some tendency for interindustrial wage differentials to increase

24. The data are available in Carlos G. Langoni, "A Study in Economic Growth: The Brazilian Case" (Ph.D. diss., University of Chicago, 1970), p. 163.

between the traditional industries like textiles, foodstuffs, and so on, and the more dynamic sectors producing consumer durables and capital goods.[25] Note as well from table 3.3 that the regional differential in wages had widened after 1968, having narrowed previously. These circumstances help to explain why the increase in real income of urban workers after 1967 may have been associated with increasing inequality among themselves.[26] The continuing post-1967 wage limitations seem to have been more effective for the unskilled than for the more qualified.

The net result of the various shifts among and within classes appears to be a dramatic increase in the inequality of the nonagricultural income distribution between 1960 and 1970. The Gini coefficient calculated directly from the respective decennial censuses increases from .49 to .56, a substantial change indeed for such a short period. The extent of the growing inequality is vividly captured by the estimated share of income received in the upper reaches of the distribution: 5.8 percent of those gainfully employed in nonagricultural activities in 1960 received 29.8 percent of monetary income; in 1970, an equivalent 5.8 percent received 37.9 percent.[27] It is difficult to hold stabilization (and subsequent) policies blameless for this outcome.

Table 3.3 speaks not only to urban incomes, but also agricultural wages. Their stagnation from 1960 on, and even after 1961, is a second significant finding. It has sometimes been argued that the reduction in urban real wages at least had a positive counterpart in improved conditions in the countryside and a reduced income differential. New policies like guaranteed

25. These data on the average level of wages and their distribution after 1966 come from the Industrial Registers and are published in IBGE, *Anuário Estatístico*.

26. Of the two changes in Gini coefficients for urban employees from first quarter 1969 to third quarter 1969 to first quarter 1970 for each region, all are positive for São Paulo and Guanabara, and one each for the Northeast and Brazil as a whole. Even more significant, in every region except the Northeast, the value for first quarter 1970 is between 4 and 10 percent greater than one year earlier, and the Northeast is characterized by little change in the average.

27. The Gini coefficients in the text exclude those economically active and reporting zero incomes. Including family workers does not change the calculated deterioration very much: .50 to .58. The result in the text seems more appropriate since no distinction is made in 1970 between zero income and nonreporting. For more discussion of the 1960 and 1970 income distributions see my "Brazilian Size Distribution of Income," *American Economic Review* 62 (May 1972): 391–402.

agricultural minimum prices, for example, did apparently alter the terms of trade in favor of the rural sector according to available indices. Yet the data here show no evidence of any sustained effect upon the fortunes of agricultural laborers except in São Paulo, and these at a rate inferior to the gain of nonagricultural employees.

Other evidence corroborates and extends this conclusion. Agricultural wages received as calculated in *Conjuntura Econômica* are constant in real terms from their initial tabulation in 1966 through 1970.[28] The 1970 preliminary census tabulation, deflated by the cost of living, indicates no increase over the decade in average monetary income for those engaged in agricultural pursuits, including proprietors, sharecroppers, administrators, and workers. While the average remained constant, and indeed inequality measured by the Gini coefficient slightly diminished, the upper extreme of the distribution tells a different tale: .55 percent of the renumerated labor force commanded 10.7 percent of the income in 1970; an almost double .95 percent in 1960 claimed a proportionately smaller 13.4 percent.[29] While inclusion of income in kind would increase the mean at both dates, and allowance for family workers would alter the distributions somewhat, the validity of the basic result is not sensitive to these adjustments. Neither rural workers nor any but the largest proprietors apparently realized significant improvement in their incomes over the decade.

These distributional consequences cannot be ignored in evaluating the post-1964 economic accomplishments. The wage policy, instead of receiving kudos for its ingenious principles, merits a rather more reserved reception for its application. The decline in urban real wages during stabilization accurately measures the degree to which the government was unable to attain its inflation targets. Such a margin did make matters easier for the government and ultimately helped to control inflation. But the social cost of the policy and its limited technical justification cannot be ignored, especially since declining real wages between 1964 and 1967 did not lead to increased employment absorption, nor is there evidence of significant response since.[30]

28. See *Conjuntura Econômica* (July 1971), pp. 84–106.

29. These results are discussed in my "Brazilian Size Distribution of Income."

30. Edmar Bacha reports statistically significant, but small, elasticities for the cost of labor in determining employment over the 1949–69 period. For industry as a whole, the value is .24. Note also that over the 1966–69 period, when costs rose slowly, the predicted employment increase is sub-

The absence of formal politics was necessary to continue pursuit of such a stabilization strategy. Wage compression of this sort would have been impossible under a freer regime. But that does not mean that successful stabilization was exclusively dependent upon income redistribution. Other options were present. More vigorous and direct action upon prices in 1964 and 1965 would have provided an additional and powerful policy instrument. So too, greater restraint upon governmental military expenditures could have relieved fiscal pressures and freed up larger tax incentives to stimulate economic activity.

The latter technically feasible alternative was foreclosed by the need to unify the one remaining significant political entity in the country, the armed forces. The importance of military wage increases was therefore considerable, and it is not surprising that Castello Branco included it as one of the principal aims of the Revolution in one of his speeches at the Superior War College:

> The policy of the revolutionary government has been that of supporting the reorganization of national power; restructuring the economy and finances of the country; . . . and adjusting the wages of the armed forces.[31]

This objective was not reduced in priority by the rapid increase in wages that had taken place previously. Expenditures for military personnel in 1961 were only a fourth of the total direct federal outlays for wages in that year, rising in the next two to about 45 percent. Thereafter in 1964 and 1965 they amounted to more than half of total wages and salaries. In the latter year military salaries represented 1.3 percent of gross domestic product.[32] The reallocation of priorities was not temporary. The military share of budgeted expenditures rose to as much as 25 percent in 1968. (From 1957 to 1963 its share had declined from 29.2 percent to 15.2 percent.[33]) The ideology of the Revolution produced its own inflationary pressures, hardly different from

stantially greater than that realized. This means a wage-constraint policy did not succeed in creating many more job opportunities. See Edmar Bacha et al., *Encargos trabilhistas e absorção de mão-de-obra*, Relatórios de Pesquisa, no. 12 (Rio de Janeiro: IPEA/INPES, 1972).

31. Inaugural lecture of Castello Branco in the Superior War College, March 1965, as cited by Ianni, *Crisis in Brazil*, p. 173.

32. Centro de Estudos Fiscais, *O sector público federal na economia brasileira*, vol. 2 (Rio de Janeiro: Fundação Getúlio Vargas, 1967).

33. Calculated from the distribution of budgetary expenses as reported in the *Anuário Estatístico*. Outlays not covered by the original budgetary authorization are therefore excluded.

those arising from previous political bargaining over the budget. What was new was the ability to impose reductions in outlay elsewhere, to reconcile divergent interests by fiat, and to pursue restrictive wage policies despite their unpopularity.

ACCELERATION OF ECONOMIC GROWTH

Thus far our concern has been with the stabilization program proper. The aftermath, the impressive growth from 1968 through the present, and the evidences of widespread institutional change has not yet fully figured. Yet it is this recent record, even more than the slowing of inflation, that has rightfully made the Brazilian experience so prominent internationally. There is a widespread belief that Delfim Neto's greater accommodation to the indigenous realities, together with the earlier Campos reforms, has provided a firm basis for continuing Brazilian development. Five years do not constitute a secular trend, however, even for those afflicted with myopia. It is therefore useful to place these current accomplishments in a broader perspective.

The Brazilian economic model now evolving is forthrightly capitalistic in inspiration. Its driving force is individual behavior guided by market signals. The role of the government is both to perfect markets, as well as to intensify the signals. The two areas that have attracted most prominent attention have been the capital market and foreign trade. Both are central to the present strategy. Improved financial intermediation is essential to the noncoercive provision of national savings adequate to higher growth rates. Incentives for exports and receptivity to foreign investment establish a continuing supply of foreign exchange to purchase imports from abroad.

In response to the stimuli of tax deductions to purchasers of stocks and of tax concessions to firms raising capital in this fashion, the securities market has rapidly developed in recent years. Within the year 1970–71 the index of stock prices quadrupled; and a technical guide to investing in the market was on the list of best sellers in July 1971. The recent decline in prices has now eliminated the previous euphoria; it has not greatly dampened the volume of transactions. While new capital raised by sale of equities shows much less pronounced increase than simple asset transfer, this external source of investment finance is clearly of some importance now.[34] The government has recently elaborated

34. For a good treatment of government policies aimed at establishing a functioning capital market see David Trubek, "Law, Planning and the Development of the Brazilian Capital Market," *Bulletin of the Institute of Finance,* NYU Graduate School of Business, nos. 72–73 (April 1971).

new tax incentives to encourage both further "democratization" of capital by extending share ownership and consolidation of national firms to enhance their competitiveness with foreign investment.

The revitalized securities market and its associated institutions do not represent the only financial innovation. The creation and rapid growth of the National Housing Bank is also important as a source of savings and determinant of investment. The bank's special characteristic is its growing revenue base, financed by compulsory contributions from payroll taxes to the reorganized social security system. Resources in turn are committed to finance residential construction, which has responded handsomely to the availability of funds. Yet in its earliest phases, since applications for mortgages lagged behind supply of savings, the bank's most important contribution was to finance the federal cash deficit by purchase of government bonds.

One pillar of government policy thus is stimulation of private savings, both voluntary and compulsory, through a variety of mechanisms. Even the recent Programa de Integração Social, a nominally redistributive channel, is projected to increase net private savings by an average of 7.5 percent annually over the next five years.[35] Another government priority is emphasis upon exports as a mechanism for financing foreign exchange requirements. Generous allowances, largely in the form of excise tax rebates, are conceded to exporters of manufactures. A recent estimate calculates the total effect of the incentives as enabling an export price as much as 40 percent lower than for domestic sales without prejudicing profits. This differential is due more to the subsidy component inherent in the rebates than to simple exemption from indirect taxes.[36] In response, exports of manufactures neared $500 million in 1971, and they are continuing their spectacular growth in 1972. They now account for about a fifth of total exports, compared to less than 5 percent in 1964. For all exports, the policy of continuous devaluation to accompany internal inflation has considerably reduced the risks of loss, and

35. This is the percentage increment in savings assuming the 1970 private rate remained constant. See Affonso Celso Pastore and José Roberto Mendonça de Barros, "O programa de integração social e a mobilização de recursos para o desenvolvimento," Estudos Econômicos 2, no. 4 (1972): 113–27.

36. Originally the export policy merely exempted sales abroad from internal excises. This enabled more equitable conditions of competition. Beginning in 1968 the policy was extended to include subsidy rebates that currently may amount to as much as 30 percent of the value of the product. See Carlos von Doellinger et al., Exportações dinâmicas brasileiras (Rio de Janeiro: IPEA/INPES, 1971).

this certainly has undoubtedly contributed to more aggressive participation in international markets.

The attitude toward foreign capital inflow, which both supplements domestic savings as well as satisfies exchange requirements, has likewise been positive. Net capital entry has increased continuously since 1965, and the 1971 total of much more than $1 billion constitutes half of the foreign exchange generated by exports. Preliminary indications suggest a much greater inflow in 1972. In turn, a considerable segment of the capital inflow has gone to bolster international reserves, which in mid-1972 were estimated as $2.4 billion. Reserve accumulation in turn has facilitated a more advantageous term structure of foreign indebtedness. Short-term borrowing has declined steadily since 1968 when it was the principal means of closing the current account deficit. In each of the last three years, as Brazilian creditworthiness has increased, medium- and long-term debt have been the principal instruments of foreign participation.

Consistent with the commitment to private sector preeminence, the tendency toward governmental participation in the economy has been arrested in recent years. While the share has not undergone significant reduction — at least through 1969, the last year for which national accounts data are available — its composition has. Governmental consumption relative to that of the private sector is below its pre-Revolution levels, while investment has risen. Government thus continues as a potent force in the demand for resources and has sustained aggregate demand by its infrastructure expenditures. As private capital formation recovers, however, as has occurred in 1970 and 1971, this governmental role will presumably diminish even as it already has in the realm of consumption. Casual observation, and a structure of industrial growth oriented toward consumer durables, certainly suggests that the private sector has now become the principal expansive factor.

Such a capitalistic model of development has not escaped criticism from the Left. It has been challenged in the first place by the spector of inevitable stagnation caused by underconsumption.[37] This argument, tracing back principally to Celso Furtado, is a variation upon Malthus's original theme in his famous correspondence with Ricardo. An unequal income distribution gives rise to demands of a particular character, in this case consumer durables, whose production is capital intensive.

37. Celso Furtado, in his *Um projeto para o Brasil* (Rio de Janeiro: Editôra Saga, 1968), provides an updated version of his views, followed more recently by *Análise do modelo brasileiro* (Rio de Janeiro: Editôra Civilização Brasileira, 1972).

These factor proportions reduce employment opportunities —
the elasticity of substitution is limited — and ratify the existing
concentration of income. Because the narrow range of consumers in the market must soon find their tastes satiated, the
demand for such commodities cannot grow continuously. In
such an economic environment, the potential resultant savings of
the wealthy cannot be utilized because investors, failing to
foresee a vigorous market for their product, see no reason to
expand. Hence capitalist development is inevitably limited unless an increasingly dualistic income distribution can offset the
tendency to underconsumption. The early 1960s in Brazil, and
much of the rest of Latin America, were interpreted in these
terms; and now with some modification, even the present prosperity is similarly interpreted.

Apart from the contradiction inherent in the recent vigor of
the Brazilian economy, which is now unsatisfactorily explained
away as a consequence of the more unequal income distribution,
the basic and continuing assumptions of the underconsumption
approach are not very convincing. There is no evidence in empirical studies of Brazilian consumption of the rapid decline,
with increased income, in the elasticity of demand for durable
consumers' goods. The specific objectives of such demand may
alter, as it has in other countries, from radios to televisions to
cars, and so on, but neither so abruptly nor so definitively as to
create *permanent* stagnation. Rather, with resources immobile
in the short run, there may be a tendency toward cyclical instability. Over the long run, increasing aggregate income, hold-
ing the existing inequality constant, will typically contribute to
an expanded market for these consumers' goods by permitting
lower income purchasers to enter for the first time. The presumed sharp discontinuity in purchasing capacity that would
prevent this is not reflected in the facts.[38] As means are found
to secure favorable financing of durable purchases, moreover,
the extent of the market is given a further, once and for all

38. These conclusions derive from my study of consumption patterns during the 1960s, which was based primarily upon the cross-section data collected by the Fundação Getúlio Vargas but also included the time-series demand for automobiles. The stocks of consumer durables possessed by different
income classes in Rio in 1968 shows great continuity. *Every* type of consumer
durable, including automobiles, is represented as soon as family income exceeds two minimum salaries. See Companhia Central de Abastecimento do
Estado da Guanabara (COCEA), *Resultados da pesquisa sôbre consumo
alimentar e orçamentos familiares no grande Rio* (Rio de Janeiro, 1970), p.
61. I hope to publish these results shortly in the context of a fuller exposition and critique of the underconsumptionists.

boost. New financial intermediaries have in fact been created to play such a role in Brazil, exactly as they developed in the United States in the 1920s. Rapid growth of Brazilian automobile production at rates in excess of 20 percent for the last few years is related to the diffusion of demand reinforced by credit availability. While increases at such rates cannot be extrapolated, neither can it be anticipated that the market will fail to keep pace in the future owing to long-term income elasticities less than unity.

There is another related (but contradictory) avenue of attack that is also frequently employed to reject the viability of Brazilian market-oriented growth. Because of the limited size of the market, it is argued that diseconomies of scale will inevitably increase as more complex products with correspondingly narrower demand are introduced. This implies ever-greater capital output ratios. Hence growth will become continuously more costly in terms of savings. This view sets deficient savings as the limit to high rates of growth while the previous one argues underconsumption, although both are frequently invoked simultaneously. This critique envisages growth occurring through introduction of new products on an accelerating scale. For an economy as large as Brazil, there is not much evidence that such *increasing* diseconomies over time are the rule. Moreover, one of the important attributes of the present style is its greater openness. There is no reason why import substitution must continue as in the past. Those products Brazil cannot produce efficiently can be imported. For these reasons, the prospect of reduced growth from this side is not particularly menacing.

Both analyses attempt to relate the inequality of the income distribution and a limited market to stagnation. The wish may be father to the thought. Greater inequality undoubtedly and necessarily brings with it a different mix of goods and services, and hence a different structure of growth. The resultant pattern may not be desirable socially, nor even maximize the rate of growth. But inequality does not preclude growth altogether by inevitable internal contradiction, any more than growth requires inequality to be sustained.

In the face of the recent Brazilian expansion, many have abandoned their earlier adherence to these variants of the underconsumption approach in favor of an alternative interpretation. For them the present model of development is "fascist-colonial," self-sustainable but inevitably repressive and subordinate to American imperialism.[39] Yet such a designation ignores the full

39. Ianni, *Crisis in Brazil*, develops his arguments along this line.

implications of the rapid rise of exports that has occurred in recent years, a rise that continues to be central in the present growth strategy. Increased exports are a means of significantly *reduced* dependence upon the United States. They obviate the pressures for capital import to equilibrate the balance of payments. They provide the foreign exchange necessary to amortize past debt without resort to "swaps" and other potentially destabilizing short-term capital inflow. They permit selectivity in the acceptance of foreign investment and emphasis upon the transfer of technology as its raison d'être. They encourage competition among the advanced countries that assures more equitable distribution of the gains from trade. Note that the recent surge in exports has been accompanied by a dramatic decline in the share of the United States in Brazilian trade and a significant diversification in composition.

Exports of manufactures have special advantages. They can help to create greater decentralization of decision making and closer dependence upon national policies by multinational firms. Branches of the same international firm find themselves in a competitive situation with world market, regardless of original intention. Even when home office directive succeeds in suppressing such a possibility, the contest continues among different firms whose ability to compete depends upon the national site of production. Of the recent rapid growth of Brazilian exports of manufactures the largest share derives from the international firms and is directed to the Latin American market.[40] It remains to be seen whether this initial experience will lead to more aggressive and continued penetration of the markets of the industrialized countries themselves.

Industrial exports also provide an entry for the winds of competition too frequently absent in monopolistic national markets. More efficient firms benefit from the increased foreign demand relative to the less efficient. Thus a process of natural selection, less painful than that deriving from competitive imports but equally effective, can increase the average productivity of the economy. The need to match the rate of increase of efficiency abroad to retain markets provides a stimulus to technological change that may be more powerful and sure than the limited competition within national borders. It also provides pressure for domestic policies that can help to maintain productivity growth.

Much depends, of course, upon the maintenance of this export

40. Carlos von Doellinger, "Exportações Brasileiras: Diagnóstico e perspectivas," *Pesquisa e Planejamento* 1 (June 1971): 119 ff.

orientation and upon the feasibility of sustaining recent rates of increase. In the absence of a growing stream of foreign exchange receipts, the commitment to an open economic model could not be sustained. For while capital inflows can substitute in the short-term, the ability to service and amortize that debt depends upon export earnings. In particular this is the case now, since much more of the recent entry of capital has taken the guise of finance rather than equity participation. Private direct investment did not recover its level of the late 1950s and early 1960s until 1969. But then it declined again in the next two years. Total plant and equipment expenditures of United States subsidiaries have remained constant from 1968 through 1970 after recovery from their earlier troughs. Projections to 1972, based upon reports of individual firms, suggest much larger future commitments, and it is conceivable that direct investment will again become prominent.[41] Even were it to do so, accumulated debt obligations still necessitate buoyant exports. As of June 1972, the debt was estimated at $7.8 billion, after having almost doubled in three years. On a net basis, thereby discounting the large increase in reserves, the increment since 1969 still has been $1.6 billion, required to finance the growing current account deficit.

Export promotion is a policy that therefore is peculiarly consistent with the multiple objectives of the government. It provides a margin of confidence to assure potential investors that their present loans can be repaid. Yet at the same time it caters to nationalist sympathies both by demonstrating the unique ability of Brazilian industry to compete internationally and also by reducing the reliance on external finance. Those nationalist leanings, as evidenced by the firm stand for higher coffee prices despite opposition from the United States, the insistence upon a 200-mile offshore limit, and the prosecution of the Trans-Amazon project despite disapproval by international agencies, cannot be dismissed. They represent a potential constraint to certain policy options like increased reliance upon foreign savings that may alter significantly the capitalistic and open qualities of the present strategy.

I shall elaborate this theme presently. Before doing so, being unpersuaded by these criticisms of the Brazilian economic model,

41. Recently published projections of investment by manufacturing of United States corporations in Brazil indicate anticipated investment rising from an actual $181 million in 1970 to $386 million in 1972. *Survey of Current Business* 51 (September 1971): 29. These projections based on previous surveys have proven reasonably accurate.

let me focus on one potential frailty that has been largely ignored. That is the capacity of the economy to maintain its current momentum without cyclical interruption.

Cyclical processes have received little attention in developing
economies, largely because maintenance of aggregate demand
is assumed. The variations in growth in Brazil over the last
decade suggest, however, that it may be appropriate to view
the present economic boom in just such a context. Three distinct periods of real growth characterize recent development:
1957–62, 1963–67, and 1968– . The first corresponds to vigorous (average annual rates of 9.3 percent) industrial growth oriented toward import substitution. The second features the overriding influence of anti-inflationary policy, reduced capital formation, and a dramatic slowing in industrial expansion (2.4
percent); it was exactly such an experience that fostered belief
in stagnation as the outcome of diminished import substitution
possibilities. Finally, since 1968, growth has been accelerating,
and matches again the rapid increments of the late 1950s and
early 1960s.

There is more to this pattern than the inevitable perturbations caused by the mounting inflation and balance of payments
deficits and policies to deal with them. The import substitution
process by its very nature reinforces the susceptibility of the market to cyclical influences. Import substitution introduces new
lines of domestic production, either by replacing existing imports or feeding upon repressed demand. Such activities therefore experience initial rates of growth higher than those possible
over the longer term. This is true, of course, of new goods more
generally, where diffusion of knowledge concerning the product
and diminishing price provide an effect equivalent to the stimulus of repressed demand for import substitutes. The former is
the basis for logistic curves of growth of individual industries
as they have been observed in developed economies. The analogy
is not exact, however. First, import substitution typically involves much larger initial investments than accompanies the introduction of new goods because the market is already well
established. Import substitution activities therefore account for
a greater share of capital formation than would new products.
Moreover, in the specific instance of Brazil, the capital requirements of the industries implanted — durable consumer and capital goods — were already above average, because of the modern
technology and its associated economies of scale.

Second, import substitution is, virtually by definition, a
bunched process. Many new activities are undertaken within a

short interval through the stimulus of policy measures making domestic production more attractive. Again there is a parallel with innovations more generally, as Schumpeter emphasized, but again the specific incentives to import substitutes tend to exaggerate the phenomenon. Finally, and perhaps most important, the flexibility of resources in response to price signals and the accuracy of governmental policy — both of which are necessary to counteract the inherent cyclical tendencies of the process — are far less likely to be found in developing economies undergoing import substitution. Accompanying inflation and balance of payments problems mask the problem until too late, and aggregate policies are more likely to emerge than those directed toward rectifying the sectoral imbalances and rigidities that inherently characterize the surge of industrial growth.

In Brazil, this model seems to have been played out to its fullest. The import substitution investment boom of the late 1950s was soon followed by deceleration of product growth in the early 1960s and a diminished incentive to invest. The previous high, but continuously unattainable, rates of growth had become a benchmark against which the present was weighed. Because much of the newer investment was interrelated, with the final import-substituting products using new import-substituting inputs, the cumulative effect was magnified. Because much of it was foreign financed, the ultimate balance of payments crisis was intensified. Cognizance of the substantial existing excess capacity became increasingly widespread as growth rates failed to be maintained, just as disappointed holders of growth stocks become aware of price-earnings multiples in excess of 50 only when stock prices cease to rise. Thus by 1961 the growth rate in investment in capital equipment (as distinguished from construction) had already perceptibly slowed from its 1957–60 pace, even before increases in output turned down. When in 1962, the rate of expansion again was a disappointing 4 percent, the lack of dynamism in the industrial sector was further reinforced.[42]

Against such a cyclical backdrop, inadequately understood, policy making was made more difficult and ultimately failed. Government expenditures continued to mount on current account, and the rapidly mounting deficits had inflationary rather than growth consequences because the real sector was readjusting to

42. For the unpublished decomposition of investment into its major components, see Langoni, "A Study in Economic Growth," tables 66–68. The information really necessary to test the cycle model, involving sectoral investment, is not available.

a different structure of demands after the first bloom of import substitution. Then as inflation accelerated, there were periodic attempts to employ restraining monetary and fiscal policies. These were ineffective against the inflationary expectations that had cumulated, and when they proved unsuccessful, they were followed by a further round of stimulation to offset the short-run negative production effects of stabilization. Adding to the problem was the need to restrain imports and curtail domestic income, owing to servicing obligations on the debt incurred to finance the import substitution process. The worst of all worlds was experienced — continually slowing real growth, progressively higher inflation, and an insoluble balance of payments deficit.

After 1964, and for reasons associated both with the anti-inflationary policies and the overhang of prior capital accumulation, the economy grew only slowly. In 1965 investment in equipment was below its 1961 level. The proportion of total investment in product had declined to 12 percent, of which the public component was the largest share. Precisely in such a situation, as was elaborated earlier, an expansive and consistent monetary policy properly implemented could yield increases in real product without proportional consequences upon prices. Ultimately such a course was pursued in 1967 and contributed to the initiation of a recovery that has continued through the present.

An essential feature of this recent growth has been a low marginal capital-output ratio. While investment has grown more rapidly than product itself, its proportion to output is now estimated, without firm statistical basis, at no more than 20 percent. Thus substantial increases in productive capacity are yet to come and will undoubtedly serve as a basis for continuing expansion in the near future. The crucial question is whether excessive capital accumulation and foreign debt can be avoided this time.

Even without the imbalances introduced by import substitution, there is still an impressive variance in the fortunes of the diverse components of the manufacturing sector. São Paulo industrial sales growth by two digit sector in 1970 ranged from −1 percent to +45 percent! Automobiles continued their expansion while appliances reacted to their strong increase in 1969 by remaining stable. Foodstuffs grew at close to the average 13.1 percent, but clothing and shoes failed to increase. The variance in the national results is no smaller.[43] With both high and vari-

43. *Visão*, 14 February 1971, p. 154; *Conjuntura Econômica* (February 1972), pp. 28–36.

able rates, the sensitivity of private investment to cyclical influences cannot be dismissed. Nor can a debt requiring amortization and servicing to the extent of a third of export proceeds be casually disregarded. Amid the present euphoria such caution finds few adherents; takeoff is much more in vogue than cycles. But who, in the wake of the rapid growth of the Brazilian industrial park a decade ago, would have ventured that the economy possessed such structural weaknesses as later became apparent?

Yet because the government is more ready to respond to such tendencies, in terms of its resources and its information, and because underlying fiscal, monetary, and commercial policies are much more sound, I look for another more probable source of difficulty this time. The problem of adequate savings to satisfy investment requirements looms on the horizon. Up to the present, with excess capacity inherited from the past, growth has been inexpensive. Economic wisdom has consisted of encouragement to demand rather than austerity. To sustain continuing rates of growth on the order of 9 or 10 percent, however, will almost inevitably require much higher rates of savings than have been historically achieved in Brazil. Magnitudes of 25 percent now seem more necessary than the 15 percent of the 1950s. Such savings can come only by postponement of current consumption or by increased reliance on external sources.

Perfection of the capital market and provision of reasonable returns to savers are the basic elements of the government's strategy to evoke private resources; fiscal adequacy and limitations upon consumption outlays are the counterpart in the public sector. To the degree that domestic savings respond, the implicit political judgment regarding the divergent interests of present and future generations that is inherent in present policies will probably attract little comment. Should they not, however, these priorities and the question of income distribution will take center stage. Even now the debate appears to have begun. The apparently technical instruments applied to elicit domestic thrift have significant distributional implications. In deciding how much saving, the government can choose between augmenting private or public sources. In encouraging the former it can offer higher interest rates to individuals or incentives to corporations; in fostering the latter, it can opt for higher taxes or lesser public services. Very different wealth configurations and distributions of the benefits of growth result. What is disguised behind the veil of economics during rapid growth will reveal its true political character quickly as problems arise.

Reliance upon external sources of savings will not adequately blunt the issue. For it will inevitably reactivate nationalist aspirations to which present policies of export growth and more limited capital inflow have so far proved an effective answer. Already the government has had to respond to its critics. Foreign savings will also expose the economy to an important source of instability, a situation that was experienced a decade ago. Economic strategists of the present government are aware of the aggravating role earlier played by debt servicing requirements. The Central Bank has established a special unit to monitor the debt on an ongoing basis. Measures restricting short-term inflow have been taken. Thus far the burden of the debt has not weighed at all; but neither has capital inflow become a significant source of savings. Note, moreover, that foreign capital partially substitutes for domestic; a dollar of external investment does not add a dollar to total savings because some potential domestic accumulation is diverted to consumption instead. Debt obligations can increase without a proportional effect upon growth.

The discontinuity of the increase in savings necessitated by continuing growth at high rates will therefore almost inevitably call for a series of decisions going beyond the technical. The present political structure may not be sufficiently flexible to respond adequately. Failure to confront and mediate among the alternatives could easily permit a resurgence of inflation as a temporary equilibrating mechanism. Monetary correction would amplify and sustain such an outbreak. Commitment to solutions that worsen still further the income distribution such as even more attractive tax incentives can avoid that specter but may not be feasible any longer. There are signs that the Médici government has begun to recognize that welfare is not only a matter of relatives, but also of absolutes. For those at the bottom of the income distribution an immediate increase through redistribution can easily be better than a small share in even a rapidly increasing total. In 1960 a fourth of Brazilian *families* had an annual income, including imputed income in kind, of less than $420, and a decade later, the proportion is not much smaller despite intervening growth.

Present policies, while they seem to have succeeded in conciliating divergent interests up to now, are not in fact adequate to the task of offsetting the distributional consequences of significantly increased private savings. The Programa de Integração Nacional (PIN), also known as the Trans-Amazon project in its original guise, is unlikely to make more than a marginal contribution to the problem of poverty in the Northeast. Designed to attract the poor farmer from the Northeast and thus to treat both the problem of severe regional disparity and the special plight of the landless and small landholders, PIN is an ironic return to the Furtado strategy of outmigration. It is thus a recognition of the limited success that the 34/18 tax incentive program has had. The latter, by allowing deductions of up to 50 percent of tax liabilities on the condition of investment in industrial (and later agricultural) ventures in the Northeast, mobilized substantial investment. But by its very nature, modern industry even with growth rates in excess of 10 percent could not by itself resolve the problems of the region. Limited employment opportunities were created, and the predominantly agricultural population continued at levels of productivity incompatible with reasonable incomes.

Indeed, the prosperity and growth of recent years have succeeded only in increasing the regional contrast. The data of table 3.3 earlier showed both how nonagricultural incomes since 1968 have risen relative to agricultural and how the recent expansion has been more beneficial to São Paulo than to the Northeast. During the years of recession in the Center South, investment was more rapid in the Northeast and the differential in income probably modestly reduced. Now, however, the tendency seems again to have been reversed, as employment data also verify.[44]

The efficiency of colonization as solution to these distressing problems may be seriously doubted. The number of families to be relocated initially is discussed in the order of meager thousands, while the surplus in the Northeast is reckoned in the hundreds of thousands. Cost of relocation, quality of the land, and the very ability to attract large numbers of migrants remain in doubt. In turn, PIN is partially financed by a redirection of 30 percent of the existing tax incentives. Thus, whatever its impact, it is to some extent diluted by a compensating reduction in the resources destined for the Northeast and Amazon regions.

Simultaneously, the states and municipalities in the Northeast especially have been hurt due to the halving of the Fundo de Participação in early 1969. This had originally been set up to distribute 20 percent of Federal tax receipts. Since division among states was inverse to income, the Northeast had been favored by the establishment of the fund. Moreover, while all municipalities in the country received their quotas on the basis of population, the *relative* contribution in the Northeast from the distribution of the federal funds was larger owing to their smaller receipts.

44. *Visão*, 14 February 1971, pp. 171–74, based on the *Pesquisa Nacional por Amostra de Domicílios*.

In addition to reducing the total amount of resources made available in this fashion, the government tied state and local expenditure more closely to execution of federal plans.

Underlying the reduction of the fund was the desire to increase the resources at the disposition of the federal government and thereby offset inflationary pressures. Waste in public expenditure was also alleged — mayors with new cars and municipios with illuminated plazas.[45] Such centralization carries with it important political ramifications. If local priorities and allocation decisions are no longer important, neither is a system to elicit local sentiments. This tendency has now reached its highest expression in the direct choice of governors by the president. The atrophy of the political system makes regional redistribution that much more difficult to achieve. Seen from the center, the objective easily becomes maximization of total growth, and reduced sympathy for regional concerns. Even PIN, designed to ameliorate regional disparities, has diverted resources from regional agencies.

Ultimately the problem in the Northeast, which has not yet been satisfactorily addressed, is its low-productivity agriculture. Within the Zona da Mata serious efforts at agrarian reform are still stymied. Better distribution of income and larger output are consistent to the degree that increased productivity is attained by the landless workers and owners of minifundia. Yet the government seems unwilling to disrupt traditional land tenure or to introduce modern inputs — fertilizer, seeds, technical knowledge — on the necessary scale. Indeed, taken as a whole, the policies of minimum prices, agricultural credit, and improved commercialization have probably benefited the wealthier farmers at the expense of the poor. It remains to be seen how the newly implemented Proterra program alters the outlook. This new land reform cum agricultural modernization program is designed specifically for the Northeast, and it is to be financed by 20 percent of the tax incentives formerly applied to private sector investment. It thus will command resources previous reform attempts lacked. One might question whether a serious commitment is intended, however. The Minister of Agriculture has made it clear that this policy is not directed to the rural proletariat: "The principal objective of Proterra is to create medium-

45. The reluctance to accept consumer sovereignty in this context is in sharp contrast with the willingness to accede to individual purchases of automobiles. It is not altogether obvious, whether as demonstration effect or for pure satisfaction, that illuminated plazas do not represent an important increase in welfare.

sized rural enterprises capable of revitalizing regional agriculture and not the distribution of land between thirty million *nordestinos.*" [46] For the rest there is only the dubious prospect of out-migration to Amazonia.

Another important redistributive instrument of the government is the Programa de Integração Social (PIS). Its objective is to improve the lot of urban workers. A fund financed by employers has been created — initially through tax reduction — in which workers will possess shares proportional to their years of service and salaries. Upon certain specified occasions — marriage, construction of a house, retirement, becoming an invalid, and death — the worker can draw on the fund. The net inflow into the fund is estimated to amount to more than $500 million in 1974 and to continue to grow thereafter.[47]

If there is legitimate question concerning the ability of PIN to treat regional disparity adequately there must be even greater doubt about the capacity of PIS to ameliorate the inequality of the size distribution of income. In the first instance, the fund is destined to generate a surplus over its first years of operation, and will thereby contribute forced savings rather than augment present consumption. Even recent liberalization of worker access to their accounts probably does not alter this fact. Any redistributive aspects are therefore postponed, while the effects of wage policy are felt now. Note as well that quotas in the fund are related to salaries in positive rather than in inverse relation. Higher paid and more experienced workers receive more. An *equalizing* negative income tax scheme implies just the opposite. PIS is thus a supplement to existing social insurance schemes rather than a redistributive device. Moreover, it is far from being incident upon capital alone as is claimed. Initially it is largely financed by reduction in governmental receipts from sales taxes, on the assumption firms pass along none of the decline, but use it instead to pay their quotas to the fund. Redistribution is thus limited to the transfer from all consumers to a subset of them who gain from the fund. Over time it may be financed partially out of profits, but note then an additional anomaly — the cost of hiring labor will be increased, implying smaller employment, without an increase in worker current income.

46. From an interview with Luiz Fernando Cirne Lima in *O Globo,* September 24, 1972, as cited in David E. Goodman and Roberto Cavalcanti de Albuquerque, "Economic Development and Industrialization in a Backward Region: The Brazilian Northeast," to be published in book form.

47. Pastore and Barros, "O programa de integração social," p. 127.

This new legislation is modest indeed in the face of other government policies, oriented toward growth, that work in favor of continued concentration of income. Income tax incentives are a prime example. By granting exemptions whose value varies with income, it makes the tax less progressive in its operation: obviously those who pay little or nothing at all receive no advantage. By using such incentives to channel private resources to the capital market, or even to the Northeast, rather than supplying public savings directly, the government is guaranteeing future income streams to those whose present incomes are highest.

In general, the position of the government has been to favor profits as a source for the savings necessary to finance capital formation. Wage restraint, initially an anti-inflationary instrument, increasingly has become useful to this larger objective as expansion has accelerated. Underestimation of the productivity term in the wage formula (like the earlier discrepancy between the inflationary residual and reasonable expectations) works against the labor share even in the period of rising real wages. This incomes policy is effective because the Brazilian labor movement no longer exists to protest and because growth rather than welfare has become the measure of success.

It is not surprising that a centralized regime committed to capitalist development should have provoked little in the way of serious distributive policies. An essential role of a free and broad political system is to counteract the excesses of a free market by establishing popular priorities. In its absence the interests of the masses are ignored in favor of goals and instruments, implicitly political as we have seen, imposed by others. It is not ignorance nor lack of patriotism that has caused the most literate of the working class in Guanabara and São Paulo to express its opposition to the government when the opportunity has presented. It is legitimate concern with their immediate lot, too little heeded since 1964. The expansion, while an impressive accomplishment, must also be gauged by those who gain and lose.

There is widespread belief that a modernizing and rapidly growing Brazil requires the political stability of military rule. Just as orthodox stabilization policy was apparently necessary to combat inflation, so centralization and income concentration are now regarded as essential to development. Yet just as we now understand that the money supply could stimulate output rather than prices, and that inflation rates of 20 percent can be tolerated, so we may come to appreciate that political institutions for the expression of priorities and choice of instruments may be necessary for transforming growth to welfare. Indeed, in generating the consensus needed to confront successfully the problem of maintaining high investment and savings rates, broader participation may be a contribution to sustained growth itself.

For perhaps the most likely source of the required capital is the government itself. The burgeoning revenues of the federal government and present cash budgetary surplus attest to the potential. So too do the resources commanded by state-associated enterprises. Maintenance of high levels of taxation can provide a lever for alleviating at least the most blatant abuses of inequality: a proper redistribution of 5 percent of product could bring all families below a minimal poverty standard up to it. Direct governmental savings set up no claim on private wealth to the detriment of the future distribution of income. Yet it is not easy to imagine channeling of such large quantities of resources for the market to do with them what it chooses. Social austerity brings with it inevitably the need, and opportunity, for social valuation. Through such adaptation the Brazilian model may yet become the miracle not merely of capitalistic and outward-directed growth but of successful dedication to consistent increases of income of its poor as well as its rich. Up to the present the accomplishment cannot be claimed.

Appendix

This appendix sets out in more exact terms the orthodox and heterodox inflation models discussed in the text. The models are identical except in their description of the mechanism of price determination. Common to both is the following equation for equilibrium in the money market:

$$\frac{M}{P}\left(Y, i, \frac{\dot{P}^*}{P}, \frac{\dot{Y}^*}{Y}\right) = \frac{M\,(G - T, R, B.B, Cof)}{P} \qquad (3.1)$$

The demand for money is a function of real income (Y), the money rate of interest (i), and expected rates of inflation $\left(\frac{\dot{P}^*}{P}\right)$ and of real income growth $\left(\frac{\dot{Y}^*}{Y}\right)$. The rate of inflation enters because its effects may not fully show up in the money rate of interest. The expected rate of income growth is relevant because balances are acquired in anticipation of further expenditures, which in turn depend upon future income. The normal supply of money is determined by the government deficit (G-T), the acquisition of foreign exchange reserves (R), relative participation in lending by the Bank of Brazil ($B.B$), and the coffee account (Cof). The nature of the functional relationship subsumes the required reserves of commercial banks, their willingness to lend, and the net sales of securities to finance the deficit. An equilibrium condition is that the real demand for money balances be equal to the real supply.

Equation 3.2 expresses the demand for goods in the system.

$$Y = f\left(G/P, T/P, r, \frac{M}{P}\right) \qquad (3.2)$$

Aggregate demand in real terms, given that consumption responds in a predictable fashion to income, depends upon the exogenous expenditure variables, governmental outlays (G/P) and investment. The latter is not included explicitly, but is shown instead through inclusion of the real interest rate (r) upon which it depends. The level of real taxes (T/P) is included since they influence the size of disposable income, and hence consumption. Finally, the level of real money balances $\left(\frac{M}{P}\right)$ is included for its impact upon expenditure. As the value of such balances increase, so does demand. This describes the mechanism by which increases in the quantity of money are translated into increased expenditures.

Equation 3.3 ties together the nominal interest rate (i) and the real interest rate (r) through the rate of expected inflation.

$$i = r + \frac{\dot{P}^*}{P}. \qquad (3.3)$$

Equation 3.4 introduces the crucial difference between the two inflation variants. It is the supply equation of output. In the classical version, it is a simple one:

$$Y = Y_f. \qquad (3.4a)$$

Demand is equal to full employment supply, itself exogenously determined by the size of the labor force and capital stock and the character of technology.

The second version of equation 3.4, relevant to the heterodox alternative, treats supply differently. It makes it fully responsive to demand, with prices varying according to mark-up over unit cost.

$$P = g \left(\frac{Y}{Y_f}, \frac{\dot{P}^*}{P}, r \right) \cdot h(w, i, T, c) \qquad (3.4b)$$

Thus the price level P is some multiple of unit wage costs (w), of financial costs, here measured for simplicity by the nominal interest rate (i), unit tax burden measured by (T), and costs of foreign inputs (c).

The mark-up is determined by three variables. The first of these is capacity utilization (Y/Y_f). It plays a dual role. At high levels, price is influenced positively by obvious demand pressures and hence opportunities for profits. But economies of scale enter to offset it somewhat. On balance, one would expect positive variation. At low levels of capacity utilization these two forces contend in opposite fashion, and again on balance, there is probably some negative tendency. The rate of expected inflation $\left(\frac{\dot{P}^*}{P} \right)$ is directly associated with the mark-up factor — the higher the anticipated future price rise, the higher are prices charged today relative to costs. The third variable, the real interest rate, influences the way in which capacity enters. The real interest rate, measuring the cost of working capital, enters in the very determination of what constitutes full capacity output because inventory availability influences the potential scale of production. The result follows from the imperfect substitution of other productive factors. A given real demand at high interest rates will thus represent more of a pressure on prices and tend to lead to larger mark-ups. Such a phenomenon in part explains the resistance of prices in 1965 and 1966, which were years of conversion to high real interest rates.

These two different sets of equations each have the same four endogenous variables, P, r, i, and Y. In this simplified version, expectations are given exogenously. In fact, of course, past inflation influences current anticipations and makes for a cumulative process. Since our purpose is to focus upon the differences between orthodoxy and heterodoxy, such an extension is here unnecessary.

Figure 3:1 diagrammatically presents the essentials of the equation systems and permits us to contrast their working. In the second quadrant the aggregate demand relationship is plotted against r. For a given governmental outlay and real balance, demand decreases with r due to declining investment. As real balances and government expenditures are higher, the curve shifts outward to a new position. In the third quadrant we have the demand for money, $\frac{M}{P}$, plotted against i, real output given. As i rises, $\frac{M}{P}$ falls, and its reciprocal, which is here graphed, rises. Note that the difference between r and i reflects the expected inflation rate, $\frac{P*}{P}$. In quadrant four is the supply of money, here presented as an exogenous variable. In this presentation, it is the angle of the line that measures the changing supply of money; as it moves closer to the P axis the quantity is increased.

Finally, in the first quadrant we have the supply equations. That for the orthodox system is easily represented: it is merely a straight line at height $Y = Y_f$. There is no inherent relationship between Y and P except that which emerges indirectly in the equilibrium situation. The alternative supply equation explicitly establishes such a relationship. Here we see price rising only slightly over a wide range of output, and then become elastic at different capacity levels depending upon the real rate of interest.

The essential differences between the two systems can be seen by examining the consequences of monetary restraint. We start from a full employment situation with some inflation. Now the money supply is reduced to being price increases under control. The former equilibrium is necessarily altered. An immediate impact is an increase in both money and real interest rates (with P not yet changing), and for demand to be reduced as real money balances are reduced. So far, the description is common to both systems. The differences emerge when prices begin to adjust. The consequence of such pressures in the orthodox scheme is ultimately to force the equilibrium price level down to P_1, the only

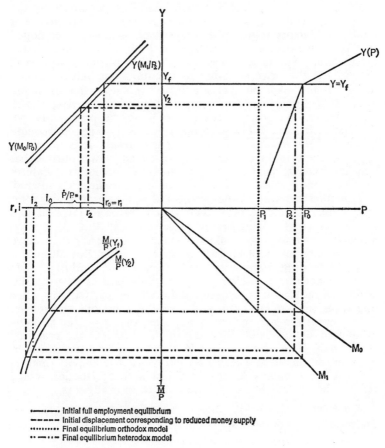

Figure 3:1

one compatible with full employment. (In the process inflationary expectations also may be altered thereby reducing the spread
between i and r, but this is not shown in this figure.)

But in the heterodox model, P is reduced much less, and at the
expense of real output so that the new equilibrium has higher
prices, P_2, and lower income, Y_2, compared to the orthodox results. That new equilibrium is found as a result of appropriate
shifts in the aggregate demand function and the demand for
money until a new and compatible alignment is found. The
first round reduced demand, and the final equilibrium configuration are shown in the figure.

Note, then, that if the system is really as portrayed by the second equation set, and orthodox policies are applied, not totally satisfactory results will be achieved. It can only be hoped that the price determination equation itself will be altered due to changing expectations over time. Orthodox policy *can* work therefore if the price equation in quadrant one can be shifted to the left and made more elastic. It is in this sense that orthodox policy is a clumsy and costly, but still possibly effective, instrument. Heterodox policy focuses as well on the price equation, but more with an eye toward direct controls; it is generally more tolerant of the residual inflation that may result. It is unwilling to accept the combination of higher prices *and* lower output that may characterize continuing application of orthodox measures in a heterodox world until expectations are sufficiently altered.

This interpretation of the problem of stabilization policy after 1964 must compete with another, which argues in favor of lags as the principal villain of the piece.[48] Under this alternative, monetary restraint takes hold somewhat more slowly than originally assumed and typically with some oscillation. But ultimately it works, and its temporary ineffectiveness has nothing to do with the nature of pricing behavior. The data can hardly discriminate satisfactorily between these effects, particularly when one takes into account instability of the functions themselves. In any event the government policy after 1967 has been strongly influenced by its belief in cost inflation; policy was practiced accordingly. The heterodox model developed here can thus perhaps be considered as a formalization of what later policymakers thought the economy looked like, just as the orthodox model reflects the basic belief of the Castello Branco advisors.

48. See Robert A. Mundell, "Growth, Stability and Inflationary Finance," *Journal of Political Economy* 73 (April 1965): 97–109.

4 The Effect of Changes in the Distribution of Income on Labor, Foreign Investment, and Growth in Brazil

SAMUEL A. MORLEY AND GORDON W. SMITH

During the years from 1968 to 1971 Brazil recovered from the stagnation of the mid-1960s, and this success has been used by the current Brazilian government as a basis for support and legitimacy. Yet there are many who are both critical of the regime and skeptical about the long-run durability of the present growth pattern. They foresee problems in three key areas — adequacy of demand, denationalization of Brazilian industry, and labor absorption.

Among the skeptics the best known are the "stagnationists," identified with the Economic Commission for Latin America and Celso Furtado.[1] This group believed that the import substitution process in Brazil was essentially completed by 1962. Industrialization had not brought the hoped-for benefits. Labor absorption had been low because of the highly capital-intensive nature of the new industries.[2] It was reasoned that this type of capital-intensive industrialization had led to an increase in the inequality of the distribution of income. Given the higher saving propensity of the rich, this in turn should lead to a Keynesian-type stagna-

The authors gratefully acknowledge the research computation assistance of the Program of Development Studies at Rice University in the preparation of this chapter.

1. See Economic Commission for Latin America, "Rise and Decline of Import Substitution in Brazil," *Economic Bulletin for Latin America* 9 (March 1964): 1–61; Celso Furtado, *Subdesenvolvimento e Estagnação, na América Latina* (Editôra Civilização Brasileira, 1967); Celso Furtado, *Obstacles to Development in Latin America* (Anchor, 1970).

2. See Werner Baer and Michael Hervé, "Employment and Industrialization in Developing Countries," *Quarterly Journal of Economics* 80 (February 1966): 88–108. Werner Baer, "Import Substitution Industrialization in Latin America," *Latin American Research Review* 7 (Spring 1972): 95–122; Albert Hirschman, "The Political Economy of Import Substituting Industrialization," *Quarterly Journal of Economics* 82 (February 1968): 1–33.

tion.[3] Baer and Maneschi have presented a variant of this stagnationist approach in which they claim that there are economies of scale in capital so that a lack of demand results from a lack of investment opportunities.[4]

A quite different approach is taken by Georgescu-Roegen.[5] He argues that the pattern of growth through import substitution has led to an industrial structure producing goods for the rich. Any equalization in the distribution of income would lead to underutilization of capacity in luxury goods industry and consequently a low rate of industrial growth. According to this argument, since the regime is basing its claim for support on its ability to guarantee a high rate of growth, it is forced to follow an income distribution policy favoring the rich. Among the undesirable aspects of this panorama is the probability that it will lead to a progressive denationalization of Brazilian industry, since foreign firms dominate the dynamic luxury consumer goods sectors.[6] It should also lead to a continuation of the low rate of labor absorption. Critics of the regime assert that these implicit contradictions in the growth strategy (regressive income distribution, denationalization, and low labor absorption) may eventually lead to unbearable social pressures and the overthrow of the regime.

Central to these stagnationist analyses is the belief that the distribution of income is an important determinant of the structure of demand and in turn of labor absorption and foreign investment. In this chapter we explore how important the distribution of income really is. Toward this end we have made an estimate of consumption patterns by income class and then, using an input-output growth model, performed simulation experiments in which we systematically varied the distribution of income and calculated the resulting structure of growth throughout the economy. Note that such an experiment does not forecast the future. Rather it indicates the direction of change that alternative distribution policies would have.

We find that the variations in the distribution of income that

3. Furtado, *Obstacles to Development,* pp. 154–56.

4. Werner Baer and Andrea Maneschi, "Import Substitution, Stagnation, and Structural Change: An Interpretation of the Brazilian Case," *Journal of Developing Areas* 5 (January 1971): 177–92.

5. Nicholas Georgescu-Roegen, "Structural Inflation — Lock and Balanced Growth," *Economie et Sociétés, Cahier de L'I.S.E.A.* 4, no. 3 (Librairie Droz) (March 1970).

6. Samuel Morley and Gordon Smith, "Import Substitution and Foreign Investment in Brazil," *Oxford Economic Papers* 23 (March 1971): 120–35.

one might expect to occur in a functioning market economy do not cause a significant variation in the structure of growth. Increasing regressivity does raise the growth rate of manufacturing as the critics have predicted, but by only a small amount. We were surprised to find that the predicted rate of growth of employment in manufacturing should at least equal that of the population and that labor absorption in manufacturing is positively related to regressivity. Finally, rapid denationalization does not appear to be a danger. The foreign share grows slightly in all our experiments, and the rate of growth is quite insensitive to variations in the distribution of income.

METHODOLOGY

In order to test the hypothesis that growth patterns are sensitive to the distribution of income, we simulated the growth of Brazil under different assumed changes in the distribution of income. Our experiments compare different growth trajectories in which the government is assumed to alter the distribution of income by a tax-and-transfer scheme that creates differential rates of growth for different income classes. The growth paths are not constrained by capital in existence because induced demand for capital is endogenously satisfied on each final growth path by new investment. Capital goods are an intermediate product required to satisfy a given bill of final demand. In other words a more capital-intensive growth path will, ceteris paribus, have a higher rate of growth of total output.

We did not investigate the effect of our experiments on the external sector. If we had imposed balance of payments equality, we would have been forced to vary the import substitution parameters to meet it. As in the case of capital goods we assume that potential imports can be produced domestically and therefore an increased demand for imports leads to a higher rate of growth of domestic production. To simplify matters we assumed that capital inflows met differences between exports and imports. Removing the assumption would slightly accentuate the relationship between growth and regressivity, assuming that the upper class demands more imports than the lower.

Thus the only real constraint on the growth rate is the availability of labor. Given the paucity of data on this subject we did not explore the constraint. One does not generally think of labor as scarce in an underdeveloped economy, although a scarcity of skilled labor may exist. We are assuming that none of our strategies demands more of some labor type than is available.

The model that we chose for the simulations is a linear input-output growth model adapted from van Rijckeghem.[7] Growth for any industry is definitionally equal to a weighted average of the growth rates of the various categories of final and intermediate demand, where the weights are each category's share in the total sales of the industry in question. Thus the effect of a change in the distribution of income may be direct — it changes final consumption demand for the product. Or it may be indirect: a change in the output of some other sector affects the growth rate of sector i, because sector i is a supplier of sector j. By using an input-output table we capture the indirect backward linkages from final demand to each industry and thus obtain a more complete estimate of the relationship among changes in income distribution, final demand, and the structure of growth.

Formally the growth identity for each industry can be written

$$s_i = \sum_j d_{ij}x_{ij} + d_{ic}c_i + d_{ig}g_i + d_{iz}z_i + d_{ie}e_i \qquad (1)$$

where

s_i — growth rate of total supply in industry i
d_{ij} — percentage of total sales of industry i going to industry j
x_{ij} — growth of demand by industry j for intermediate product of industry i
d_{ic} — percentage of total sales of industry i consumed
c_i — growth rate of consumer demand for output of industry i
d_{ig} — percentage of sales of industry i bought by government
g_i — growth rate of government demand
d_{iz} — percentage of sales of industry i to satisfy investment demand
z_i — growth rate of investment demand for i
d_{ie} — percentage of sales of industry i exported
e_i — growth rate of exports

The d_{ij}'s are obtained from an input-output table by dividing each item in a row by the row sum. Thus

$$\sum_j d_{ij} + d_{ic} + d_{ig} + d_{iz} + d_{ie} = 1.00.$$

Setting exogenous import substitution targets allows us to convert the growth rate of total supply into a growth rate of domestic supply.

$$s_i = \pi_i x_i + (1 - \pi_i)m_i \qquad (2)$$
$$m_i = u_i s_i$$

7. Willy van Rijckeghem, "An Intersectoral Consistency Model for Economic Planning in Brazil," in *The Economy of Brazil*, ed. H. S. Ellis (Berkeley and Los Angeles: University of California Press, 1969).

where

$(1 - \pi_i)$ = relative importance of imports in total supply.
u_i = import substitution target ($u_i = 1$ indicates no import substitution).
m_i = growth rate of imports.

Assume that the demand for capital goods by each sector is a log-linear function of output (i.e. an accelerator relationship). Assume also that the composition of capital is invariant in a sector. This allows us to write:

$k_{ij} = \tau_j x_j$
k_{ij} is the growth rate of capital goods
    supplied by sector i to sector j.
τ_j is the capital output elasticity in sector j.

The growth rate of investment is related to the growth rate of capital by:

$$z_{ij} = k_{ij} + k'_{ij}/k_{ij}$$
$$= \tau_j x_j \quad \text{(under constant rates of growth)}$$

For each sector producing capital goods we calculate the growth in investment as a weighted sum.

$$z_i = \sum_{i=1}^{n} E_{ij}\tau_j x_j \qquad (3)$$

E_{ij} is the percent of total sales of capital goods by sector i to sector j.

Substituting (2) and (3) into (1) we have a system of n simultaneous equations that we solve for the growth rates of each industry consistent with the growth rates in final demand.

$$(4)$$

$$
\begin{bmatrix} x_1 \\ \bullet \\ \bullet \\ \bullet \\ x_n \end{bmatrix} =
\begin{bmatrix} \dfrac{\pi_1}{1-(1-\pi)\mu_1} & -a_{11}d_{11}-d_{12}E_{11}\tau_1 \cdots -a_{1n}d_{1n}-d_{12}E_{1n}\tau_n \\ & \\ -a_{n1}d_{n1}-d_{n2}E_{n1}\tau_1 \cdots & \dfrac{\pi n}{1-(1-\pi_\mu)\mu_n}-a_{nn}d_{nn}-d_{n2}E_{nn}\tau_n \end{bmatrix}^{-1}
\begin{bmatrix} f_1 \\ \bullet \\ \bullet \\ \bullet \\ f_n \end{bmatrix}
$$

$$\| \\ [D]$$

x_i = growth rate of industry i.

$f_i = d_{ic}c_i + d_{ig}g_i + d_{ie}e_i$ = growth rate of final demand for industry i's products.

The ij element of $[D]^{-1}$ tells the effect of a 1 percent change in the growth rate of final demand for industry j on the rate of growth of industry i. (It is the elasticity of output i with respect to the final demand of j.)

Now a change in the distribution of income has its effect through c_i, the growth rate in the consumer demand component of final demand for the output of the ith sector. c_i may be written as the weighted sum of the growth rates of demand for product i by different income classes, where the weights are the share of total consumer demand for product i stemming from each income class. In turn, the growth in demand by each class is a function of the growth of its income.[8]

$$\Delta C_i^t = \sum_{r=1}^{n} \beta_i \alpha_{ir}^{t-1} \gamma_r C_i^{t-1} + h C_i^{t-1}(1 - \beta_i)$$

$$\frac{\Delta C_i^t}{C_i^{t-1}} = \beta_i \sum_{r=1}^{n} \alpha_{ir}^{t-1} \gamma_r + h(1 - \beta_i) \qquad (5)$$

C_i^t is consumption demand, product i, time t.

$\beta_i =$ income elasticity of demand for product i, assumed equal for all income classes.

$\alpha_{ir}^{t-1} = \dfrac{C_{ir}^{t-1}}{C_i^{t-1}}$, the share of the rth income class in total consumer expenditures on good i, time $t - 1$.

$\gamma_r =$ growth rate of income of income class r.

$h =$ rate of growth of population, assumed to be 3% for all income classes.

Equation (5) says that the growth rate in consumption is equal to the population growth rate plus the income elasticity times a weighted income growth rate, where the weights are the shares of the various income classes in total consumption. The α_{ir} are dated because over the course of the simulation the shares change as the income distribution changes.

To see the effect of different redistribution patterns on aggregate demand we allowed growth rates across different Brazilian income classes to vary, such that the overall growth rate of disposable income was a constant 7 percent (4 percent per capita).

8. We assume that the demand for the ith good by the rth class is the following: $\left(\dfrac{C}{P}\right)_r = \left(\dfrac{Y}{P}\right)_r^{\beta_i}$.

Each income redistribution experiment produces a different vector of final demand, which in turn generates a different pattern of industrial growth. In matrix notation equation (4) becomes:

$$[X] = [D]^{-1}[F] \qquad (6)$$

Each column of X gives the sectoral growth rates required by the jth column of $[F]$, the matrix of growth rates of final demand. Each column corresponds to a different income distribution experiment.

The method of comparing growth rates that we are using here economizes on necessary information, particularly on production technology. It allows us to make projections without detailed knowledge about capital output ratios and production functions. Changes in technology over time are easily handled by varying the input-output elasticities, d_{ij}, and changes in capital intensity can be investigated by varying the Υ_j. Also the method is very flexible in investigating different policy assumptions about import substitution, export growth, or government purchases.

Our method seems to be a good way of focusing on demand, but it ignores one important feedback, namely changes in relative prices. Rapid growth may cause large changes in relative product prices leading to substitution by consumers and producers. We leave out this possibly large influence on the final pattern of growth.

DATA INPUTS

In carrying out our experiments we required a distribution matrix for Brazil, estimated growth rates for government expenditure and exports and consumer income elasticities for each sector. For all of these inputs we relied heavily on van Rijckeghem.[9] The distribution matrix was derived from a 1959 input-output table. We assumed that government expenditures would grow at 6 percent in all sectors and exports would grow at 4 percent in all sectors other than agriculture and mining where the growth rates were set at 5.6 percent and 13.4 percent respectively. On import substitution, we assumed $u_i = .8$ for metals, machinery, and chemicals and $u_i = 1$ elsewhere. That is, we have domestic supply growing more rapidly than imports in only three sectors.

Our consumption income elasticities were drawn from cross-

9. Van Rijckeghem, "An Intersectoral Consistency Model."

section consumption functions estimated by van Rijckeghem from consumer budget studies. Unfortunately, the budget studies are not disaggregated in a manner comparable to the industrial classification, so that elasticity estimates are quite tentative. In particular, the disaggregation could explain van Rijckeghem's estimate of 1.08 as the income elasticity for consumer durables. This very low figure could also reflect the nature of the period in which the budget survey was done. In 1961–62 the consumer durables industry was still a semi-infant characterized by high prices, low product quality, and the exclusion of competitive imports. These factors would tend to reduce the share of expenditures by the high-income class and thus the observed income elasticities. Drawing on other recent work on consumer demand, we have set the income elasticity of consumer durables at 2.00.[10] The final elasticities for each sector are reported in table 4.2.

The basic data on consumption patterns and income distribution are drawn from the 1961–62 and 1962–63 Fundação Getúlio Vargas (FGV) budget survey. The strengths and weaknesses of this survey are fairly well known (see appendix 4.1).

The FGV data are reported by expenditure class and nine family annual income groups, ranging from about $200–250 and below to an open-ended class beginning at $6,250. We aggregated the original nine income classes into three for our experiments (see table 4.1). We also found it necessary to reclassify some

Table 4.1. Income Classes Used in the Simulations

Class	Family Income[a]	Income (%)	Families (%)
Lower	$875 and below	18.5	41.3
Middle	$876 to $3,000	46.5	48.0
Upper	Above $3,000	35.0	10.7

[a] We used an exchange rate of CR$400/$ for the period, very close to the pseudo-free trade rate calculated by Joel Bergsman. See his *Industrialization and Trade Policies* (London: Oxford University Press, 1970), p. 45.

of FGV's expenditure classes in order to fit better the industrial census groupings we used. The methods employed are explained in appendix 4.2.

10. For some recent estimates of price elasticities of demand for durables and other goods, see A. S. Goldberger and T. Gamaletsos, "A Cross-Country Comparison of Consumer Expenditure Patterns," *European Economic Review* (Spring 1970), pp. 357–99, esp. pp. 375–85.

In our simulations, we have assumed that the FGV sample characteristics for each region are exactly representative of the universe: The distribution of families by income class, the average family size, and the distribution of expenditures in each income class all are assumed exact microcosms in the sample. This enables us to "blow up" the sample to the universe and then aggregate across regions, yielding an estimate for Brazil as a whole (see table 4.1). Obviously, this procedure is far from ideal. In particular, the share of income accruing to the upper class seems unusually low.[11]

The data on consumption patterns by income groups are interesting in themselves, reflecting Brazil's blatant dualism. (See tables 4.2 and 4.3.) Fully 10 percent of the families in the blown-up sample had annual incomes below $400. These people, the major part of whom are members of the rural masses in the Northeast, are irrelevant for the "modern" economy. Almost 60 percent of their expenditures went to food, and practically none for the products of import substitution industries. Even purchases from such industries as textiles and clothing form a miniscule part of total expenditures (4 percent) for this subsistence-oriented group. It is almost certain that the relative size of this "rural proletariat" is significantly underestimated.[12] At the other extreme we find approximately 10 percent of Brazilian families with incomes of $3,000 or more. These people are concentrated in the Rio-Saõ Paulo area and appear to be the main buyers of import substitutes and capital-intensive consumer durables.

11. For example, our 35.0 percent estimate for the income share of the top 10.7 percent of Brazilian families compares with W. R. Cline's 48.0 percent for the top 10 percent of active nonagricultural workers in 1960 (see W. R. Cline, "The Potential Effect of Income Redistribution on Economic Growth in Six Latin American Countries," Woodrow Wilson School Research Program in Economic Development, discussion paper no. 13 (August 1970), p. 66) and A. Fishlow's 42.1 percent for the top 11.0 percent of economically active families, also for 1960 (see Albert Fishlow, "Brazilian Size Distribution of Income," *American Economic Review: Papers and Proceedings* (May 1972), p. 392).

12. No studies were made by FGV of consumption patterns in the rural Northeast, clearly the poorest segment of Brazil. As a result we were forced to use Minas Gerais as representative of the Northeast. This must overstate the actual income of the Northeast. Second, as we noted in appendix 4.2, all of the rural samples seem to have included too many farm people of higher incomes. This, too, would bias downward our estimate of extremely poor Brazilians.

Table 4.2. Exogenous Parameter Values

	Final Demand Shares			Elasticities and Growth Parameters		
	d_{ic}	d_{ig}	d_{ie}	β_i	g_i	e_i
Vegetable product	0.4465	0.0193	0.0340	0.5200	0.0600	0.0560
Animal product	0.4603	0.0845	0.0300	0.5200	0.0600	0.0400
Electricity	0.1744	0.0640	0.0000	1.0100	0.0600	0.0400
Commerce	0.5355	0.0862	0.0751	1.0000	0.0600	0.0400
Services	0.6024	0.0000	0.0000	1.2000	0.0600	0.0400
Wastes	0.0000	0.0000	0.0000	0.0000	0.0600	0.0400
Fuels	0.1138	0.0438	0.0012	1.9400	0.0600	0.0400
Packaging	0.0000	0.0000	0.0000	0.0000	0.0600	0.0400
Mining	0.0000	0.0140	0.0000	0.0000	0.0600	0.1340
Nonmetallic	0.1159	0.0401	0.0037	1.0900	0.0600	0.0400
Metals	0.0347	0.0770	0.0001	1.0900	0.0600	0.0400
Machinery	0.0768	0.0998	0.0030	1.0900	0.0600	0.0400
Electric machinery	0.4111	0.0521	0.0002	2.0000	0.0600	0.0400
Transportation equipment	0.4251	0.0755	0.0009	2.1200	0.0600	0.0400
Wood	0.0351	0.0138	0.0025	1.0900	0.0600	0.0400
Furniture	0.7642	0.0000	0.0000	1.0900	0.0600	0.0400
Paper	0.0361	0.0228	0.0000	0.7300	0.0600	0.0400
Rubber	0.3976	0.0101	0.0012	1.9400	0.0600	0.0400
Leather	0.1075	0.0023	0.1609	1.0100	0.0600	0.0400
Chemicals	0.0250	0.0208	0.0474	1.0100	0.0600	0.0380
Drugs	0.7724	0.0273	0.0023	0.9000	0.0600	0.0400
Cosmetics	0.8921	0.0384	0.0001	0.5950	0.0600	0.0400
Plastics	0.6482	0.0093	0.0003	1.0900	0.0600	0.0400
Textiles	0.5742	0.0060	0.0062	1.0100	0.0600	0.0400
Clothing	0.9579	0.0127	0.0007	1.0100	0.0600	0.0400
Food	0.6463	0.0069	0.2171	0.5200	0.0600	0.0440
Beverages	0.8592	0.0000	0.0005	1.0300	0.0600	0.0400
Tobacco	0.8166	0.0000	0.0101	0.4700	0.0600	0.0400
Publishing	0.5371	0.0466	0.0027	1.2700	0.0600	0.0400
Miscellaneous	0.7522	0.0848	0.0033	1.0000	0.0600	0.0400
Construction	0.4039	0.0557	0.0000	1.9800	0.0600	0.0400
Transport	0.5435	0.1558	0.0796	1.7400	0.0600	0.0400

RESULTS OF THE INCOME DISTRIBUTION EXPERIMENTS

Patterns of Growth

Our experiment is intended to test the effect of changes in the distribution of income on the pattern of growth. Table 4.4 focuses on the manufacturing sector, where the issues of employment and domination by foreign investment are most acute. Table 4.5 shows the yearly growth rate of output for all sectors. The results lend no support to the stagnationist position. On the contrary, the more regressive the distribution scheme, the higher the rate of growth of the economy, of manufacturing, and of employment in manufacturing. This is due in good part to the importance of consumer durables, especially automobiles and their supplier industries — rubber, machinery, metals, and fuels — in the budgets of the rich. This supports the Georgescu-Roegen hypothesis that the type of industry built in Brazil during import substitution industrialization (ISI) would grow most rapidly under regressive distribution schemes, because it sells to the upper class. In part the result stems from the induced demand for capital goods to supply upper- or middle-class wants. Since capital needs are not a constraint, but simply another demand for output, capital intensive growth strategies imply a greater demand for labor and a more rapid growth in output.

In our minds another interesting result is the striking stability in the growth patterns across experiments. Despite rather violent redistributions of income, the sectoral rates of growth of output and employment show little variation. Going from the most progressive to the most regressive experiment only changes the average growth rate of manufacturing 2.2 percentage points per year. Within manufacturing there is a subgroup of industries that is dynamic in all experiments, with the exception of the most progressive, experiment 7. It is composed of metallurgy, machinery, electric machinery, transportation equipment, rubber, and publishing. Except for the last, these are the industries producing capital and intermediate goods. Their output is demanded on all growth paths. Thus even if final demand is subject to fairly large variance, that variance is damped by intermediate and capital goods production.[13]

The reader may be wondering whether this stability is because our redistribution schemes were too cautious. We do not think

13. The variance in the final demand vector is relatively greater than that in the final growth rates vector indicating that backward linkages damp output variation.

Table 4.3. Total Consumption Share Matrix

Share of Consumption by Each Income Class

	<99	100–149	150–249	250–349
Vegetable product	.0090	.0179	.0931	.1112
Animal product	.0093	.0194	.0953	.1095
Electricity	.0086	.0178	.0738	.0807
Commerce	.0000	.0000	.0000	.0000
Services	.0035	.0099	.0582	.0821
Wastes	.0000	.0000	.0000	.0000
Fuels	.0008	.0045	.0293	.0529
Packaging	.0000	.0000	.0000	.0000
Mining	.0000	.0000	.0000	.0000
Nonmetallic	.0007	.0052	.0317	.0512
Metals	.0000	.0000	.0000	.0000
Machinery	.0010	.0047	.0313	.0629
Electric machinery	.0008	.0050	.0310	.0596
Transportation equipment	.0000	.0430	.0022	.0063
Wood	.0069	.0160	.0714	.0674
Furniture	.0008	.0043	.0302	.0582
Paper	.0053	.0128	.0742	.0843
Rubber	.0000	.0009	.0019	.0054
Leather	.0023	.0088	.0455	.0728
Chemicals	.0000	.0011	.0017	.0047
Drugs	.0067	.0087	.0671	.0948
Cosmetics	.0074	.0154	.0845	.0981
Plastics	.0008	.0045	.0293	.0529
Textiles	.0016	.0070	.0394	.0635
Clothing	.0023	.0082	.0447	.0747
Food	.0097	.0190	.0982	.1132
Beverages	.0045	.0049	.0309	.0606
Tobacco	.0058	.0187	.0935	.1141
Publishing	.0006	.0020	.0216	.0351
Miscellaneous	.0057	.0030	.0233	.0525
Construction	.0022	.0048	.0175	.0304
Transport	.0027	.0081	.0415	.0719

NOTE: Rows sum to 1.0. Column headings are yearly income in thousands of cruzeiros.

Table 4.3 (*continued*)

350–499	500–799	800–1199	1200–2499	>2499
.1722	.2338	.1580	.1483	.0565
.1700	.2343	.1556	.1478	.0588
.1289	.1970	.1492	.2142	.1299
.0000	.0000	.0000	.0000	.0000
.1359	.2042	.1583	.2338	.1141
.0000	.0000	.0000	.0000	.0000
.1122	.2458	.2081	.2306	.1156
.0000	.0000	.0000	.0000	.0000
.0000	.0000	.0000	.0000	.0000
.1161	.2404	.2111	.2361	.1075
.0000	.0000	.0000	.0000	.0000
.1206	.2822	.2026	.1962	.0984
.1203	.2751	.2064	.2064	.0953
.0063	.0673	.0647	.4016	.4085
.1493	.2191	.1511	.1731	.1458
.1252	.2703	.2039	.2039	.1030
.1499	.2261	.1727	.1984	.0762
.0317	.1131	.1053	.4759	.2658
.1198	.2136	.1814	.2504	.1053
.0314	.0941	.1102	.4794	.2774
.1585	.2297	.1518	.2148	.0679
.1582	.2313	.1595	.1803	.0653
.1122	.2458	.2081	.2306	.1156
.1172	.2274	.1918	.2463	.1058
.1219	.2175	.1824	.2384	.1100
.1756	.2364	.1530	.1390	.0558
.1163	.2138	.1878	.2544	.1267
.1997	.2163	.1443	.1519	.0567
.0821	.1553	.1846	.3112	.2073
.0924	.1957	.2231	.3197	.0846
.0406	.1245	.0969	.2441	.4390
.1292	.2024	.2297	.2093	.1052

Table 4.4. Rates of Growth of Manufacturing and
Foreign Enterprises in Manufacturing under
Different Redistributions of Income

Redistribution Scheme	Annual Rate of Growth of Manufacturing[b]	Annual Rate of Growth of Share of Foreign Manufacturing[c]	Rate of Growth of Employment[d]
Growth in middle class, lower-class share constant			
7–4.7–10[a]	.0742	.0073	.0480
7–9–4	.0672	.0015	.0464
Growth in upper class, at expense of lower class			
3–6.3–10	.0762	.0072	.0494
9–6.2–7	.0692	.0042	.0421
Growth in middle-class share, upper class constant			
2–9–7	.0729	.0041	.0490
9–6.2–7	.0692	.0042	.0421
Most regressive			
0–7–10.7	.0783	.0080	.0510
Most progressive			
.246–3–3	.0566	.0009	.0312
Constant growth			
7–7–7	.0705	.0042	.0446

[a] Rate of growth of disposable income of lower, middle and upper classes, respectively.

[b] Annual rates of growth for all columns were calculated according to the formula

$$G^t = \Sigma a_i{}^t \gamma_i.$$

γ_i is the average growth rate of industry i, from table 4.5. $a_i{}^t$ is the share of industry i. Starting from a 1965 base, annual revisions were made in the share by

$$a_i{}^t = \frac{a_i{}^{t-1}(1 + \gamma_i)}{1 + G^{t-1}}.$$

An average rate of growth G is derived from the annual growth rates by solving

$$(1 + G)^{10} = \prod_{t=1}^{10} (1 + G^t).$$

Base year weights for labor and output were taken from Fundação IBGE, *Industrias de Transformação Dados Gerais Brasil — 1964/65* (Rio de Janeiro, 1967). For foreign manufacturing we took the market share estimated in Samuel Morley and Gordon Smith, "Import Substitution and Foreign Investment in Brazil," *Oxford Economic Papers* (March 1971), table 5, calculated the 1965 profits in each sector accruing to foreign firms, assuming profits were equal for foreign and national firms, then calculated the share of total foreign profits in each manufacturing sector.

[c] Rate of growth of foreign share $= \frac{(1 + G_F)}{(1 + G_M)}$ where G_F is foreign growth rate and G_M is growth rate of total manufacturing.

[d] Assumes labor-output elasticity equal to its observed level in the 1959–62 period. This is a crude adjustment for labor-saving technical change.

so. For example, in our most regressive scheme the upper-class share rises from 35 percent to 49 percent and the lower-class share falls from 18.5 percent to 9.4 percent over ten years. In the most progressive scheme (experiment 7) the lower-class share rises from 18.5 percent to 44.3 percent, while the real income per capita of the other two classes is held constant. These are changes which exceed, we believe, any change that is ever likely to occur in practice in the absence of revolution.

Looking more closely at the disaggregated growth rates in table 4.5, we see that when we shift from the most progressive to the least, experiment 7 to experiment 6, the growth rate of most products rise. Those whose growth rate is positively related to progressivity can be called necessities. They are cosmetics, food, tobacco, and both sectors of agriculture. A significant and expected pattern is the dependence of transportation equipment and rubber on the fortunes of the upper class. Any policy that increases the rate of growth of the upper class will increase the growth rate of the automobile industry and its suppliers, rubber, machinery, and metals. There are many products that, though not necessities as we have defined that term, grow more rapidly under a middle-class-oriented distribution policy, even if that means a redistribution away from the upper class. Compare the experiments with the growth rates 7–4.7–10 percent and 7–9–4 percent. We find that electric machinery, furniture, leather, textiles, clothing, and beverages increase their rates of growth when the middle-class share grows. This suggests that it is the middle class which is the principal market for household durables and clothing, an impression that is confirmed in tables 4.2 and 4.3. In the aggregate, this positive growth effect of progressivity is swamped by the negative effect on the important transportation industry.

Growth in Foreign Investment

An integral part of Furtado's diagnosis of the Brazilian growth pattern is a prediction of progressive denationalization of Brazilian industry.[14] He argues that the industrialization process has left Brazil with a tendency toward income concentration and an orientation toward luxury products like automobiles and consumer durables. But these are the products in which foreign firms are dominant.[15] If Brazilian industrial growth is led by such industries, then the foreign share should increase significantly over time. Such a development pattern would implicitly

14. Furtado, *Obstacles to Development*, pp. 154–55.
15. See Morley and Smith, "Import Substitution and Foreign Investment."

Table 4.5. Projected Growth Rates in Various Redistribution Experiments
(Percentages)

	(1) 7-4.7-10	(2) 7-9-4	(3) 3-6.3-10	(4) 9-6.2-7
Vegetable product	5.23	5.66	5.27	5.46
Animal product	4.90	5.44	4.89	5.22
Electricity	6.73	6.47	6.86	6.52
Commerce	6.57	6.32	6.63	6.41
Services	7.46	7.40	7.63	7.33
Wastes	8.31	6.94	8.56	7.44
Fuels	7.83	7.85	8.15	7.65
Packaging	5.90	6.08	6.01	5.94
Mining	6.72	6.39	6.93	6.43
Nonmetallic	8.31	6.64	8.53	7.28
Metals	8.14	6.70	8.34	7.27
Machinery	8.30	7.32	8.51	7.67
Electric machinery	9.21	9.23	9.76	8.92
Transportation equipment	11.63	7.40	11.77	9.36
Wood	7.85	6.60	8.07	7.05
Furniture	6.20	6.82	6.64	6.28
Paper	6.85	6.54	7.04	6.57
Rubber	10.82	7.83	11.21	8.97
Leather	6.38	6.53	6.58	6.34
Chemicals	7.06	6.97	7.28	6.88
Drugs	6.41	6.93	6.53	6.63
Cosmetics	5.21	5.74	5.24	5.49
Plastics	6.52	6.65	6.92	6.34
Textiles	6.86	7.07	7.18	6.78
Clothing	6.89	7.15	7.15	6.87
Food	4.67	5.20	4.65	4.99
Beverages	7.03	7.08	7.37	6.83
Tobacco	4.52	5.12	4.51	4.88
Publishing	8.05	7.11	8.35	7.34
Miscellaneous	7.03	6.93	7.35	6.76
Construction	8.93	6.51	9.11	7.52
Transport	7.86	8.37	8.21	7.93

Table 4.5 *(continued)*

(5) 2–9–7	(6) 0–7–10.7	(7) 24.3–3–3	(8) 7–7–7
5.53	5.21	5.51	5.48
5.20	4.79	5.54	5.21
6.75	6.95	5.82	6.60
6.52	6.69	6.00	6.44
7.64	7.73	6.61	7.44
7.91	8.86	5.46	7.61
8.25	8.32	6.31	7.86
6.15	6.04	5.55	6.02
6.81	7.07	5.35	6.57
7.70	8.86	5.27	7.43
7.64	8.62	5.52	7.40
8.06	8.74	6.15	7.81
9.90	10.02	6.72	9.27
9.62	12.37	6.08	9.45
7.47	8.35	5.30	7.20
7.08	6.79	4.85	6.56
6.93	7.18	5.54	6.70
9.77	11.80	5.11	9.26
6.71	6.67	5.61	6.47
7.29	7.40	5.88	7.03
6.85	6.51	6.46	6.70
5.55	5.17	5.66	5.52
7.08	7.11	4.75	6.61
7.36	7.31	5.61	6.98
7.34	7.25	5.99	7.03
4.96	4.55	5.32	4.98
7.46	7.55	5.46	7.06
4.85	4.40	5.26	4.87
7.91	8.63	5.41	7.54
7.36	7.54	5.32	6.97
7.89	9.52	5.15	7.65
8.57	8.32	6.82	8.16

contradict the nationalistic goals and aspirations of the regime, and it could be a potential source of future problems.

Our experiments confirmed the positive association of the foreign share with the regressivity of the income distribution. But the effect is weak. This finding is partly the result of the stability in the growth patterns over the various experiments. Another factor responsible is the nature of the foreign sector, which is a microcosm of Brazilian manufacturing with the important exception of automobiles. Look at table 4.6. It does not

Table 4.6. Weights Used in Calculating Aggregate Growth Rates
(Base year 1965)

Industry	Employment Share (by men)	Profit Share	Output Share	Foreign Investment Share
Nonmetallic	7.2	3.2	4.0	2.0
Metals	12.8	10.2	10.9	7.4
Machinery	3.9	2.2	3.0	3.5
Electric machinery	4.4	3.9	4.9	6.1
Transportation equipment	7.1	9.4	9.1	21.8
Wood	4.1	1.4	1.7	0
Furniture	2.5	1.1	1.3	0
Paper	2.6	2.3	2.3	2.2
Rubber	1.2	1.7	2.0	4.8
Leather	1.2	.8	.8	0
Chemicals	5.2	13.7	12.9	14.8
Drugs	1.9	1.2	2.3	2.7
Cosmetics	.7	1.1	1.2	2.2
Plastics	1.3	1.2	1.3	1.2
Textiles	16.5	11.1	11.3	10.3
Clothing	4.9	2.6	2.7	0
Food	13.8	28.5	21.9	18.0
Beverages	2.6	1.8	2.2	.5
Tobacco	.9	.9	1.1	2.0
Publishing	3.4	1.2	1.8	0
Miscellaneous	1.9	.8	1.2	0
TOTAL	100.0	100.0	100.0	100.0

appear to be true in Brazil that foreign firms locate only, or even principally, in sectors with high demand elasticities. According to our rough calculations about 60 percent of foreign investment profits come from the nondynamic or vegetative part of manufacturing. In several cases, notably tobacco and drugs, the foreign firms dominate sectors whose growth rates are positively correlated with progressivity. But those firms are overshadowed in the aggregate by the 25 percent of foreign investment associated with the automobile industry.

One could probably show that there is a new and an old foreign investment sector. The latter is located in the final consumer goods that underwent import substitution early. We would speculate that the foreign investment in machinery, consumer durables, and automobiles, i.e. the high income-elasticity goods, is more recent, that it is the product of the import substitution phase of the 1950s. When we look at the overall Brazilian industrial structure, the impression we now get is of foreign firms spread throughout, with a slight and undoubtedly growing concentration in the fastest growing parts of industry. It is because foreign firms are so widespread that their relative growth rate is so insensitive to changes in final demand.

The figures in table 4.4 show the estimates of the annual growth rate of the foreign share. They were made on the assumption that the foreign share of each industry would remain at its 1965 level. This may be a conservative estimate although a recent study suggests that foreign investment has been growing slower than manufacturing as a whole during the last few years.[16] Our results suggest that the foreign share will grow slightly over the next ten years, with the gain ranging from .01 percent to .8 percent per year. Since the 1965 base year share of foreign investment is about one-third, this annual growth rate implies that the share will grow by less than 3 percent in absolute terms over ten years. This undramatic change in share, coupled with the insensitivity of the growth pattern to changes in demand, suggest to us that the problem of denationalization will not be a particularly significant one in the future. The era of rapid growth of foreign investment in Brazil came during the import substitution era of the 1950s when entirely new foreign-dominated industries like automobiles and consumer durables were being established. Given the current industrial structure, we can now forecast a more balanced growth, and with it a general stability in the share of foreign firms.

16. U.S. Department of State, Airgram A529, "Foreign Investment in Brazil" (Rio de Janeiro, December 28, 1970), p. 7. From year end 1966 through year end 1969 total additions to foreign investment are given as $.5 billion. Since the stock is estimated at around $3.5 billion in 1966, this is a three-year growth rate of less than 15 percent, far less than the growth rate of Brazilian industry.

Labor Absorption

Our experiments generated an unexpected implication about the demand for labor. As table 4.4 shows, in each experiment the rate of growth of labor in manufacturing adjusted for technical change (assumed to be Harrod-Neutral) exceeds the rate of growth of population by a significant amount. Is this optimistic result believable and if so, why do our estimated growth rates for labor differ so markedly from the actual experience during the 1950s, when industry had roughly the same rate of growth we are projecting? If one looks at the patterns of employment and growth during that period, he is struck by the tremendous rates of apparent technical progress in certain sectors. The difference between the annual rate of growth in labor and output in transportation equipment is 22 percent! For machinery the difference is 32 percent! Textiles registers an absolute decline in employment, although this may be explained by the exclusion of household production in the 1960 census.

We would argue that the industrialization of the 1950s was unbalanced and intentionally capital intensive. New products such as synthetic textiles, consumer durables, and automobiles were produced internally for the first time. There were all capital-intensive products. It is conceivable that this process will continue, but given the small share of goods now imported, it is much more likely that future industrial growth will come from an expansion in internal demand rather than substitution of capital-intensive imports. If future industrial growth is generated by the natural expansion of income and demand, we see no reason why the apparently labor-saving trend of the 1950s should be expected to continue.

How do changes in the distribution of income affect the relative growth rate of labor? Surprisingly it turns out that the more progressive the distribution, the *slower* the increase in the share of labor. The quantitative effect of progressivity is small, but its direction is unmistakable. This finding reflects two things. First, in Brazil, capital goods and consumer durables are relatively labor intensive.[17] Second, more regressive experiments have higher growth rates of all variables so it is not surprising that

17. Our definition of durables includes transportation equipment, metals, electric machinery, machinery, furniture, rubber, and wood. These industries employ 36 percent of the manufacturing labor force and produce 32.9 percent of its output. Nondurables are all other sectors except plastics, chemicals, and nonmetallic minerals. This group employs 50.4 percent of the labor force and produces 48.8 percent of output.

the growth in employment also is higher. The reason for the higher growth rates is, as indicated earlier, the increase in demand for capital goods associated with distribution schemes favoring either of the top two classes. Paradoxically, it is precisely *because* of the extra capital goods demanded, which after all have to be produced, that output and employment growth rates are positively related to regressivity.

We have been looking at three particular aspects of the future that are potential sources of instability and trouble for the Brazilian government, namely the maintenance of an adequate rate of growth, denationalization of Brazilian industry, and labor absorption in manufacturing. We have found that plausible variations in income distribution had surprisingly little effect on the pattern of growth. This is partly because of the failure of demand to change substantially when income is transferred from one class to another and partly because of the influence of intermediate production. Brazilian industry has a well-developed intermediate and capital goods sector. Different patterns of final demand tend to produce similar growth in intermediate and capital goods production. If our results are valid they have three implications. First, labor absorption in, and denationalization of, Brazilian industry are not very sensitive to changes in the distribution of income, nor is either likely to be a major problem in the foreseeable future. Second, the stability of growth rates across our experiments means that the Brazilian government could afford a quite highly progressive redistribution without jeopardizing its growth goal or unduly penalizing important industries like automobiles or consumer durables. In other words, on the economic front we do not see the necessity of repression of the lower portions of the income profile or undue favoritism to the upper. Third, the hope that some internal economic contradiction will bring down the current Brazilian government is not justified, a conclusion also reached by Philippe Schmitter elsewhere in this volume. Brazil has a well-balanced economy capable of a long period of satisfactory growth.

This is not to say that there are no problems but rather that the problem never has been a potential lack of demand or stagnation. We can more easily imagine Brazil confronting saving constraints than oversaving. Her problem is more likely to be an excess of investment opportunities relative to savings rather than a lack of them. The difficulty is not a matter of too much saving and too little spending, but exactly the reverse.

Appendix 4.1: Characteristics of the Fundação Getúlio Vargas Budget Survey

1. The coverage of urban areas is quite extensive. All regions of the country are represented.
2. Unlike many such surveys, it did include small interior towns, as well as large capital cities. Thus, something like a representative sample is more closely approximated.
3. Unfortunately, the rural sample seems biased in favor of farm operators (higher income), and the expenditure figures, collected as they were through interviews rather than from written records, must be quite rough.
4. The exact method by which the sample was drawn has never been clarified in print, although oral tradition has it that the sample bears *some* relation to census data. The method of sampling may seriously impair the validity of this data for our purposes.
5. The surveys covered a period of violent inflation and rather violent changes in relative prices. These were not "normal times." Quite apart from the survey procedure one can make a good case that 1961–63 is not a very good period to use in analyzing the 1970s. Consumption shares, particularly those of new industries such as consumer durables or automobiles, were probably depressed by the high prices and lack of availability of many products. Protection was high, industries were new, quality was low, and costs were still suffering from the initial inefficiencies facing new enterprise in less developed countries. As relative prices and costs fell, the share of expenditures on these products must have risen in relative terms, since their price elasticity was almost certainly greater than one. This factor will tend to bias downward the estimated impact of regressive income redistribution policies on the pattern of industrial growth.
6. The rural survey was completed a year after the urban survey. While the income classes were somewhat altered, the inflation between the two years must distort our estimated expenditure patterns by income class. This difficulty is lessened by our aggregating the nine reported classes down to three. Nonetheless, one should not use our estimates as a proxy for the distribution of income in Brazil.

Appendix 4.2: Making the Budget Studies Consistent with the Industrial Census

The consumption figures published by the Fundação Getúlio Vargas (FGV) in their budget studies are not disaggregated in a manner consistent with the industrial classification used by the IBGE. There is an excessive disaggregation of services and too great an aggregation in other budget items. In order to disaggregate we used the detailed expenditure breakdowns that were published for each city in FGV, Pesquisa sobre Orçamentos Familiares "Ponderações" (Rio de Janeiro, 1961–62). This publication gives detailed expenditure information for each city for each of the consumption classes reported in the urban and rural surveys. By assuming that the consumption patterns within each of the consumption classes was the same for each income class, we could take the shares for the city as a whole as representative of each class, and thus regroup consumption expenditures into the industrial classification. The general reclassifications were the following:

Maintenance was broken down into electricity, wood, and employee salaries (which were excluded). Food was divided between expenditures on animal and vegetable products. Household articles was divided into furniture, nonmetallic minerals (ceramics and glass), electric machinery, and a part of textiles (rugs) and plastics. Cleaning materials was subdivided into paper and soap. The latter was combined with personal care articles to form cosmetics. Manufactured clothing and textiles was broken into leather, clothing, and textiles. Health was divided between medical services and drugs. Services was the sum of expenditures on restaurants, rent, cleaning, personal care services, part of health, recreation, education, and a part of travel. The other categories of the budget survey have direct crossover to the industrial classification. Expenditures on owned automobile was broken into rubber and fuel.

5   Associated-Dependent Development: Theoretical and Practical Implications

FERNANDO HENRIQUE CARDOSO

Almost everyone, victors as well as vanquished, was taken by surprise by the ease with which the Brazilian populist regime was overthrown in 1964 and by the nature and extent of the subsequent military rule. In the impassioned aftermath of 1964 much of the discussion concerning the nature of the new military regime revolved around the rather sterile debate as to whether the military movement was a "coup" or a "revolution." Later a more serious analytic discussion ensued as to whether the 1964 coup should be seen as a "restoration movement," as one very able foreign observer, Philippe Schmitter, has called it.

Those who emphasize that the current authoritarian regime has many roots in the Estado Nôvo period are correct in some respects. However, a central thesis of this chapter is that the regime established in 1964 is not simply a return to the past. I will attempt to demonstrate that the regime represents a fundamentally new political restructuring of the polity and that this restructuring is closely interrelated with basic economic and social changes that became significant in the late 1950s and are now occurring at an even more rapid rate.[1] Furthermore, I contend that most analytic discussions concerning the nature and future of the current Brazilian regime have neglected or incorrectly interpreted the implications of these changes and that all too frequently analysts do not take into account, either theoretically or empirically, the dynamic, mutually shaping, *interrelationship* between politics and economics.

This chapter thus has three main goals:

1. It attempts to analyze the context in which the new regime emerged and to emphasize what is particular to it. My analysis stresses the dynamic process by which new forms of national

1. This essay was already written when I received Alfred Stepan's book on the changing pattern of military intervention in Brazil. In his book Stepan shows the effects of the overall changes I discuss on the military institutions and consequently on the type of intervention they exercise at present.

political power and new international economic forces have inter-
acted and resulted in the emergence of what I call the new
"associated-dependent development" in Brazil.

2. It attempts to show that some of the major analytic interpretations of the new regime, such as those found in the writing
of Celso Furtado, Hélio Jaguaribe, or Cândido Mendes, have
(despite their frequent brilliance) contributed to the conceptual
confusion concerning the regime and its relationship to the "associated-dependent" model. I argue that these interpretations
give overly static, mechanistic views of the relationship between
the economy and the polity. They err either on the side of excessive *economic determinism,* which does not take into consideration the full implication of "associate-dependent development,"
or on the side of excessive *political voluntarism,* which does not
take into consideration any economic constraints on political
elites or sufficiently consider internal contradictions within the
political elite.

3. Keeping in mind the dynamic interrelationship between
politics and economics, it attempts to suggest the range of possible futures for the Brazilian development model and to offer
some useful insights both for people actively involved in politics
and for analysts.

THE NEW MODEL OF "ASSOCIATED-DEPENDENT DEVELOPMENT":
POLITICAL AND ECONOMIC IMPLICATIONS

As I asserted before, the new bureaucratic-authoritarian political regime is closely related to the changes in the pattern of
economic development in Brazil and in the balance of political
forces on which that development was based.

During the Kubitschek administration (1956–61) the older
model of economic development was undermined and lost its
force. That model, which had emerged in the 1930s — with the
Volta Redonda steel plant, if one wishes to refer to a landmark
and a symbol — gained momentum during World War II and
became the predominant policy in the second Vargas government
(1950–54). In essence that policy orientation concentrated on
strengthening the role of the state as investor, particularly in the
expansion of heavy industry and in the formation of an infrastructure for the production of durable consumer goods. That
policy orientation, as has now been well documented, was more
a short-term response to practical problems than a coherent set
of projections based on a nationalist ideology. Yet it had important effects on the style of economic development. It helped
shape a development pattern in which, in descending order of

importance, the state, native Brazilian capital, and foreign capital (mainly to finance public undertakings) were the main propellers of economic growth.

With Kubitschek's policy of rapid industrialization and the expansion of the urban middle-class market for manufactured goods, a redistribution of influence began to take place. There was a noticeable change in the groups attempting to influence economic policy decisions, as well as changes concerning the control of the investment process. The social bases of the populist regime (whether in its authoritarian stage under the Estado Nôvo or in the later democratic periods under Kubitschek, Quadros, and Goulart) began to correspond less and less to the class sectors controlling the productive forces. To this increasing incongruence in the internal arrangements relating the economic structure to the social and political structures, one must add the effects of changes in the organization of the capitalist economy at the international level. To put it succinctly, international corporations began to diversify not only the lines of production and economic activity under their control, but even the geographical distribution of their plants. For the purposes of our argument, the essential factor is that international capitalism became more interested in establishing productive units such as factories and plants in the periphery, that is, in the underdeveloped countries.

In the three largest countries in Latin America — Brazil, Mexico, and Argentina, all of which have sizable domestic markets — United States direct private investment has gone increasingly into the manufacturing sector. (See table 5.1.)

In Brazil the level of foreign private investment in the dynamic industrial sectors has been so high and so sustained that the state sector and national entrepreneurs clearly no longer play a dominant role in such key decision-making centers as the capital goods and durable consumer goods industries. (See table 5.2.) This growing industrial power of foreign-owned manufacturing firms which sell to the domestic market also means that foreign firms are the main advertisers in Brazil. According to a 1967 *Visão* article, for example, the twelve major advertisers in Brazil (as measured by the accounts of the principal advertising agencies) were: Willys Overland, Sydney Ross, Volkswagen, Gillette, Gessey Lever, Nestlé, Ford, Rhodia, Fleishman and Royal, Coca-Cola, Shell, and Colgate Palmolive.[2] They thus have a great potential influence on organs of opinion such as newspapers, weekly

2. *Visão* (São Paulo, September 1967), cited in Fernando Magalhães, "El perverso 'milagro económico Brasileño,'" *Panorama Económico*, no. 265 (Santiago, Chile, November–December 1971), p. 34.

Table 5.1. United States Direct Investments in Manufacturing
as a Component of Total United States Direct
Investment in Latin America
(In percentages)

Years	Total for Latin America	Argentina	Brazil	Mexico	Other Countries
1929	7	25	24	1	4
1940	8	20	29	3	3
1946	13	39	39	21	6
1950	18	45	44	32	7
1952	21	50	51	43	1
1955	22	51	51	45	7
1956	22	51	50	46	8
1959	17	43	53	47	7
1960	19	45	54	49	8
1961	20	43	54	50	7
1962	22	51	56	51	8
1963	24	55	59	55	8
1964	26	57	67	59	9
1965	29	62	67	64	11
1966	31	63	68	64	12
1967	32	63	67	66	13
1968	34	64	69	68	14

SOURCE: F. Fajnsyler, *Estrategia industrial y empresas internacionales: Posición relativa de América Latina y Brasil* (Santiago: Naciones Unidas, CEPAL, November 1971), p. 204. This study is based mainly on official U.S. figures published in *Survey of Current Business.*

Table 5.2. Source of Capital for the Ten Largest Firms
in Each Economic Sector in Brazil, 1968
(In percentages)

Sectors	Foreign Capital	State Capital	Brazilian Private Capital
Infrastructure	17.2	73.1	9.7
Intermediate goods	34.6	52.0	13.4
Capital goods	72.6	–	27.4
Durable consumer goods	78.3	–	21.7
Nondurable consumer goods	53.4	6.4	40.2
Commerce	7.0	–	93.0
Services	8.2	–	91.8

SOURCE: Unpublished research study prepared by ADECIF in Rio de Janeiro and published in *Jornal do Brasil,* 20 April 1970.

magazines, and television, much of whose revenue is dependent upon advertising.

The general consequences of these new trends in international capitalism have been (1) increased interdependence in production activities at the international level, particularly if we look at the world economic system from the standpoint of influence on decision centers, and (2) a modification in the patterns of dependence that condition, or set constraints and limits to, the development policies of the countries located at the periphery of the international capitalist system.[3] It is true, as table 5.1 indicates, that the state, public enterprises, and local capitalists have retained some role and influence. But there has been a basic change in the main axis of the power system. The dynamic basis of the productive system has shifted. The result of these basic changes is that groups expressing the interests and modes of organization of international capitalism have gained disproportionate influence. From the perspective of our argument, it does not matter greatly whether the industrial firms are owned outright by foreigners or are owned by Brazilians associated with foreign corporations, for in either case they are linked to market, investment, and decision-making structures located outside the dependent country.

Another crucial factor in understanding the current political-economic model in Brazil is that the antipopulist sectors of the military and the technocracy, which had been relatively uninfluential in the populist model of development, gained in influence as the new economic trend emerged. Given their ideological affinity to the new holders of economic power, and the similarity of their policy orientations, they have played an important and often decisive role in the creation of the present regime. The antipopulist sectors of the military and technocracy have taken upon themselves not only the modernizing function in administration, but also much of the repressive function in the social and political realm.

In the same process the older ruling sectors have lost their

3. On the new patterns of dependence, see my study (with Enzo Faletto) *Dependencia y desarrollo en América Latina* (México: Siglo XXI, 1970). For an up-to-date analysis on the effect of the policies adopted by the multinational corporations on the Latin American economies, see F. Fajnzylber, *Estrategia industrial y empresas internacionales: Posición relativa de América Latina y Brasil* (CEPAL, 1970) and *Sistema industrial y exportación de manufacturas: Análisis de la experiencia brasileña* (CEPAL, 1970). Also, Anibal Pinto and Jan Kñackál, *El sistema centro-periferia veinte años después,* 3rd ed. (CEPAL, 1971).

relative power position in the total structure. Not only the traditional agrarian sectors (*latifundiários*), but even industrial and merchant interests that have not adapted to the changed conditions under which the expansion of the market is now being sought and to the redirection of governmental economic and financial policies have found themselves politically at a disadvantage in the new regime.[4] As a parallel process, there has been a nearly complete erosion from below of the power groups and structures on which the previous system was based. The more traditional, bureaucratic component of the middle classes has lost prestige and influence. The position of the career politicians, generally identified with the dominant classes in the previous arrangement, has also been extensively undermined. These politicians had served to express, at the overt political level, the class alliance in terms of which power had been organized since the Old Republic (1889–1930). This alliance had survived (though not without important changes in its internal structure) and had made the "national-populist" development model viable for some time. In the case of the other component of the alliance — the more integrated sectors of the working class — marginalization was no less marked. Consider the complete disappearance from the political scene of the union leaders who mediated between these workers and the state.

My main hypothesis to explain such sweeping changes in the relative power positions of all the major political actors is that the accumulation process required that the instruments of pressure and defense available to the popular classes be dismantled.[5]

4. For an analysis of these changes, with particular reference to the ideological expressions of the whole process through which some sectors redefined their interests, see my *Ideologias de la burguesía industrial en sociedades dependientes: (Argentina y Brazil)* (México: Siglo XXI, 1971).

5. I am making only general remarks about the structural roots of the 1964 crisis. Of course, the picture is very complex and could not be adequately sketched within the limits of this chapter. It is, however, appropriate to point out the factors behind the institutional crisis, which has been called the end of the import substitution process. It had become necessary to restructure the mechanisms of accumulation at a higher level, one that would be better adjusted to the advances already accomplished in the development of the productive forces. This restructuring would require, among other things, keeping down the wage level and therefore dismantling an array of union and political organizations through which, in the populist period, the wage earners were able to resist part of the pressure for accumulation. In this sense, Morley and Smith's statement in this volume that from the economic point of view repression is not necessary is a purely formal one. Historically, it *was* necessary. Of course, once a regime has become established

This the 1964 coup did immediately, through repression. The bourgeoisie paid a price. By accepting military intervention at first in order to destroy the influence of the workers, it ultimately contributed to the creation of a situation in which a return to civilian control of the political process proved impossible. In other words, in its attempt to contain the "pressure from below," the bourgeoisie supported measures that essentially destroyed its own direct political expression. It is true that the bourgeoisie never had effective political organization and pressure instruments. Now, however, not only the political party system but all other forms of political action open to the bourgeoisie became dependent on contacts and alliances with the military and technocratic groups that alone controlled the state apparatus. Whatever the long-range implications, this much can be said: The bourgeoisie lost all leverage to shape its more immediate political interests.

However, in order to understand a political model, it is not sufficient to direct attention to the social and economic pillars that support it. It is also necessary to describe the particular mechanisms through which it generates and organizes power, the mechanisms that make it viable as a relatively stable political structure.

The current Brazilian development model has caused great analytic confusion. As we shall see in greater detail later, some analysts have asserted that the economic interests of foreign capital are now dominant and that this means that there is no room either for political maneuvering or national development in Brazil. Others believe that the military leaders have acquired a position of such great power that, free of external constraints or internal contradictions, they can and have imposed their own development model on Brazil.

I will attempt to demonstrate here that these observers are mistaken in their assumptions about the high degree of autonomy and internal coherence of the dominant economic and/or political interests. They do not understand the dynamics of the

and accepted, and as long as it seems that it will go on functioning without social and political pressures, it is possible to imagine, idyllically, that repression is unnecessary. However, this is a naive, static view of an historical process. Without repression those pressures may grow, eventually affecting the very "rationality of the system." For an analysis of the structural process underlying the political crisis of 1964, see the essay "Raizes estruturais da crise política brasileira," in my book *Mudanças sociais na America Latina* (São Paulo: Difusão Européia do Livro, 1969), orginally printed in *Les Temps Modernes* (Paris, October 1967).

process that I call associated-dependent development when they assert that it entails stagnation.

Before discussing their work in detail, I should clarify what I see as some of the crucial characteristics of the model of associated-dependent development. The phrase was chosen deliberately to combine two notions that traditionally have appeared as separate and contradictory: development and dependence. In my view, changes in international capitalist organization have produced a new international division of labor. The moving force behind these changes is the multinational corporation. Assuming as it does the immersion of industrial capital into peripheral economies, the new international division of labor puts a dynamic element into operation in the internal market. Thus, *to some extent,* the interests of the foreign corporations become compatible with the internal prosperity of the dependent countries. In this sense, they help promote development. Because of this factor, the growth of multinational corporations necessitates a reformulation of the traditional view of economic imperialism which holds that the basic relationship between a developed capitalist country and an underdeveloped country is one of extractive exploitation that perpetuates stagnation. Today, the massive investment of foreign capital aimed at manufacturing and selling consumer goods to the growing urban middle and upper classes is consistent with, and indeed dependent upon, fairly rapid economic growth in at least some crucial sectors of the dependent country. Development under this set of conditions implies, quite obviously, a definite articulation with the international market (the same thing happens, of course, in the relationships among advanced economies). Development in this situation also depends on technological, financial, organizational, and market connections that only multinational corporations can assure.

In many Latin American intellectual circles the idea that associated-dependent development is in some important sense *dynamic* will be considered a controversial, revisionist assertion. Let me add at this point that this path of development entails costs. The data generated during the Brazilian "boom" based on associated-dependent development support the hypothesis that this pattern of development is based on a regressive profile of income distribution (as Fishlow's data in Chapter 3 show), emphasizes luxury consumer durables as opposed to basic necessities (see table 5.3), generates increasing foreign indebtedness (see table 5.4), and contributes to social marginality and the underutilization and exploitation of manpower resources.

Table 5.3. Total Output of Key Selected Goods in Brazil:
Average Annual Change, 1964–70
(In percentages)

Type of good	Total output	Per capita output	Urban per capita output
Foods	1.8	−0.8	−3.8
Textiles	0.1	−2.5	−5.4
Clothes	1.8	−0.6	−4.9
Automobiles	14.3	11.7	8.8

SOURCES: Based on data developed by IPEA (Brazilian Ministry of Planning) and ANFAVEA (The Association of Brazilian Automobile Manufacturers), cited in Fernando Magalhães, "El perverso 'milagro económico brasileño,'" *Panorama Económico* (Santiago de Chile), no. 265 (November–December 1971), p. 20.

Table 5.4. Foreign Debt and Reserves of Brazil
(Millions of U.S. dollars)

Period	Debt	Reserves
1963–64	3,161	–
1967	3,372	199
1968	3,917	257
1969	4,403	657
1970	5,295	1,187
1971[a]	6,000	1,378

SOURCES: Banco Central de Brasil and *Visão* (Rio de Janeiro, September 1971). Cited in Fernando Magalhães, "El perverso 'milagro económico brasileño,'" *Panorama Económico* (Santiago), no. 265 (November–December 1971), p. 16.
[a] As of 30 April 1971.

Having thus sketched out some of the most useful empirical and theoretical considerations for understanding the extraordinarily complex and complicated model that has emerged in Brazil, I will now examine in greater detail the works of the major Brazilian analysts, whose interpretations are basically at variance with mine.

THE INDETERMINACY OF ECONOMIC DETERMINIST MODELS: CELSO FURTADO AND HÉLIO JAGUARIBE

Much of the confusion surrounding the conflicting interpretations of Brazilian development since 1964 is rooted in the failure to draw fully the theoretical and empirical implications of the dynamic interdependence between politics and economics. This interdependence is implicitly denied in the linear arguments that are in essence economic determinist or political voluntarist. Oddly (but predictably, since interdependence is denied) the same theorist may shift from a position of traditional economic determinism (where he neglects the impact of politics) in attempting to describe the actual working of the system, to a position of political voluntarism (where he neglects the constraints imposed by the economic system) when he suggests a strategy for surmounting the present situation. The works of Celso Furtado and Hélio Jaguaribe, though often extremely valuable, are both flawed in precisely this way. In both cases these conceptual flaws are compounded because they cloud their perception of the process that I call associated-dependent development, and thus they do not take into consideration the full economic and political implications of the process.

Celso Furtado, in his analysis of the Brazilian political model, rightly points out one peculiarity of what he calls the military state: its bureaucratic character.[6] Yet his analysis starts from the assumption that the military state would have social stability as its major goal and that the consequence of preserving the status quo would be slow development. The economic model corresponding to this political project would be reduced to urban-industrial investment in favor of agricultural production. Through a "horizontal expansion of the economy" ("pastoralization") it would be possible to absorb manpower without altering the production functions, that is to say, without continuing to absorb modern technology. Such policies would make it possible to keep social pressures at a low level.

When Furtado wrote his influential analysis he was undoubtedly reacting to an existing ideological tendency within the 1964 movement that could be interpreted as advocating such a model. Yet, as Furtado himself admits, the reality of Brazilian development was more complex. To begin with, the army bureaucracy, in control of the state apparatus, was likely to be inadequately responsive to the pressures of a rather highly differentiated society with comparatively high interclass mobility. Precisely for that reason, he adds, the middle class — a particularly effective political actor in the new situation — would probably react in one (or a combination) of three ways:

6. Celso Furtado, "De l'oligarchie à l'état militaire," in Les Temps Modernes, no. 257 (Paris, October 1967). It appeared in Portuguese in Brasil: Tempos modernos, ed. Celso Furtado (Rio de Janeiro: Editôra Paz e Terra, 1968), pp. 1–23.

1. Fight for a return to formal democracy
2. Attempt to mobilize mass support, with a particularly effective appeal to youth and student groups as a starting base, but aiming especially at the rural masses, in opposition to the military state
3. Infiltrate the military by means of an ideological appeal stressing "authentically national" development, which, of course, would also attract some sectors of the middle class

The last alternative, authentically national development, is advocated by Furtado himself in his book *Un projeto para o Brasil* [a project for Brazil].[7] His ideas, however, did not gain much influence among the groups controlling the state. There clearly has also been no significant movement either toward a return to democracy or toward the mobilization of massive opposition.

Within the structure of Furtado's argument we are thus left with the "pastoralization" model as an estimate of the probable course of evolution of the new Brazilian regime. It is an estimate following from the kind of economic determinist, linear reasoning we have alluded to. In essence, it contends that the military state's policies are strictly determined by the social groups on which its power is based. In the Brazilian case, Furtado is implicitly assuming that base to be oligarchical and dependent. This seems to be inferred from the fact that the sectors of the bourgeoisie prevailing after the coup favor a pattern of development that is both associated with and dependent on international capitalism. As a consequence, social stability is valued as a goal and ruralization is the means to achieve it. Caught in cross-pressures from the latifundiários, international capitalism, and local entrepreneurs, the military state chooses the line of least resistance, which it understands to be that which will cater to the pressures from all these groups while presenting the least danger to its own integrity. The latter part of the chosen course of action implies keeping order, and particularly the hegemonic position of the armed forces.

In fairness, it must be said that Furtado has not really relied on this kind of prognosis. He estimates that the degree of social and economic differentiation already attained would make much more likely a model that is economically more dynamic and politically more flexible. That is why he then turns to speculation on the chances of a pattern of development that would be eco-

---

7. Celso Furtado, *Un projeto para o Brasil* (Rio de Janeiro: Editôra Saga, 1968).

nomically autonomous and politically more open. In the model
he proposes, development would be based on the ability of the
state, fueled by the middle class, to contain the excesses of international capitalism and promote development along national or
autonomous lines. What he is really suggesting then is a return
to the earlier nationalist development model politically adapted
to a situation in which the other element of the coalition, populism, has been wiped out. The new coalition and its policies
would be nationalist and technocratic. A major prerequisite for
its viability would be the enactment of an income redistribution
scheme that would broaden the market without endangering the
accumulation process.

Furtado's proposed development model found few powerful
supporters. The key middle-class actors in the model — the local
entrepreneurs and the sectors linked to the state — have chosen
a different path, as we shall see shortly. Any model comprises,
of course, an analysis of the existing situation and a set of goals
to direct action. However, Furtado's propositions lean much too
heavily toward the latter. They neglect the economic realities
of the new model of associated-dependent development and place
almost exclusive reliance on political voluntarism. Its lack of
appeal must be attributed to the anachronistic undertones of his
version of a national-developmentalist ideology based on the
assumptions that a politically capable middle class exists and
that it would be interested in supporting that ideology or model
of development.

Before discussing in greater detail the issues raised by Furtado,
let me turn to Hélio Jaguaribe, another important political analyst who has also explored the possibility of an authentically national route to development.[8]

According to Jaguaribe, there are three fundamental political
alternatives for a development process under optimal conditions.
Each, to be applicable, is dependent upon a specific set of conditions:

1. "National capitalism." This depends on an alliance among
   the progressive sectors of the national entrepreneurs, the
   middle class, and the proletariat, under a neo-Bismarckian
   style of leadership by the head of state and unified into
   a national party for development.

8. Hélio Jaguaribe, "Stabilité sociale par le colonial-fascisme," *Les Temps
Modernes*, no. 257 (Paris, October 1967). Quotations in the text are from
the Brazilian edition "Brasil: Estabilidade social pelo colonial-fascismo?" in
Furtado, *Brasil: Tempos modernos*, pp. 25–47.

2. "State capitalism." By means of a coup, power comes to be controlled by the progressive sectors of the military and technocracy, which weld themselves together into a coalition approximating a "party of national revolution." Their leverage in this process is the state apparatus itself.

3. "Developmental socialism." This presupposes a revolutionary takeover by an elite willing to mobilize the masses and to resort to socialist means of accumulation and control.

Before 1964, it seems that Jaguaribe's prescription for Brazil, given his judgment of the existing social and political conditions, was the national capitalist development model. After that date, by virtue of the changes that had taken place, he seems to have inclined toward the state capitalist model.

However, the political model that Jaguaribe believes will actually become institutionalized is "colonial-fascism." Unfortunately, since his main purpose is to argue how unviable this trend is, he has not fully elaborated the colonial-fascist model. He did, however, suggest some of its characteristics in the Brazilian case.[9] Colonial-fascism, he says, depends at least on the following:

1. Strengthening the state, not in order to make possible a significant extent of interference and control of the economy, but in order to preserve stability, which of course depends on maximum use of coercion capabilities

2. Close integration, political as well as economic, of Brazil with the Western system as it is being structured by the United States

3. Reliance, under state supervision, on the market: control of the economy must be, as far as possible, in the hands of private economic units

This model would permit — as it did in fascist Italy and Germany — economic development without changes in the social structure. However, given the dependent character of the Brazilian economy, the local bourgeoisie, unlike its German or Italian counterpart, would be unable to place the economy on a dynamic growth plane. It would also be impossible to establish an appropriate coalition between entrepreneurs and a middle-class party, which he sees as the political axis of the typical fascist model. Instead entrepreneurs ally with international capitalism.

9. Jaguaribe, "Brasil: Estabilidade social pelo colonial-fascismo?" pp. 25–47, esp. pp. 33–34.

Hence the "colonial" in his description of this type of fascism. In the Castello Branco government's economic policies and its concentration of coercive powers, Jaguaribe perceived a clear trend toward colonial-fascism. The fundamental prerequisites for this model's functioning were apparently being deliberately prepared by government policies. Yet Jaguaribe does not think the model can work in Brazil. For one thing, "the colonial-fascist model would in a few years aggravate the disequilibrium between population growth and the opening up of new employment opportunities, at all occupational levels, to such an extent that the new ruling classes would soon be compelled to enforce some sort of apartheid, that is, to prevent peasant immigration into the cities, where they would become explosive marginal masses." Secondly, "the dominant economy needs raw materials from the dependent economy . . . and cannot induce any dynamic effect on it . . . as long as the dependent economy does not develop a domestic market. . . . Yet the colonial-fascist model aims precisely to prevent the social changes required for the development of such an autonomous and endogenous economy." [10]

In short, Jaguaribe believes that the military regime will not be able to maintain itself if it keeps a colonial-fascist orientation, since this makes it impossible to overcome the structural impasses just mentioned. Thus, given that, in the long run, the military regime is incompatible with the complexity of the urban-industrial sector, political and socioeconomic changes will certainly take place once the fear that led the industrialists and the middle class to accept the colonial-fascist model vanishes. The options will then probably be limited to two: either the military will reinstate into power-controlling positions the social groups that are presently marginalized (in which case, of course, some will wish to assume civilian political roles through the political parties and so on) or the military themselves will transform the fundamental nature and meaning of the regime.

Initially, in 1967, Jaguaribe believed that the first hypothesis was more likely. Now he seems to regard the second — the regime changing itself from within — as a better approximation of reality.[11]

Let us now take a closer look at the two analytical schemes we have discussed thus far. Both start from the assumption that the economic model now being developed is not (or is insufficiently)

10. Ibid., pp. 43, 44.

11. See, for example, his, "Enfoques sôbre a América Latina: Análise crítica de recentes relatórios," presented to the Bariloche meeting of the Consejo Latinoamericano de Ciencias Sociales (CLACSO), November 1970.

dynamic. Celso Furtado speaks of pastoralization and stagnation, while Jaguaribe describes the Brazilian fascist model as colonial. According to Jaguaribe, today's metropolis-colony relationships can still be described in terms of an international division of labor in which the colony specializes in exporting raw materials, and such a relationship must be seen as an obstacle to development. Viewing the Brazilian economy as nondynamic suggests two consequences. One is that the guarantors of the regime, the military, pursue a goal of social stabilization that requires economic stagnation. This follows from the assumed correspondence between the regime's social basis — the agrarian oligarchy — and its economic interests. The military, then, is nothing but the instrument of the oligarchy, regardless of the military's own corporate interests. The second consequence of this view is that the solution to the impasse must be to come back to a pattern of authentically national development, based, of course, on the assumption that the system's lack of dynamism derives from its dependent character. However, once it is realized that the Brazilian bourgeoisie, or its hegemonic sectors, has opted for the pattern of associated-dependent development, the basis for autonomous development must be sought somewhere else. Among the other possible candidates, the middle class is the strategic actor. Certain functional groups, specifically some sectors of the military or the governmental technocracy, both identified with the middle class in their social characteristics, come to be seen as decisive. These, then, would be the actors charged with the responsibility of carrying forward the project of authentically national development.

It is time to pause and ask: how much of this is an objective attempt to analyze real, existing tendencies, and how much is simply the preferred, normative model? An objective analysis would show, in fact, a very different picture. Associated-dependent development is *not* without dynamism; it is *not* based on ruralization at the expense of industrialization; it does *not* reinforce the old division of labor in which some countries only exported raw materials and imported manufactured goods.

On the contrary, the distinguishing feature of the new type of dependency that is evolving in countries like Brazil, Argentina, and Mexico is that it is based on a new international division of labor. Part of the industrial system of the hegemonic countries is now being transferred, under the control of international corporations, to countries that have already been able to reach a relatively advanced level of industrial development. I have elsewhere called this process an "internationalization of the internal market," in contrast to the previous stage of import substitution industrialization.[12] The latter was significantly controlled by the local bourgeoisie and by the state.

It is clear that both Celso Furtado and Hélio Jaguaribe are familiar with this process. They have not, however, come to terms with all of its implications, as one can perceive from their description of the major political actors and the policies they should be willing to carry out.

The model of associated-dependent development does have a dynamic character. It does allow for economic growth and social mobility, at least for the urban-industrial sector. Undoubtedly it does not prevent class attrition, it does almost certainly have a "marginalizing" effect, and it does not reduce inequality; on the contrary, it is based on concentration of income and increasing relative misery.

The task of the informed critic is not to deny or obscure these characteristics of the associated-dependent model of development. Instead, he must take them fully into consideration to make realistic assessments and identify the social groups that might be able to carry through an alternative model.

In Furtado's and Jaguaribe's analyses, the hope for an authentically national pattern of development, once pinned on the nationalist entrepreneurs, is now pinned on the middle class, and particularly on the military sector of the middle class. However, my analysis of associated-dependent development shows that the middle-class groups have, if anything, exerted pressure toward associated-dependent development. Rather than looking forward toward a "capitalism without capitalists," they have in practice favored growth through private capital, whether Brazilian or foreign, while other investment areas are reserved for the state itself.

What is the role of the military in this process? What did they initially intend and what has actually happened? Is there any reality to the idea that they might themselves replace the dependent-associated, bureaucratic-authoritarian models of development and rule with other models as is occasionally suggested by such authors as Furtado and Jaguaribe?

The Castello Branco "project" was politically and economically liberal, though its liberalism was qualified, of course, by the circumstances of an underdeveloped country: a strong executive, political party representation (appropriately purged to prevent pressures from the Left), and a combination of market mecha-

12. See Cardoso and Faletto, *Dependencia y desarrollo en América Latina.*

nisms with strong state regulation, strengthening private business, and opening the national economy to international capitalist investment and connections. The model had not foreseen either bureaucratic modernization or the steep rise in the participation of the public sector in the economy. Governmental policies of the Castello Branco period seemed to expect a massive contribution of foreign investment, which did not materialize. The government clearly intended to abide by its promise to restore democratic forms after purging the populist element. An illustration of this intention was Castello Branco's pledge to respect the electoral calendar, despite the risks this might imply for the regime. Finally, the Castello Branco model called for the army to refrain from exercising its overwhelming corporate influence on political decisions. This model in theory would benefit the party system and therefore the bourgeois sectors represented in it.

However, the military did not implement this model. They did, of course, share the goal of a strong executive, but they placed it under their direct control. This was accomplished, for example, by changing the organization and role of the military and civil offices of the presidency; broadening the scope of the National Security Council and particularly the latter's General Secretariat; creating a national intelligence service; and establishing security departments in all the ministries and state enterprises. In short, the aim was to establish ever-tighter linkages between the planning and control agencies of the executive and their counterparts in the armed forces, especially the chiefs of staff. Through these coordination devices, they sought to achieve greater control over all the key economic sectors and to accelerate economic growth. Thus the military came to accept as their own the goals of centralization of the administration and the repression of all forms of social protest. Making the state apparatus more efficient and increasing repression developed side by side. Both were justified by the doctrine of national security. Dismantling workers' organizations and achieving a high degree of "political tranquillity" should, quite naturally, make it possible to catch up again on the development process or, if you will, on capitalist accumulation on a greatly amplified scale. Thus, pursuing what at one level can be seen as their own policies, the military have in fact placed the model of dependent-industrial development on a sound, dynamic basis.

The military's actual policies, then, can be appropriately characterized as social stability with economic change. Yet even here one must qualify what is to be understood by stability. The term does refer, of course, to the maintenance of a class society, but it does not preclude mobility. Mobility occurs and is in fact ideologically encouraged, as long as it does not become associated with political mobilization. The policy is, in this sense, one of modern conservatism. Its aim is to keep socially open a politically closed society, while trying to accelerate capitalist economic growth through a combination of public and private enterprise.[13]

The main features of the present power arrangement, then, are the disproportionate amount of power held by the military (and, in a subordinate position, the technocracy) vis-à-vis the internationalizing bourgeoisie and the military's implementation of policies that entirely satisfy the internationalizing bourgeoisie's interests. This explains the complacent apathy of the urban middle class, not to mention the contentment and euphoria among those members of it who are beginning to enjoy the benefits of development through their employment in large private or public enterprises.

Thus an agreement has been reached between the Brazilian bourgeoisie and the state. The former has momentarily relinquished its political-control instruments (political party system, elections, and so on) as well as the instruments of symbolic-ideological definition and diffusion (freedom of the press, habeas corpus, doctrinaire pluralism, liberal education), all of which have become rather closely responsive to state pressures and military control. In the trade-off, civil society has contracted and the state has mushroomed, particularly with respect to the regulation of economic life. But in the process, the military implicitly assumed an identity between the economic interests of the entrepreneurs and the general interests of the nation. They defined some areas in which private business would be preferentially encouraged to act. Thus structured, this system does have a dynamic element built into it; the question of its durability does not concern us here. The system does have considerable social costs, but it has also opened up very promising opportunities for the

13. It is necessary to keep in mind the objective difficulties involved in the institutionalization of this model. First, there is the limited room afforded for social mobility by such an intrinsically marginalizing development process. A second difficulty involves the position of rural workers. The populist phase was not very different in this respect. It too managed to keep its unstable equilibrium and to go on with accumulation for some time thanks to the economic overexploitation and political marginalization of the rural workers. The present bureaucratic-authoritarian regime, however, will find this problem to be an even greater obstacle to the maintenance of its chosen course of development.

absorption of the modern sectors of the middle classes, linking
them through self-interest to the international bourgeoisie. This
is an important political fact.

Can this situation be described by seeing the state as an "executive committee" for the international bourgeoisie and the
military as the latter's armed hand? If this description were accurate, political analysis would be simple. The social process
would be conceived as a noncontradictory continuum or at best
as a continuum in which the only contradiction would be that
between the dominant classes, harmoniously integrated with the
state, and the dominated classes, excluded from the state and
hardly a part of an ongoing society. It seems more accurate, however, to underscore that the relative degree of stability achieved
in the alliance among the military, the bourgeoisie, and the
middle classes is the contrivance of a development model and a
political regime in which their interests are balanced as against
more serious enemies. This balance could be achieved, quite obviously, because their internal contradictions were not as antagonistic as the threat of a development policy generally favorable
to the popular classes.

Let us come back to a question raised at the beginning of this
chapter. Are we justified in inquiring about the possibly revolutionary economic consequences of the 1964 coup? Would it not
seem more apt to describe it as a victorious counterrevolution?
The answer is not simple. Clearly, the 1964 movement, through
conscious intention and by virtue of its own dynamics, did seek
and was able to impose its conception of order through repression.
In this sense, its consequences were clearly reactionary. Was it,
however, integrally counterrevolutionary? It is interesting to note
here, despite the appearance of triviality, that some of its main
actors assert this to have been the case, since they regard the
previous regime as revolutionary. It is true that, from 1963 to
March 1964, the Brazilian situation could be described as pre-
revolutionary. The state seemed to be in partial decomposition,
and the level of mobilization might have reached a point where
the existing capabilities of the political system would have been
unable to control it. Yet, it is quite unlikely that the final outcome would have been a fundamental social revolution, given
the lack of adequate means to achieve it: clearly defined goals,
a nonopportunistic strategy on the part of the left-wing groups
prevailing at the moment — in short, organization to capitalize
for its own benefit on the decomposition of the state apparatus.
The populist alliance through which some sort of attempt was
made to bring together the masses, middle-class groups, and the

national entrepreneurs was itself dependent on the state. It was caught up in a web of interests and relationships ultimately based on an economic foundation that was not only intrinsically nonrevolutionary, but also backward. Furthermore, one of the structural anchorages of that alliance was the nonincorporation of the rural population, leaving it politically unorganized and economically overexploited. This made it possible to count on the support of the conservative clientelistic parties, particularly the Social Democratic party (PSD).

The 1964 coup forced out the national-bourgeois sector as well as the statist developmentalist groups that had until then been in a hegemonic position. The deposed groups were replaced with the bourgeoisie's internationalized sectors, which are necessarily more dynamic and more "modern," because they are in essence part of the international capitalist system of production. The new economic policies and administrative reforms unleashed the productive forces of "modern capitalism," and the entire economic system became intimately linked to the international capitalist system of production. In other words, the relationship between the hegemonic world centers and the dependent economy was, and is increasingly being, restructured in accordance with new patterns of international economic organization. As emphasized at an earlier point in this study, however, this situation does not preclude the possibility of industrial and financial development in the peripheral dependent state. The urban-industrial pole, which had been growing at a fast pace since the Kubitschek period, now became dominant in the development of Brazilian capitalism.

It is hardly necessary to point out that primary exports — raw materials and agricultural products — still retain a major place in the economy. But even in these areas, new, associated forms of production involving international monopolies and local enterprises have appeared. Not even public enterprise is excluded from this new scheme of things, as attested by the mining consortia in iron and manganese. Other characteristically subordinated aspects remain, particularly foreign indebtedness and technological dependence, and foreign firms have acquired greater control over the private industrial sector.[14] The internal market

14. See tables in the text, where evidence for some of these assertions can be found. However, since my purpose here is to emphasize a process of qualitative change in the development model, understanding the policy approach to development problems is more important at this point than any figures to indicate concrete results. It is necessary to observe, for example, that the public enterprises have "privatized" themselves: they issue stock

has become essential to foreign businesses themselves. In addition, the policy aimed at diversifying exports has produced a reduction in the relative weight of the traditional primary items (almost exclusively produced by local entrepreneurs) in favor of industrial or semiprocessed minerals, both expressing the new patterns of association. Public enterprises function more and more like private corporations, enjoying the same freedom and aiming at the same results. The role of PETROBRÁS (the state oil monopoly) in the establishment of the petrochemical industry is suggestive in this regard: PETROBRÁS works in association with international and local firms, although it acts as the lead partner in the consortium. Association mechanisms like this have reduced conflict between public enterprise and private business. It has thus been possible to forge a modus vivendi, if not an effective political alliance, between functional middle-class groups (such as the military, the technocracy, and the bureaucracy), despite their nationalistic values, and the representatives of the international and the Brazilian internationalized bourgeoisie.

Given the picture just sketched, is there any meaning in reviving, as Furtado and Jaguaribe do, nationalist ideals based on the assumption of an active, local entrepreneurial sector bound up with a state structure that serves as a bridge to the popular masses? Is it not true that the economic assumptions of the nationalist model — autonomous state enterprise and equally independent, native, private capital — no longer hold? Is it not anachronistic to go on thinking of the Empresa Pública (public enterprise) as the moving force behind that model? And if what I suggest is true, what can we now conceive as the political role, present and potential, of the nationalistic middle-class sectors? One answer suggests itself promptly: unless they confine themselves to an ideology that cannot be expected to offer any effective political choices, they will be compelled to redefine the content of their nationalism. That redefinition is already under

---

shares, aim to make profits, and associate themselves with other, private business. In this context, indicators or conjectures (like those of Morley and Smith in this volume) concerning *actual purchase* of local businesses by foreign businesses, or the evidence that net foreign investment has diminished, which seems questionable, do not in any case invalidate my argument. The point at issue is that, in the present phase, it is the *internationalized sector* — whether it is made up of Brazilian, foreign, or mixed businesses, does not matter — that experiences the fastest growth. Moreover, foreign businesses utilize a substantial amount of internal, i.e., local savings for their expansion. Consequently, incoming capital is not a clear-cut indicator to measure the internationalization of the market.

way. In all likelihood, we will soon be unable to understand, in the light of the pre-1964 experience, what is now meant by nationalism.

It is in this limited sense that we are entitled to refer to the dynamic economic consequences of 1964 as a revolution. A bourgeois economic revolution did take place, brought into being by a reactionary political movement. It was economically revolutionary to the extent that it pushed the local bourgeoisie to adapt to the beat of international capitalist development, thereby establishing an effective subordination of the national economy to modern forms of economic domination. Modernization of the state machinery and the changes introduced in the public sector of the economy fall into the same context of integration into the international capitalist system.

Undoubtedly those who believe that the native bourgeoisie in dependent countries can carry through a bourgeois revolution, infusing the latter term with the meaning it has as a description of the French or American revolutions, will call attention to still existing "structural obstacles." These, they will claim, reduce the scope and meaning of the economic changes that have been occurring in Brazil since 1964.

I do not believe that the Brazilian bourgeoisie, a child of dependent capitalism, can stage a revolution in the strong meaning of the term. Its "revolution" is limited to integrating itself into the scheme of international capitalism, to associating itself with international capitalism as a dependent and minor partner. The Brazilian bourgeoisie will, and does, struggle to make the most of it. But it faces an objective limitation: capitalist accumulation in dependent economies does not complete its cycle. Lacking "autonomous technology" — as vulgar parlance has it — and compelled therefore to utilize imported technology, dependent capitalism is crippled. Dependent capitalism must thus bear all the consequences of absorbing capital-intensive, labor-saving technology; but that is not the main problem. It is crippled because it lacks a fully developed capital-goods sector. The accumulation, expansion, and self-realization of local capital requires and depends on a dynamic complement outside itself: it must insert itself into the circuit of international capitalism. The latter, of course, does develop the capital-goods sector without which the expansion of the consumer-goods sector (including durable goods) in dependent countries can hardly be imagined.

It was this limited transformation to a dependent capitalist economy that the 1964 coup made possible. In order to accomplish it, it was necessary to repress the working class, to keep down wages, and at the same time to broaden the channels of accumulation. In the process it removed — even though some instability may remain in this respect — the ideological and organizational factors that tended to work against the formulation of policies of association between the state, local private enterprise, and international trusts.

THE FRAGILITY OF POWER-ELITE MODELS: CÂNDIDO MENDES

To claim that a new economic power base has come into being and that a political modus vivendi among the dominant classes is again possible is not to say that political conflicts among the groups in power have ceased to exist. Even less does it mean that opposition forces have altogether disappeared. But here again, the more ambitious attempts to analyze the present Brazilian regime have failed, and once more this failure must be credited to an underlying linear construction of events. Or it may be attributed to what looks like the opposite error: the analytic models proposed have been so heavily based on the apparent power relationships prevailing in each particular presidency that the models crumble and must be rebuilt after each political zigzag that forces the government in power to alter its political or economic program. More often than not, political changes have been neither foreseen nor desired by the actors themselves. And yet they must bear some relationship to the more basic, underlying structures and constraints. To make them explicit wherever possible is the task of political analysis.

Thus, rather than inquire into the conscious purposes or manifest strategies of succeeding governments, we must attempt to identify political forces, to trace the contours of the framework within which they operate, and to weigh the outcomes of their actions. Before I present my own views, I will look first at the contributions made by another major political analyst in Brazil.

Cândido Mendes, who has made perhaps the most consistent attempts to lay bare the working models of political development in Brazil, seems to have been compelled to alter his explanatory scheme at each change in government. His revisions are explained by his attempts to capture the manifold political facets of the regime through ad hoc interpretations. Thus, the Castello Branco government was for him a "paradigm" of the power-elite model.[15] That elite, so the argument ran, had been formed among the members of the Superior War College, which

15. See Cândido Mendes, "Sistema político e modelos de poder no Brasil," *Dados*, no. 1 (Rio de Janeiro, 1966), pp. 7–41. See also the articles cited in n. 16.

trains both military and civilian personnel. These men formed a homogeneous group, conscious of its historical responsibility and armed with an effective political ideology inspired by the "doctrine of national security." Thus it was able to formulate, and started to implement, a national development model. That model corresponded to the notion of a modernizing autocracy, and as such it implied a consistent program of social and economic reform. For Cândido Mendes, the power-elite model, as practiced by the *castellistas*, prevented personalization in the exercise of power. The president had preserved for himself maximum coercive capabilities, but he did not in fact apply them, limiting himself to skillful use of threats rather than actions. Thus the model made it possible to avoid a thorough, formalized dictatorship.

According to Cândido Mendes, the power-elite type of regime, as exemplified by Castello Branco, has two main characteristics. First, it refuses to broaden the scope of political compromise through incorporation of other groups into the limited circle of power holders. This maintains the circle's own "purity" and prevents it from being disfigured or diluted. Second, the regime rejects consensual legitimation, which it might achieve through the manipulation of symbols with strong mobilizing appeal.

Thus the Castello Branco regime must be seen as a specific instance of the power-elite type, with regard to its structure or mode of exercising power. It consciously adapted that pattern to the task of instituting a democratic, technically reformed governmental structure. It sought to achieve this goal through strategically conceived economic and political reforms. That is why the military elite allied itself to the technocratic elite. This, as Cândido Mendes puts it, "made it possible for the *castellistas* to insulate themselves as a ruling group . . . from any objective determination, whether of class or any other social denominator, in order to retain exclusive access to the highest level of governmental decision." [16]

16. Cândido Mendes, "O govêrno Castello Branco: Paradigma e prognose," *Dados*, nos. 2/3 (Rio de Janeiro, 1967), pp. 63–111. Note that in his more recent study, "Elite de poder, democracia e desenvolvimento," *Dados*, no. 6 (Rio de Janeiro, 1969), pp. 57–90, Cândido Mendes insists that the Castello Branco government did not attempt to "authenticate" itself, that is, it remained faithful to the particular form in which legitimation does or does not occur in power-elite regimes. Precisely by doing this, the government was caught in a situation in which political validation became exclusively a function of its economic development model, which in turn depended on a number of factors lying outside the country's boundaries.

In an earlier study, Cândido Mendes had described the Castello Branco regime in more realistic terms.[17] Though emphasizing its characteristically power-elite type, based on a military-technocratic alliance, he also called attention to the fact that the army, particularly after Costa e Silva became the presidential candidate, began to take an active role in the shaping of major decisions. Thus, he wrote, the political model "could be described as a 'technocracy' in an authoritarian state." Its overall function was "to provide the necessary institutional conditions for economic planning . . . through an extremely centralized arrangement."

The power-elite model became less tenable when Costa e Silva came to power. Therefore Cândido Mendes reinterpreted it. Of course Costa e Silva's election was "inevitable, given the inner logic of the existing system." [18] The election served to legitimate the regime's natural course, in the sense that Costa e Silva's candidacy "was identified with the military's consolidation of their own position, as a strengthened and restored force, ready to take up a competitive and polarizing role in the exercise of the power functions which, taken together, make up the present Brazilian state." [19] Thus continuity was assured, despite eventual differences about policy coloration and even despite the fact that Costa e Silva's coming to power had "from a technical point of view, a populist cast, as a rigorously objective representation of a given stratum of the nation, namely the army." Despite all of these departures from the power-elite model as posited before, "he should find no difficulty in placing himself formally within the previously established line (or policy range)." [20]

In short, despite the obvious difficulty in reconciling the new features of the Costa e Silva period with the power-elite model — the ambiguity in the quotations above seems quite telling — Cândido Mendes continues to insist that the interpretation remains valid. The role of the army, he says, supports his contention. Acting as a status group and keeping major policy within its range of control, it guarantees the necessary conditions of the power-elite model's applicability. Yet, according to Cândido Mendes, the Costa e Silva government could evolve in the direction of a Bonapartist regime. That is, a populist caudillo could

17. Mendes, "Sistema político e modelos de poder no Brasil," p. 9.
18. Ibid., p. 17.
19. Ibid.
20. Ibid. By "formally" Cândido Mendes means effective policy choices, since "this formal element would even include the commitment to uphold the economic models followed by the Castello Branco government."

spring up from the military. A change in this direction would imply a drastic policy reorientation, involving a scheme of income redistribution and an extension of the power pact to incorporate other actors. The latter element in Cândido Mendes's speculation is accounted for by the existence (at the time he was writing) of the Frente Ampla, which was quite active as long as it managed to maintain itself. Incorporation of other political actors would also require some way of preventing a return to tutelary intervention of the *dutrista* type.[21] On the other hand, a Bonapartist solution would only make sense if it implied a deeper commitment of the armed forces in the regulation and management of the society. That is, it would require an extensive utilization of the military's "managerial" inclination (as exemplified, among other things, by General Albuquerque Lima's performance in the Interior Ministry at that time). Were these conditions to come about, it could well be possible for the military to shape the regime into a Nasserist pattern.[22]

Again, we seem to have the kind of analysis that starts with the intention of constructing an analytical model and then moves toward a rationalization of de facto situations, evolving into a thinly disguised normative view. In this case, hopes are pinned on military nationalism as an alternative to the development model that has already been put into practice. Yet, as mentioned before, Cândido Mendes did stress (probably too much) the privatizing character of economic policy under the Castello Branco government. He had also attempted to describe the "power vacuum" that led to the emergence of the military regime.[23] What social forces, then, would give the nationalist alternative the support it would need?

Here the misconceptions regarding the political process have their roots in a much too serious reading of the actors' political platforms and cover ideologies. Unlike the authors discussed in the first part of this chapter, who tended to overstress structural constraints, Cândido Mendes seems to think that the power-elite regime functions in a social vacuum. Hence his fundamental assumption that the elite — president, technocracy, and military groups at the top — operates "technically." Celso Furtado and Hélio Jaguaribe tended to exaggerate the weight of the socio-economic basis of political life. In Cândido Mendes's interpreta-

21. After the name of Army Marshal Eurico Gasper Dutra, Vargas's war minister under the Estado Nôvo and later president of Brazil (1946–50).

22. See Mendes, "O govêrno Castello Branco," esp. p. 110.

23. See Mendes, "Sistema político e modelos de poder no Brasil," esp. pp. 14–15.

tion, on the contrary, the political actors act out a story that is purely ideological. The political logic that they follow is assumed to have nothing to do with the social and economic structure.

An analysis of the Castello Branco government and its "paradigmatic" character, however, should not take as a starting point the ideal-typical coherence of its purposes, but rather the insurmountable difficulties it faced in its attempt to convert them into actual policy. An important case in point is the Second Institutional Act, issued in October 1965 in response to government defeats in key state elections. There was an external conditioning factor (external to the power elite, that is), and it was this factor that made the act necessary. The troops, opposed to the idea of abiding by a self-imposed electoral calendar, imposed a ukase on the president. He had little choice but to accept the situation and broaden the "power pact" — broaden it to such an extent that the package bargain included military imposition of the Costa e Silva candidacy as successor. Why? Why is it that the Castello Branco governing elite insisted on elections and legality? Which forces pressured the president in this direction? Which opposed it? Perhaps by asking simple and straightforward questions like these, we can bring back into the picture the real nerve of the political process — conflict.

Any view that rationalizes de facto political processes, picturing them as the unfolding of an elite's conscious will, bears the burden of subjectivity. A more objective approach stresses the conflicts among groups within the arena of organized power as well as the conflicts between these groups and those located outside the arena who attempt to make their views felt and to change prevailing orientations. Let us keep in mind, for a moment, only one aspect of the contradictions faced by the Castello Branco government. The political outlook that was identified with his own personal views and that found considerable support in the political parties focused attention on "institutionalizing" the Revolution. In other words, the Revolution aspired to some sort of legitimacy that would ultimately reflect itself in a rule of law, or lawful state. In the army, however, there were groups — the so-called hard-liners — who pressured for radicalization, for carrying the repressive anticorruption measures much further. Given their aims, they naturally wanted strict military control over the decision-making machinery. Very likely these groups embodied two broad tendencies, which might or might not coincide in the same persons. Both were anticommunist, but one was nationalistic while the other was more concerned with moralizing. Both placed themselves together to the right of the government, and both were constantly on the watch for occasions to hold the government in check. Their faits accomplis were often sufficiently vigorous to threaten a crisis situation. In addition, there was, outside the centers of power, the "opposition." Toward the end of the Castello Branco term, it was made up of the MDB (the Brazilian Democratic Movement, which had been created to act as an opposition in the political-party game) and of various remnants of the pre-1964 regime and party system.

After the election of Costa e Silva, as mentioned earlier, a trend became clear. The army acted more and more as a corporate group, seeking to occupy the state apparatus, which had been modernized by the Castello Branco government. At the same time, the regime admitted into its ranks parts of the once assertive "national (local) bourgeoisie." This group was represented in the government by virtue of the prestige enjoyed by some nationalists (who were apparently partly responsible for the movement favoring the Costa e Silva candidacy).

The most significant feature of the period, however, is neither the marshal-president's paternalism nor his populistic impulses. There was no change, despite official declarations to the contrary, in economic policy on the *arrôcho salarial* (tightly keeping down the wage level). The insignificance of the self-styled Nasserites is underscored by the fact that their main representative, the minister of the interior, lost his post as a result of a clear and direct confrontation on economic policy with the minister of finance. The issue involved far more than a mere question of official roles, because the latter was known to represent an opposite developmental model, namely, strengthening entrepreneurial organization through association of private Brazilian, public, and foreign capital. Rather, the distinguishing feature of the period is that, once more, the president sponsored a strategy of "democratic opening" (*abertura democrática*).

The president sought to reactivate the party system, reassert political freedoms, and appeal to national union. Once the overall situation began to change, opposition and protest mounted (as exemplified by the rally of "the 100,000" in Rio de Janeiro, initial scattered guerrilla actions, the MDB's beginning to act as a serious opposition party, constitution of the Frente Ampla, and so on). And again, an opposition force *inside* the power system checked the government's course; the "young officers," nationalist and *ultra* sectors of the army, brought pressure to bear on the top officeholders, and the Fifth Institutional Act was issued. Now the situation changed drastically. The act virtually transformed the president into a dictator, under surveillance by the military. Now it was the army, as an institution, making its own pressures initiated by the ultra sectors.

The scene was repeated once more durin·; the Costa e Silva period — without, of course, public demonstr..·ions of opposition and protest — when attempts were made to "rc constitutionalize" the regime. These attempts originated within the *cúpula pala-ciana* (the presidential inner circle) and were apparently supported by the "political class" — civilian politiriau: and remnants of the previous regimes. Reconstitutionalizat·on did not come about, seemingly because of Costa e Silva's illness and immediate succession. Be that as it may, opposition to tl.e new attempts at reconstitutionalization had already grown and another political crisis was gathering. quite aside from the president's illness.

In the meantime two other factors emerged that completely changed the stage. One was economic — essentially the resumption of a steady rate of economic growth. The other was distinctly political — *armed* opposition beginning toward the end of 1968 and increasing in 1969.

In a sense, however, the picture remained the same until the end of Costa e Silva's period. The government, with some support from the army and from the political parties, aimed to institutionalize the Revolution. At the same time, a chain of actions and reactions from left and right, mutually conditioning each other, functioned as a veto on the strategy sponsored by the governmental leadership. Behind these pressures and counterpressures, economic policy decisions followed a relatively autonomous course. Interest groups somehow got the governmental favors and decisions they needed and returned them in the form of support, if not specifically to the governmental leadership, certainly to the regime itself.

Now, let us ask, what kind of regime is this? Costa e Silva's succession, through the election of Médici, made it possible to see quite clearly the way the system works. Depite nationalist pressures and despite the prestige enjoyed within the army by Albuquerque Lima, the fundamental decision to put aside the latter's candidacy had the following features:

1. It was limited to the upper stratum of the military bureaucracy (four-star generals).
2. It was based on bureaucratic criteria of hierarchy and corporate representation.
3. It was intended to prevent a crucial risk to the army arising from fragmentation caused by the proliferation of tendencies and factions. This risk would clearly have

existed had the nationalist tendency prevailed; by the same token it would have led to the crystallization of an opposition.

4. It was, therefore, a mechanism to reconcile diverging tendencies within the army itself.

And, most significantly, once the decision was made, it was accepted in the name of hierarchy, discipline, and cohesion by the losers, even though they probably had a majority among the lower echelons.

Thus it was the armed forces, as an institution, that increasingly came to control the state. That is, a military bureaucracy came to control the state apparatus, itself a bureaucracy, which had been modernized in previous administrations. The result of this process was the consolidation of a *relatively stable* model of bureaucratic domination.

I have emphasized relatively stable, and with good reason. It is true that the regime has been able to generate effective policies and to keep order. It has not, however, solved its fundamental problems, particularly those of a distinctly political nature. It has not devised means to broaden and firmly establish its legitimacy in the society at large. For the time being, the risks of bureaucratic rigidity can be compensated for by the fact, discussed above, that the economy, including its public sector, has been cast into a more clearly entrepreneurial pattern. Administration has become more "technocratic." And, more basically, the bureaucratic-authoritarian nature of the regime does not mean that it fails to pursue the policies in which various social groups are interested. Not only the internationalized bourgeoisie, but also the military as a group and the rising middle classes (that is, professionals and skilled white-collar workers) have benefited from them. As long as the economy maintains its present growth rate, it is even possible that some sectors of the lower strata (workers in the more modern sectors, and so on) will share in the prosperity. This, of course, is quite likely to the extent that the government decides to pursue redistributive policies. The situation of these workers may be ameliorated even to the point of increasing their relative share of the total income.

The overriding goal as conceived by the military is to strengthen the state in order to guarantee national security. I have argued that there is no direct and necessary conflict between this goal and the development model that is being put into practice. The scheme even allows some room for nationalist pressures, as long of course as the "associated" nature of development is maintained and as long as a strong state is agreed upon as one of the major elements in the model.

To sum up: the regime is autocratic; its mode of organization is military-bureaucratic. It does have a dynamic economic foundation. There are undoubtedly limitations in both respects. There are political limitations — fundamental political problems that the regime has not solved. There are also economic limitations, for the model can be no more dynamic than the measure allowed by the dependent-associated development pattern.

AUTHORITARIANISM AND DEMOCRACY

This association between an increased growth rate and authoritarianism has encouraged the notion that they bear an intimate and necessary relation to each other. In this view, authoritarianism is seen as a prerequisite for economic development. It is not important to examine the whole argument nor review the evidence at this point. There is no doubt, however, that this belief has been enthusiastically adhered to in many quarters. As one can easily imagine, it has found supporters among the military, but it is by no means limited to military circles. Entrepreneurs, technocrats, and various segments of the rising middle classes have also found these notions congenial to their own interests and experience. Among the generally nationalistic ultra groups the authoritarian argument sometimes takes the form of a self-styled Nasserism. Ranged against these views, generally speaking, we find the remnants of castellista groups, as well as opposition groups without access to the government (part of the Left, intellectuals, the church, and so on).

Given this picture, it seems particularly interesting to review briefly the argument against the authoritarians. The most eloquent defense of the politically democratic, economically dependent-associated development model has been put forward by a former member of Castello Branco's cabinet, Roberto de Oliveira Campos.[24] Borrowing language, model, and intention from such American political scientists as Apter, Almond, and Verba, he wrote: "The political option appropriate in our case — which is in fact the one accepted (*consagrada*) by the Revolution of 1964 — is a combination of participatory democracy and a strong executive. A reconciliation model is the most appropriate, consid-

24. In a series of articles published in *O Estado de São Paulo*, one of Brazil's major newspapers, under the title "The Brazilian Model of Development," June 7–24; August 1, 8, 1970.

ering that our society, at least in some regions, has already reached beyond modernization and has entered the phase of industrialization." [25] This model, he goes on to say, requires a strong executive, a functioning party system, and mechanisms of "popular reconciliation," the basis of which is elite-mass information and communication. It would thus be possible to avoid the risks involved in mobilization and autocratic systems. Information would replace coercion, making it possible to avoid committing the mistakes and paying the price entailed by either "distributive populism" or "nationalist excitation." The basis for a new consensual regime would be economic pluralism, which is the necessary condition for political pluralism and for an open society. Through the improvement of the channels of social mobility, such as the educational system, this society would come into its own.

Once more, we have an argument that conceives of the political sphere as strictly conditioned by the economic (if there is a pluralist economic structure, there must be political pluralism), associated with a normative perspective. Simple as they are, the facts of the matter indicate that the regime relies more on coercion than on information, despite economic pluralism.

Let us now turn to a final question. Does the existing level of coercion indicate that the Brazilian regime is not only bureaucratic, but also totalitarian? Tendencies in that direction do exist, but they are not dominant. The state officially sticks to a "democratic" doctrine. In this sense, the present situation lacks two fundamental components of the totalitarian model: an ideology and a mobilizing political party. It remains an economically developmentalist military-bureaucratic autocracy. Will it undertake the big leap forward toward a totalitarian state?

Once again, looking for an answer only at the ideological level will not do. If we emphasize the actual power balance instead, an important fact to be taken into account is the tendency for the older political interests to regroup themselves. They place themselves around the stabilizing axis of the military and state bureaucracy, in the political parties consented to by the regime. They of course submit to the centralizing and stabilizing tendencies of the regime, as the nomination of state governors by the president has clearly shown. On this occasion, the state legislatures perform the same ritual function as the national Congress, which elects the president after the choice has been made somewhere else. Yet economic policy decisions do seem to be made in a circle

25. This quotation is from the article printed in the June 17, 1970, *O Estado de São Paulo*, p. 5.

enjoying considerable autonomy vis-à-vis the political power centers. In that circle, entrepreneurs do participate, on a quasi-corporative basis.

This decision-making system, taken as a whole, is therefore both bureaucratic-centralized and accessible to the entrepreneurs. It has been able to generate policies and to define goals quite effectively and simultaneously to legitimate itself in the society at large through the symbolic appeal of strengthening the Fatherland. At another level, perhaps a more basic one, the regime seeks to gain legitimacy (or, as Cândido Mendes would put it, authentication) through economic achievements. In a peculiar parody of those analytical schemes that posit a strict conditioning effect between economy and polity, the only answer given to protests against repression comes in economic development figures. The language of human rights is in this sense translated into GNP growth rates.

However, the system does have potential destabilizers, two of which must be mentioned. One is internal: the system's inability to control the forces of repression within its own structure. The other is external: sporadic armed opposition. Most important of all, the regime has not created an effective institutional form, so that each succession is bound to become a crisis point.

At the beginning, from the Castello Branco period on, there were the veto groups, the ultras. Their actions, as mentioned before, almost invariably have a critical, conditioning effect on the political process as a whole. In addition, there is now the repressive apparatus and the left-wing armed opposition groups. Neither of these extremes seems capable of generating viable political strategies and goals. Yet both can and do reciprocally condition the regime's course. They are able to hold it in check under specific circumstances. To the extent that they make a more open political arena rather unlikely, they reduce the regime's ability to absorb opposition groups. They lessen the regime's ability to generate policies satisfactory to those interested in "critical" or "qualified" participation, that is, those who oppose the regime but would rather retain some diffuse influence than propose clear-cut policy alternatives.

The possibility that coercion increases at the expense of information, to put it euphemistically, does exist. The possibility of keeping that tendency within limits will depend on the ability of some groups within the government, or of outside groups like the church, to neutralize the spiral of political violence. Let me assert that I do not believe in inevitability. If totalitarian tendencies exist, they can be reversed.[26] But I have no doubt that reversing them will require a vigorous reaction, within and without. The regime may well be coming to an impasse. Despite the economic accomplishments and despite the well-meaning disposition on the part of some who support it but would like to see it evolve toward "reconciliation," the fact is that forces opposed to this course of evolution have placed themselves in strategic locations.

I do not think that the outside opposition, armed or verbal, has any ability to cause the regime's breakdown. Quite the contrary, the regime is gaining strength. It benefits from the economic accomplishments, so that the situation can be described as bourgeois consolidation in the context of a developmentalist-bureaucratic regime. Behind all this lies the tragic fact that the power elite, as well as the opposition intellectuals, are unable to formulate realistic alternatives to the basic problems. Economic and urban development has mobilized the "masses," but it has not filled the historical vacuum of a society and culture in which they have never been organized, never politically educated, never enabled to claim their fundamental rights on an equal footing: bread as well as freedom. If this is true of that part of the population that has already been reached by the benefits of economic growth, it is of course even more so of the vast majority, which has thus far hardly been touched by the transformations of the last decades.

A long march awaits the Brazilians, a slow, patient march, before the nation will be able to be rebuilt politically for a people whose symbols, organizations, and hopes were crushed by the same power elite which, from the heights of its vision of the state and the nation, thought that, launching an autocratic process of development, it would bring the country one step closer to a regime of reconciliation. We have all paid the price of this elitist vision. It is to be hoped, at least, that the intellectuals will not invent other myths, whether Nasserist or not, which are as incapable as the present ones of producing viable policies for the

26. This is not to say that the alternative to totalitarianism must be a democratic overture. It may well go only so far as stabilizing itself as an authoritarian regime. In any case, even those who talk about "opening up" toward democracy seem to conceive of this only in terms of broader and more effective participation of the bourgeoisie and of the middle classes in the political process. They do not seem very interested in allowing the reconstitution of popular representative organizations. The latter therefore seems only a remote possibility in the present horizon of political choices.

participation of the popular classes in politics. Without this participation, any "technical" formula for mass mobilization will lead to mass manipulation, and perhaps to an increase in the accumulation of wealth, but will not bring about political development favoring the majority and increasing the quality of life.

PART III

THE POLITICAL FUTURE
OF AUTHORITARIAN BRAZIL

6 The "Portugalization" of Brazil?

PHILIPPE C. SCHMITTER

The seizure of power by the Brazilian military in 1964 was hailed in some circles as an act of almost unparalleled importance in the history of the "Free World." Now, with eight years of hindsight, this evaluation seems to have been right, but for entirely the wrong reasons. The course of events has moved in a direction opposite to that predicted by these self-proclaimed defenders of the West — away from democratic liberalization toward the institutionalization of permanent authoritarian rule. Whether deliberately or not (and we shall see there is growing evidence of intent), Brazil's military rulers have followed policies that have deprived most political actors of their autonomy, narrowed the arena of "permissible" political choice, and sought to eliminate all alternative system outcomes except self-perpetuation in power. In so doing, they have revived a developmental-political model that once seemed to have been historically discredited.

Portugal, by previously demonstrating the viability and longevity, as well as the costs, of such a response to the stresses of modernization-cum-development, has provided the archetype for this distinctive system of authoritarian political domination. Thus the concept of "Portugalization" can be applied to the process by which such rule is institutionalized.[1] The interrogation

1. By coining and using the concept, "Portugalization," I do *not* mean to imply that the present political outcome emerging in Brazil was determined long ago either by the pattern of economic exploitation imposed by Portuguese colonization or by the content of political values transmitted through some common "Lusotropical" cultural heritage. There is, however, something to be said in favor of both lines of argument. See Marvin Harris, "Portugal's Contribution to the Underdevelopment of Africa and Brazil" and Roger Bastide, "Lusotropicology, Race and Nationalism, and Class Protest and Development in Brazil and Portuguese Africa," both in *Protest and Resistance in Angola and Brazil*, ed. R. Chilcote (Berkeley and Los Angeles: University of California Press, 1972), pp. 209–42. See also S. Stein and B. Stein, *The Colonial Heritage of Latin America* (New York and London: Oxford University Press, 1970).

For a preliminary discussion of the process of Portugalization in Portugal itself, see my "Corporatist Interest Representation and Public Policy Making in Portugal," paper presented at the American Political Science Association

point in the title of this essay is meant to suggest that other outcomes may not yet be completely foreclosed, although their
probability is rapidly diminishing. Full institutionalization has
not yet been accomplished; unresolved structural incompatibili-
ties persist; elite values and popular aspirations have not yet
adjusted to the emerging authoritarian model. This essay is, in
fact, dedicated to the proposition that through an analysis which
is deliberately speculative and evaluative it may be possible to
convince Brazilians of the likely and longer-term political consequences of the course they have taken. Perhaps this will stimulate them to resist such a fate, which ironically so few of them
desire or deserve.[2] Unfortunately, there are few signs that the
trend toward Portugalization or the institutionalization of another model of authoritarian rule will be stopped. That intoxicating mixture of unrealistic optimism and realistic improvisa-
tion, so well captured by Fernando Pedreira in the phrase "historical opportunism," seems once again to have its tenacious
grip on the course of Brazilian political development — good
intentions and courageous political action to the contrary notwithstanding. I am afraid that one of the current slogans of the
regime, "ninguém segura êste pais" — "No one holds back this
country" — may well be correct, even if it means the country
cannot be held back from permanently unrepresentative rule.
In an atmosphere in which popular euphoria is so deliberately
cultivated and in which the present regime has so successfully
contrived to identify its interests with those of the state and the
nation, critical commentary on governmental policy and performance — especially by foreigners — can easily be converted and
distorted into an alleged affront to national honor, an attack on
the country's legitimate aspirations, and/or an act of *lèse majesté*.
Probably in vain, I can protest that I do not wish to "hold
Brazil back" from its developmental and world power objectives.
I will, however, question whether the course presently being
taken is likely to produce these outcomes, at least without in-

(APSA) Meetings, Washington, D.C., September 1972. Also Hermínio Martins,
"Portugal" in *European Fascism*, ed. S. J. Woolf (London: Weidenfeld and
Nicolson, 1968), pp. 302–36 and Manuel Lucena, *L'Evolution du système
corporatif portugais à travers les lois (1933–1971)*, 2 vols. (Paris: Institut des
Sciences Sociales du Travail, 1971).

2. Each successive post-1964 military regime has publicly committed itself
to democratization (and then followed policies antithetic to that end). For
the most recent of these, see President Médici's pledge for a "construção de
uma sociedade politicamente aberta" in his speech to the Superior War College (ESG). *Jornal do Brasil*, 11 March 1970.

curring long-run social and political consequences that seem incompatible with the values of the Brazilian people.

In evaluating the course of the government since 1964, I have deliberately chosen to use monitors of system performance that the "revolutionary" actors have themselves selected and, in large part, provided. I propose to meet them (partially) on their own grounds — in the arenas of governmental policy and societal performance of their preference. I will not berate and condemn these governments for the actions they are best known for in the world press — repeated violations of universal human rights and of their own "self-imposed" constitutional norms. These acts of arbitrary arrest, loss of political rights, press censorship, restrictions on the right of assembly, dismissal of academics, forced exile, physical intimidation and torture have been abundantly and convincingly documented. I will accept (or better, suspend my disbelief in) the regime's contention that these "measures of exception" were either unwillingly forced upon them by an extremist-terrorist minority and/or engaged in by small local groups of police and military "enthusiasts" without the knowledge or connivance of central authorities. In fact, as I shall argue, this sort of indiscriminate terror and arbitrary action on the part of public officials is inimical to the successful institutionalization of authoritarian rule. Intensive and extensive espionage, an efficient "National Information Service," as it is called in Brazil, can accomplish the same function of incapacitating and inhibiting regime opponents at a much lower and less visible cost.

My evaluation will begin with an examination of certain *policy outputs,* the pattern of decisions by the political system to appropriate and allocate resources, and *policy outcomes,* the net or concatenated result of a multiplicity of outputs plus contextual factors that alter the global performance of the system. A given regime can be held rather directly responsible for changes in the former (for example, for increases or decreases in educational or military spending), but it can hardly be entirely credited or blamed for the latter (for example, gross rates of economic growth or inflation). Here the analyst is compelled to consider the "counterfactual alternative": might the same outcome have ensued in the absence of any change in public policy?

Subsequently, I will seek to relate these policies and their indirect consequences to the future configuration of the political system as they feed back into social, economic, cultural, and political processes to strengthen or weaken the existing distribution of public power and private privilege. I will ask (or better, often speculate in the absence of reliable data), who has benefited and who is benefiting from this regime? How is this distribution of public and private goods likely to affect the nature of Brazil's future polity? In particular, I will identify from previous research certain major structural components of the *sistema*, the system of populist authoritarian rule created by Getúlio Vargas during the 1930s and 1940s, and then ask how they are faring under military rule.

SOME INTERPRETIVE DIVERGENCES

The major theme of this essay has already been hinted at. In order to understand the dynamics and probable consequences of military dictatorship since 1964, one must consider it in relation to previous authoritarian rule in Brazil — even though that rule was of a different variety. Simply put, my argument is that the military "revolutionaries" seized power in reaction to the decay (and imminent demise) of that previous authoritarian sistema, and subsequently have sought (admittedly a bit fitfully and perhaps even unconsciously), to purge that sistema of certain of its contradictory elements, especially its "semicompetitiveness" and its "populism." In so doing they have much more closely approximated pure authoritarian rule as exemplified by Spain and Portugal.[3] The relative ease and success of their efforts at "purification" can partially be explained by the fact that they were able to build upon preceding institutional structures and behavioral dispositions.

Such an interpretation conflicts with the much more orthodox one that stresses the aberrant and discontinuous nature of the Revolution of 1964. According to this version, Brazil in 1945 broke with its "semifascist" authoritarian past (which is also viewed as an aberration), and began anew its "experiment with democracy," as exemplified by the adoption of a new liberal constitution, the establishment of a competitive party system, and the revival of an active legislative process. The ensuing years saw a gradual, incremental expansion in political (i.e. electoral) participation and a progressive democratization of institutions. The country was seen as moving firmly and ineluctably along the liberal-pluralist course as traveled previously by North America and Northern Europe.[4] The 1964 *golpe* was due, at least in part,

3. Juan Linz, "An Authoritarian Regime: Spain," in *Mass Politics*, ed. E. Allardt and S. Rokkan (New York: Free Press, 1970), pp. 251–83. Also my "Corporatist Interest Representation and Public Policy Making in Portugal."

4. This theme, albeit with qualifications, has been most cogently and extensively presented in Thomas Skidmore, *Politics in Brazil, 1930–1964: An*

to a conjunctural "crisis of participation," but the implication of this "analysis" (rarely spelled out by its North American exponents, but explicitly put forth as a justification by some of the successful *golpistas*) is that military rule is merely an expedient, a short interlude during which the problems of assimilation and institutional distortion (especially the clash of a populistic president and a clientelistic congress) will be resolved. Once past this aberration, Brazil will again be restored to its "natural" historical course of liberal-pluralist political development.

A second general analytical perspective, much diffused among "radical" scholars, applies orthodox Marxist categories to the 1964 golpe and stresses its counterrevolutionary nature.[5] In effect, these analysts argue that it is an attempt to "turn the clock back," rather than merely to "reset it to the correct hour." The military, according to this version, seized power as the instrument of a coalition of urban and rural, national and international, capitalist interests, which had been radicalized (or better, "reactionized") by the emergence of a revolutionary nationalist threat. Not simply the product of a political cultural conflict between "traditional" and "modern" Brazil, the crisis was generated primarily by the *conscienciação,* the growing consciousness, of the masses and the polarization of class struggle. The *mesoi* or middle sectors were swung to the counterrevolutionary camp by a combination of fear of proletarianization exacerbated by inflation, economic dependence upon the dominant capitalist class, and hysterical anticommunism fed by United States propaganda and the Brazilian mass media. Again, there is a clear implication that ultimately the masses cannot be denied and that military rule will be a futile and temporary expedient.

Despite their different readings of the underlying cause of the 1964 crisis (and, more particularly, their divergent interpretations of the Goulart regime), both the liberal and radical perspectives are fundamentally optimistic in the long run. Both insist on the "extraordinary," "discontinuous," or "transient" nature of present-day authoritarian rule. They even specify why military rule is likely to become inviable and who will compel the military

Experiment in Democracy (New York: Oxford University Press, 1967). For a study that emphasizes the gradualist, "North European" nature of electoral expansion, see Joseph L. Love, "Political Participation in Brazil, 1881–1969," *Luso-Brazilian Review* 7 (December 1970): 3–24.

5. For the most detailed and articulate statement of this position, see Octávio Ianni, *Crisis in Brazil* (New York: Columbia University Press, 1970). For a more polemic statement, see Miguel Arraes, *Le Brésil: le peuple et le pouvoir* (Paris: Maspero, 1969).

rulers to step aside. In the liberal-pluralist scenario, the military
will be forced to return to representative democracy by the political aspirations and legitimacy expectations of the Brazilian
people, especially its middle sectors. In the revolutionary socialist
scenario, the policies followed by the military authorities and
their technocratic servants will concentrate benefits in an ever-
narrowing group, provoking a polarization of political forces
and their forcible overthrow by aroused masses. In neither
scenario can Brazil's present rulers expect to defy permanently
the postulated tide of contemporary history. They cannot stop
the structural transformation of the economy and the society,
but the more it occurs, the weaker will be the social base of authoritarian rule.

On the basis of my research on interest politics, I have speculated that both these scenarios, derived from the Western European or North American cases, may be "misspecified." I have
relied heavily for theoretical insight on Karl Marx's analysis of
Bonapartism in *The Eighteenth Brumaire* and Barrington Moore
Jr.'s delineation of a distinctive "reactionary capitalist" path to
modernization among late-developing societies (Germany, Italy,
and Japan),[6] and for empirical substance on the work of such
Brazilian scholars as Fernando Henrique Cardoso, Luciano Martins, Leôncio Martins Rodrigues, Caio Prado Júnior, and Celso
Furtado, as well as on my own study of corporatist interest representation. Drawing upon these resources, I came to the conclusion that there may be an elective affinity between certain
structural and behavioral attributes of "delayed-dependent" development and protracted authoritarian rule.

This is not the place to reiterate my entire argument. Schematically, I speculated that certain characteristics of Brazil's
delayed economic and social transformation had "conspired" to
make it highly unlikely that it would replicate either the evo-
lutionary liberal-pluralist or the revolutionary nationalist-col-
lectivist route to political modernity. On the one hand, prein-

6. Karl Marx, *The Eighteenth Brumaire of Louis Bonaparte* (New York:
International Publishers, 1963). Also of direct relevance are his *The Class
Struggles in France (1848–1850)* (New York: International Publishers, 1964);
and *The Civil War in France* (New York: International Publishers, 1940).
For a useful, intelligent summary of Marx's and others' writings on Bona-
partism, see H. C. F. Mansilla, *Faschismus und eindimensionale Gesellschaft*
(Neuwied u. Berlin: Luchterhand, 1971), pp. 137–45. Barrington Moore's dis-
cussion of "revolution from above" and "reactionary capitalism" is to be
found in his *Social Origins of Dictatorship and Democracy* (Boston: Beacon
Press, 1966), pp. 228–53, 433–52.

dustrial urbanization, proportionately low factory employment, industrialization by import substitution, dualistic stagnation in the rural sector, and heavy dependence on foreign capital and technology seemed to have obfuscated some of the major lines of interest and attitudinal cleavage that had provided the political dynamism for earlier developers. Above all, these different contextual factors tended to fragment and debilitate class consciousness or even corporate group awareness, making it difficult to establish and sustain aggressive and autonomous movements, parties, or associations. On the other hand, lengthy formal political independence, a prematurely large bureaucracy, sustained high rates of inflation and economic expansion had operated to strengthen the capacity and autonomy of preexisting state institutions. These factors enabled the state institutions to respond to emerging or latent group protest by extending the franchise "precociously," by co-opting promising (and threatening) individual leaders "preemptively," by conceding welfare benefits and governmental social protection "prematurely," by promoting widespread corruption and selective favoritism, and, of course, by exercising sporadic but effective repression of more intransigent opponents.[7]

If these "macro-speculations" are correct — if there existed some elective affinity between Brazil's delayed-dependent developmental context and authoritarian rule in the 1930–45 period, if the postwar period can best be interpreted as an attempt to adapt a basically authoritarian polity to the minimal exigencies of formal democracy without modifying its essential structures (a *democradura,* in my lexicon), if the 1960–64 period is best seen as witnessing the decay or disintegration of that *sistema* and a growing power vacuum at its center[8] — then the military regimes since 1964 (*dictablandas,* in my lexicon) must be recognized as

7. The details of this argument are traced out in my *Interest Conflict and Political Change in Brazil* (Stanford, Calif.: Stanford University Press, 1971), pp. 366–76. Recently, I have sought to test some of its assumptions through the analysis of aggregate data from 20 Latin America republics. Cf. "Delayed Development, External Dependence and Political Change in Contemporary Latin America" (Paper presented at the International Studies Association (ISA) Annual Meeting, San Juan, Puerto Rico, March 1971).

8. In passing, all this suggests that the abortive maneuverings of Jânio Quadros in 1960–61 should be interpreted as an attempt to reestablish the structure of authoritarian rule, while making it compatible with a populist social base different from that which had supported *getulismo.* This interpretive point is rather well supported by the descriptive chronology in John W. F. Dulles, *Unrest in Brazil* (Austin: University of Texas Press, 1970), pp. 101–40. Interestingly, Carlos Castello Branco, the Brasília political

basically "restorationist," not revolutionary or counterrevolutionary. As such, they are not intrinsically illegitimate. Nor are they sharply discontinuous — except with their immediate proto-pluralist or protosocialist (depending on your point of view) predecessor. They can, therefore, rely substantially upon established structures of domination and representation and draw upon prevalent "mentalities" and ingrained political cultural norms. In short, by making relatively few institutional changes and by purging the sistema of certain contradictory (i.e. libertarian) practices while maintaining a virtually identical formal façade, Brazil's military could institutionalize themselves and their hand-picked (civilian, if they please) successors in power with relative ease.[9]

Under these conditions, one would not anticipate strong resistance from bourgeois and middle-sector groups steeped in the traditions of political liberalism and angered at having "lost" something they never had: autonomous participation or hegemony over the political order. Nor would one expect working-class organizations seriously to challenge authority groups with militant demands for greater equality of access or socialization of the means of production. Instead they will be preoccupied with retaining what has already been "benevolently" granted them from above.

Instead, one would predict a pattern of participation and accommodation more characteristic of stable authoritarian rule:

columnist, has recently argued that the "frustrated activities of Sr. Jânio Quadros . . . essentially proposed a reform model *of an authoritarian stripe* that was to a certain degree realized by the Constitution of 1967" (my emphasis). All, he noted, that was presently missing from the Jânio model was a more independent foreign policy and that the Médici regime seemed to be working toward. *Jornal do Brasil,* 21 September 1970. In my terms, both Jânio and Médici have tried to establish authoritarian rule on the basis of an appeal to the *mesoi,* the urban middle masses. Cf. Francisco Welfort, "Raizes sociais do populismo en São Paulo," *Revista Civilização Brasileira* 1, no. 2 (May 1965): 39–60, for a discussion of this distinctive class base to the populist movements of Jânio Quadros and Adhemar de Barros.

9. For the first intellectual statement of awareness that the post-1964 military were seeking to impose their own institutionalized "modêlo" on Brazilian society, eschewing the roles of "military saviors" or "class instruments," see Cândido Mendes, "Sistema político e modelos de poder no Brasil," *Dados* 1 (1966): 7–41; also idem, "O govêrno Castello Branco: paradigma e prognose," *Dados* 2/3 (1967): 63–111, and "Elite de poder, democracia e desenvolvimento," *Dados* 6 (1969): 57–90. All of these have been influential in structuring my thoughts on this issue, although I tend to stress much more the element of continuity with the previous Getulian sistema and much less the differences between *castelismo* and Costa e Silva's "Bonapartism."

support from a bourgeoisie or propertied class that has willingly exchanged its pretensions to political hegemony for economic security, its "right to rule" for its "right to make money";[10] consent from a dependent, salaried, nonmanual *mesoi* whose status is protected from the proletarianizing tendencies of inflation and income redistribution and whose employment is ensured by an expanded bureaucratic apparatus of planning and control; acquiescence from a relatively privileged urban working class sheltered by minimal social legislation from displacement by *lumpen*-masses, represented from above by co-opted or appointed "leaders" and cared for by a benevolent ruler "who wants to make the lower classes of the people happy within the framework of bourgeois society [by issuing] new decrees that cheat the 'true socialists' of their statecraft in advance." [11] Complementing these variegated bases of passive social support would be an officially promoted ideology (or "mentality") stressing diffuse, non-zero-sum goals (public goods) that appear to benefit all the people simultaneously and equally: development and national grandeur.[12]

The cornerstone to this authoritarian edifice is what Marx referred to as "die verselbständigten Machte der Exekutivgewalt" — loosely translated as "the process whereby executive power becomes progressively more independent." I cannot resist citing the following paragraph from *The Eighteenth Brumaire* for its extraordinary applicability to contemporary Brazil:

> It is immediately obvious that in a country like France, where the executive power commands an army of officials numbering more than half a million individuals and there-

10. Cf. Marx, *Eighteenth Brumaire*, pp. 67, 106–07. Cardoso writes, "Not identifying subjectively with the government, because in part he is not objectively linked with it, the [Brazilian] entrepreneur draws the maximum benefit from being the economically dominant class without being the politically dominant strata," Fernando H. Cardoso, *Empresário industrial e desenvolvimento econômico* (São Paulo: Difusão Européia do Livro, 1964), p. 168. For a further theoretical exposition of the implications of this differentiation between public and private class interests, see August Thalheimer, "Über den Faschismus," in *Faschismus und Kapitalismus*, ed. O. Bauer, H. Marcuse, and A. Rosenberg (Frankfurt: Europäische Verlagsanstalt, 1967), pp. 19–38. Also R. Griepenburg and K. H. Tjaden, "Faschismus und Bonapartismus," *Das Argument* 8 (December 1966): 461–72.

11. Marx, *Eighteenth Brumaire*, p. 132.

12. In back-to-back major speeches to the Superior War College and to the Foreign Office (Itamarati), President Médici emphasized just those themes, first development and then an independent foreign policy. *Jornal do Brasil*, 11 March 1970 and 21 April 1970.

fore constantly maintains an immense mass of interests and livelihoods in the most absolute dependence; where the state enmeshes, controls, regulates, superintends and tutors civil society from its most insignificant stirrings, from its most general modes of being to the private existence of individuals; where through the most extraordinary centralization this parasitic body acquires a ubiquity, an omniscience, a capacity for accelerated mobility and an elasticity which finds a counterpart only in the helpless dependence, in the loose shapelessness of the actual body politic — it is obvious that in such a country the National Assembly forfeits all real influence when it loses command of the ministerial posts, if it does not at the same time simplify the administration of the state, reduce the army of officials as far as possible and, finally, let civil society and public opinion create organs of their own, independent of the governmental power.[13]

The eventual outcome, again using Marx's expressive phraseology, is that "the struggle seems to be ended in such a way that all classes, equally impotent and equally mute, fall on their knees before the rifle butt." [14] The essential social structural setting for this "independent executive power" is one in which sharp, class-structured conflict has emerged to the surface of political life, as exemplified by urban revolts and factory occupations (e.g. Paris, 1849; Munich, Budapest, and Torino, 1919–20) or rural violence (e.g. land seizures in the Po Valley in 1919), but in which, due to internal fragmentation and/or external dependence, *none of the warring classes is capable of imposing its model of political order upon the others.* "In reality, it was the only form of government possible at a time when the bourgeoisie had already lost, and the working class had not yet acquired, the faculty of ruling the nation." [15] Into this tense power vacuum steps the providential leader (or rides the man on horseback) and proceeds to rule and consolidate his authority by a combination of guile (playing off the divided and fearful classes against each other) and repression (incorporating the army and building an elaborate police-intelligence network). The essential point of my speculation on delayed-dependent development is precisely that this context greatly enhances the likelihood of a stalemated, impotent, nonhegemonic structure of class relations. My analysis diverges quite sharply from Marx's, however, in

13. Marx, *Eighteenth Brumaire*, pp. 61–62.
14. Ibid., p. 121.
15. Marx, *Civil War in France*, p. 56.

one crucial aspect — the permanence or persistence of such authoritarian rule. Marx clearly saw Bonapartism as something novel and modern, but as something definitely transitory. Its heterogeneity of support, its experimental and "confused groping" from one policy to another, its internal corruption and speculation "in hothouse fashion" would, he felt, lead to its rapid demise. Ultimately, Napoleon III could not sustain his image as the patriarchal benefactor of all classes — "he cannot give to one class without taking from another."

> Driven by the contradictory demands of his situation and being at the same time, like a conjurer, under the necessity of keeping the public gaze fixed on himself, as Napoléon's substitute, by springing constant surprises, that is to say, under the necessity of executing a *coup d'état en miniature* every day, Bonaparte throws the entire bourgeois economy into confusion, violates everything that seemed inviolable to the Revolution of 1848, makes some tolerant of revolution, others desirous of revolution, and produces actual anarchy in the name of order, while at the same time stripping its halo from the entire state machine, profanes it and makes it at once loathsome and ridiculous.[16]

The implication is that such policies would cause the bourgeoisie to reassert the political hegemony it had bargained away in exchange for short-lived economic security.[17]

16. Marx, *Eighteenth Brumaire*, p. 135. For an interpretation of the Brazilian Revolution that stresses the idea that its reactionary social base makes it unable to overcome structural obstacles, its inevitable association with economic stagnation ("pastoralization"), and hence, its political inviability, see Celso Furtado, *Obstacles to Development in Latin America* (Garden City, N.Y.: Anchor Books, 1970), pp. 113–200. Marx was less prone to this sort of wishful thinking, but he also overestimated the vulnerability of this type of rule, for reasons I suggest below.

17. I also diverge from those orthodox Marxist analyses, based on a faulty reading of Marx's Bonapartist model, which interpreted the rise of fascism and Nazism as the last or final stage of capitalist development, to be succeeded by, of course, revolutionary communism. Following Thalheimer, I would interpret authoritarian rule as part of the process of *installing* and consolidating capitalism rather than a symptom of its imminent demise. On the transformational role of fascism in the Spanish case, see J. Solé-Tura, "The Political 'Instrumentality' of Fascism," in *The Nature of Fascism*, ed. S. J. Woolf (New York: Vintage Books, 1969), pp. 42–50, 57. The *locus classicus* of this argument is Franz Borkenau, "Zur Soziologie des Faschismus," in *Theorien über den Faschismus*, ed. Ernst Nolte (Cologne: Kiepenheuer und Witsch, 1967), pp. 156–81.

In retrospect, Marx was wrong — at least with respect to the time perspective. Napoleon III presided over a sustained economic transformation of France and was finally removed from power over twenty years later only by defeat in international war. Since then, development in political and material technology have made it vastly easier to establish and implement a consistent set of public policies; to capture evidence of emerging opposition by social indicators and/or survey research and to act preemptively; to regiment political activity into a single official party; to "corporatize" systems of interest representation; to retain a monopoly over the instruments of organized violence; and to socialize and indoctrinate subjects through the media and mass education.

I do *not* mean to imply by the above that, given its "elective affinity" with the context of delayed-dependent development and the changing nature of political technology, authoritarian regimes once entrenched in power *cannot* be removed. I probably would not have bothered to write this piece if I held such a rigidly deterministic and pessimistic view.[18] I do believe that recognition of these proclivities and interdependencies is a prerequisite to effective strategies of resistance. No amount of wishful thinking about the libertarian ideals of the middle classes or dogmatic faith in the eschatological vocation of the proletariat will bring about a system transformation. New strategies must be devised based on the contradictions and weaknesses of this particular and distinctive type of political regime. Some suggestions along these lines will be advanced in my concluding remarks, but let us now turn to the regime's recorded policy performance.

POLICY OUTPUTS SINCE 1964

From 1964 to 1967 the Castello Branco regime reputedly issued over 6,000 decrees and decree-laws. Costa e Silva in less than two years issued more than 4,000,[19] and the present Médici regime may break even these records of "legislative" productivity. Twelve institutional acts, over 80 complementary acts (at my last

18. Here I would stress the point made by scholars of modern Germany. While the demise of the Goulart regime (or the Weimar Republic) may have been inevitable, it was by no means inevitable that "Portugalization" (or "Nazification") would succeed it. Cf. Theodor Eschenburg et al., *The Path to Dictatorship, 1918–1933* (Garden City, N.Y.: Anchor Books, 1966), p. xvii.

19. "The Law Will Rule," *Brazil 1969* (New York: Center for Inter-American Relations, 1970), p. 144.

count), one new constitution — itself amended within 24 hours — all indicate the immense difficulty in summarizing briefly the pattern of public policy followed by the 1964 revolutionary restorationists. To follow consistent threads through such a maze of decrees modifying decrees modifying decrees — not to mention the large number of "laws that never took hold" — would take me well beyond the theme of this essay. Fortunately, many of the lacunae will be filled by other authors in this volume.

I will concentrate here on some general policy arenas of special significance for the institutionalization of authoritarian rule. These all contribute in a particularly strategic manner to the "progressive independence of the executive power." They are: (1) rapid establishment of a large, stable and balanced resource base for the state apparatus; (2) increased penetration of the economy by state instruments of control and subsidization without, however, usurping the privileges and prerogatives of private enterprise; (3) heavy expenditure for external defense and internal security. Subsequently, I will discuss those more specific areas of policy which contribute to strengthening the more specialized structures of authoritarian rule, e.g. corporatism, centralization, depoliticization, monopolistic party system, and so on.

One of the paramount and manifestly proclaimed policy objectives of the 1964 revolutionaries was to restore "sanity" and "equilibrium" to the economy, as well as to purge the polity of "subversive" and "corrupt" elements. As a means to this end (or, for some, as an end in itself), they promulgated a series of policies that had the effect of restoring and slightly expanding the economic base of state authority and its penetration of the private sector. This penetrative effort, however, did not replace or even displace the established interests of capital. Supporters of the golpe who regarded it as the historical opportunity to arrest "statism" by reducing the role and resources of "interventionist" governmental institutions were bound to be frustrated. The editorials of the *Estado de São Paulo* in the ensuing years are an eloquent testimony to this frustrated liberalism.

Table 6.1 reveals the financial recuperation quite clearly. Whatever other charges can be leveled at the Goulart regime, it did preside over a substantial decline in total governmental expenditures as a percentage of GDP. From its Kubitschekian heights of 21 percent (1958, 1960), it dropped to 17.8 and 17.7 percent (1962, 1964). Expenditures at all levels of government had already increased by 1965 and by 1968 they were approximating and slightly exceeding pre-Goulart performance. Al-

Table 6.1. Government Resources, 1955–69

	1955	1958	1960	1962	1964	1965	1966	1967	1968	1969
1. Total government expenditures as % of GDP	18.2	21.3	21.6	17.8	17.7	18.9	21.1	19.9	22.1	23.4[a]
2. Federal government										
Receipts	53.5	72.4	93.1	99.0	116.9	134.2	161.5	153.7	194.0	266.9
Expenditures	61.1	91.3	105.7	128.6	161.2	168.2	165.0	170.1	190.0	252.9
Deficit/Surplus	−7.6	−18.9	−12.6	−39.6	−44.2	−34.0	−3.5	−16.1	+4.0	+14.0
3. State governments										
Receipts	48.6	61.2	84.4	93.3	109.9	118.0	128.5	142.3	178.2	—[b]
Expenditures	52.8	67.1	88.5	99.9	119.8	141.9	141.6	158.4	182.0	—
Deficit/Surplus	−4.2	−5.9	−4.1	−6.6	−9.9	−23.9	−13.1	−16.1	−3.8	—
4. Municipal governments										
Receipts	13.0	16.5	17.9	18.2	—	23.9	28.8	—	20.8	—
Expenditures	13.5	17.4	18.3	19.4	—	25.3	30.7	—	20.4	—
Deficit/Surplus	−0.5	−0.9	−0.4	−1.2	—	−1.4	−1.9	—	+0.4	—

SOURCES: Fundação-IBGE, *Anuario Estatístico do Brasil, 1955–1971*, pp. 508–09; Fundação-IBGE, *Brasil: Séries Estatísticas Retrospectivas-1970*, pp. 209–10.

NOTE: Receipts, expenditures, and deficits are given in constant 1955 cruzeiros.

[a] Based on projected estimate.

[b] Dash indicates data not available.

though I was unable to obtain concomittant data on GDP for the entire period, federal government expenditures in 1969 were up over 19 percent,[20] and for 1970, a further increase of 45 percent was planned.[21] Of special importance in table 6.1 are the figures for the government deficit. In the crisis year of 1964 almost one-third of total government spending was in the red! With the exception of a slight relapse in 1967, the so-called revolutionary authorities not only closed this gap, but were actually accumulating surpluses by 1968 and 1969. It is important to stress that this was accomplished not by a draconian liberalization program or self-imposed austerity in governmental spending, but by expanding receipts even faster than expenditures and passing some of this burden to the tax-paying public. (See table 6.2.)

Table 6.2. Total Taxes as Percentage of
Gross Domestic Product, 1955–69

1955	1958	1960	1962	1964	1965	1966	1967	1968
15.8	20.1	20.3	17.8	19.4	21.8	24.1	23.3	26.7

SOURCE: Andrea Maneschi, "The Brazilian Public Sector," in *Brazil in the Sixties*, ed. R. Roett (Nashville, Tenn.: Vanderbilt University Press, 1972), p. 189.

How, then, is this restoration being paid for? Upon whom does the increased fiscal burden rest? One of the regime's most trumpeted policies has been its imposition and stringently enforced collection of taxes on income. The specter of fearful middle- and upper-class citizens paying direct taxes for the first time has been used by the regime to enhance its socially neutral, technocratically efficient image both domestically and internationally. And there is no doubt that income tax revenue has risen — even astronomically (by as much as 70 percent in 1968 alone). However, the "rationalization" in more regressive indirect taxes has not been equally well publicized. Table 6.3 shows clearly that proportionately these have grown, while nontax revenues — for example earnings on government enterprises — shrank to nothing, and then rose again. Direct (property and income) taxes have actually decreased proportionately. The highly touted "squeezing" of the rich must be placed in context — the poor have been squeezed even harder.

20. APEC, *A Economia brasileira e suas perspectivas* 9 (July 1970): F-1.
21. The Economic Intelligence Unit, "Brazil," *Quarterly Economic Reviews*, no. 4 (1969), p. 9.

Table 6.3. Central Government Revenues, Percentage
Furnished by Tax Source, 1960–71

Nontax Revenues				Indirect Taxes				Direct Taxes			
1960	*1964*	*1968*	*1971*	*1960*	*1964*	*1968*	*1971*	*1960*	*1964*	*1968*	*1971*
9.2	6.7	3.1	13.3	54.6	60.1	74.8	63.2	36.2	33.2	21.1	23.5

SOURCE: Banco Central do Brasil, *Relatório 1971*, p. 98.

Nevertheless, important changes have been made. Not only has the regime acquired a more diversified resource base, but it has demonstrated its capability to impose new burdens on those who are its principal beneficiaries and supporters. The 1969 tax reform required *all* Brazilians to register, whether they earn enough to pay or not. It also lowered the rates for lower- and middle-income (salaried) groups. Most importantly, it adjusted downward the rates on bearer shares and offered healthy allowances for those investing in certain government-certified projects, sectors, or regions.[22] The result of all these machinations is to reduce any redistributive impact the earlier fiscal reform might have had and to place in the hands of authorities a new, powerful (if indirect) set of instruments for guiding savings and investment. In a paradoxical sense (and perverse, one might argue), they had to create a credible and efficient system of income and property taxes in order not to apply it fully — thereby increasing their potential control over the economy by deterrence.

Where, then, have these restored and augmented public resources been allocated? What has been the distribution by bureaucratic sectors of federal expenditures? And, in what way can this be said to reflect and reinforce authoritarian control over policy making?

In a recent analysis of longitudinal data on public policy outputs across 18 Latin American republics for the period 1950 to 1967, I discovered some interesting patterns of association in this regard. By examining the residual scores from multiple regressions that in effect controlled for levels of development and external dependence, I concluded that certain regime characteristics — specifically, military vs. civilian control, competitive vs. noncompetitive party systems — did have a significant independent effect upon how public monies were distributed by sector and how governmental resources were extracted. Regime types had much less effect upon such policy outcomes as overall rate of

22. "The Economy Under Control?" *Brazil 1969* (New York: Center for Inter-American Relations, 1970), pp. 10–11.

economic growth and inflation, although they were related to distinctive patterns of political instability and violence.[23]

One of the findings I have just reported for Brazil is a confirmation of what I observed at the cross–Latin American level: military, noncompetitive regimes rely more heavily on regressive indirect taxes. Another finding of my cross–Latin American study was that this type of regime tended to spend more for national-security purposes and less for health and welfare (all things being equal). Granted that "military, noncompetitive" regime is not synonymous with authoritarian regime (the former may be purely expediential or *salvacionista* in Cândido Mendes's terminology; the latter may be civilian as well as military), nevertheless the institutionalization of authoritarian rule does seem to require the support of a satisfied and unified military and the presence of a large internal police apparatus for informational and security purposes. Since another of the military, noncompetitive regime's characteristics is rigid corporatist regimentation, especially of working-class associations, we might also anticipate a relative lack of interest in (or need for concern with) steady increases in labor and welfare spending beyond some minimal degree of charitable and paternalistic attention and an occasional, co-optive-preemptive gesture of support from above.

Table 6.4 bears out these contentions. Defense spending rapidly recuperated after 1964, hitting a peak in 1967 when it was among the highest in Latin America. It has since been consolidated and has even declined somewhat, proportionately if not absolutely. Conversely, the expenditures of the Ministry of Labor and Social Security have experienced a consistent secular decline. In the 1970 budget this ministry was slated to receive less than the Ministry of Justice. Spending for the Ministry of Health has performed in a similarly dismal manner. Granted that these breakdowns by bureaucratic category are not an accurate measure of the absolute levels of spending in defense, welfare, and education, their evolution over time can be used as an indicator of proportional emphasis.[24]

23. Philippe C. Schmitter, "Military Intervention, Political Competitiveness and Public Policy in Latin America" in *On Military Intervention,* ed. M. Janowitz and J. van Doorn (Rotterdam: Rotterdam University Press, 1971), pp. 426–506.

24. Cf. Andrea Maneschi, "The Brazilian Public Sector," in *Brazil in the Sixties,* ed. R. Roett (Nashville, Tenn.: Vanderbilt University Press, 1972), esp. p. 90 where the author observes that "the expenditures of the federal government are presently available for the sixties only classified by the type of ministry and the various legislative and judiciary entities which effected them. They are not even approximately indicative of the diversity of purposes which the expenditure in each ministry has served."

Table 6.4. Federal Government Spending by Selected Ministries, 1955–69
(In percentage of federal expenditures)

Ministry	1955	1958	1960	1962	1964	1965	1966	1967	1968	1969	1970	1971[a]
Defense[b]	24.5	27.6	20.8	15.8	14.0	20.9	18.9	25.1	22.3	13.8	18.4	20.4
Education[c]	5.7	6.3	6.8	6.8	5.8	9.6	7.4	7.2	7.1	6.2	4.8	5.9
Health[d]	4.1	3.4	4.0	3.1	2.5	2.7	3.3	3.1	2.5	1.7	1.1	1.3
Labor and Social Security[e]	2.4	1.7	1.2	5.0	3.0	2.0	1.0	1.4	1.2	0.6	0.6	0.9

SOURCE: Fundação-IBGE, *Anuario Estatístico do Brasil*, 1955–1971.

[a] Budgeted rather than actual expenditures.

[b] Includes Estado Major das Forças Armadas, Ministério de Aeronautica, Ministério de Guerra, Ministério de Marinha, Conselho de Segurança Nacional (until 1962).

[c] Includes Ministério de Educação e Cultura.

[d] Includes Ministério de Saúde.

[e] Includes Ministério de Trabalho e Previdência Social, Ministério do Trabalho, Industria e Comércio (before 1960).

The figures on educational spending through the federal ministry also confirm an earlier observation of mine. Among the 18 countries of my previous study there seemed to be no significant differences in education expenditures in civilian or military, competitive or noncompetitive regimes. As table 6.4 shows, Brazilian educational expenditures perform in a surprisingly stable manner with the exception of a minor "progressive" change from 1965 to 1968. Since then, the Ministry of Education and Culture has returned to its customary 6 percent of the budget. With the increase in total government expenditures this means a higher absolute quantity of resources and, as we shall see, these have been accompanied by important qualitative changes.

POLICY OUTCOMES SINCE 1964

These are the indicators of performance by which the contemporary military rulers of Brazil wish to be judged. After weathering a period (1964–66) in which their policies of austerity and monetary sanity were associated with negative to barely positive rates of per capita growth and in which inflation continued at over 40 percent per year (incidentally, in 1964–66 there is a good deal of disparity in the data and some hints of fraudulent practice), they have broken into the clear. Whereas, before, such policy outcomes were originally held to be "regrettable and unavoidable," now the regime is doing everything it can to claim credit for the 9 to 11 percent rates of growth (and higher rates in industry) and the "contained" (20 percent) rate of inflation (See table 6.5).

It might appear patently biased to point out that their original disclaimer was well founded. For example, my longitudinal comparative research showed that growth rates are largely predictable from structural and ecological factors, such as prior level of development and degree and type of external dependence, and that regime type and even regime policy affect them very little.[25] It might also seem unfair to observe that a good deal of the economic expansion of the past three years merely has served to place Brazil back on the trendline established in the 1950s — before growth was interrupted by political-system decay and restoration.

Neither point is really relevant. Whether merited or not, the country's present rulers seem to have convinced themselves and their subjects that their brand of authoritarian rule and *only*

25. Schmitter, "Military Intervention," pp. 29–30, 53, 57.

Table 6.5. Overall Economic Performance in Brazil, 1960–71

	1960	1961	1962	1963	1964	1965	1966	1967	1968	1969	1970	1971
Annual rate of gross economic growth	9.7	10.3	5.3	1.5	2.9	2.7	5.1	4.8	8.4	9.0	9.5	11.3
Annual rate of industrial growth	9.6	10.6	7.8	0.2	5.2	−4.7	11.7	3.0	13.2	10.8	11.1	11.2
Annual rate of gross fixed capital formation (as % of GNP)	17.1	17.3	18.1	17.7	16.6	14.8	15.4	14.6	16.8	16.6	—[a]	—
Annual rate of inflation in cost of living (Rio)	29.3	33.2	51.5	70.8	91.4	65.9	41.3	30.5	22.3	22.0	20.9	13.7
Total foreign debt (in $US millions)	3910	3773	4025	3986	3874	4759	5196	3197	3677	4403	5295	6622
Balance of foreign trade (in $US millions)	−24	111	−90	112	344	655	438	213	26	26	232	−363

SOURCES: Fundação-IBGE, Instituto Brasileiro de Estatística, *Séries Estatísticas Retrospectivas-1970* (Rio de Janeiro: IBGE, 1970); Werner Baer and Isaac Kerstenetzky, "The Brazilian Economy" in *Brazil in the Sixties*, ed. R. Roett (Nashville, Tenn.: Vanderbilt University Press, 1972), pp. 105–46; "Brazil: Strong Expansion Continues," *BOLSA Review*, no. 68 (August 1972), pp. 428–33; Riordan Roett, "A Praetorian Army in Politics" in *Brazil in the Sixties*, p. 12. For total foreign debt until 1966, Marco Gomes, "Delfini Netto: A dívida como estratégia," *Opinião*, no. 5 (4–11 December 1972), pp. 7–8; APEC, *Pré Apeão 72* (Rio de Janeiro: APEC, 1972), p. 107.

[a] Dash indicates no data available.

their brand is now compatible with such high levels of global system performance. The party competition, interest-group autonomy, populist "demagogic" leadership, and ideological polarization of 1960 to 1964 have come to be associated with the inverse results. Those who would oppose the institutionalization of authoritarian rule must recognize that it may be associated for a protracted period with economic dynamism (as it was in Bonapartist France). This tends, in turn, to underwrite high levels of popular optimism about the future — especially in Brazil.[26] For example, in a December 1970 poll in São Paulo, 75 percent of the respondents felt that 1971 would be better than 1970 and 73 percent felt that 1971 would be a prosperous economic year, with "social peace" in industry (76 percent) and an increase in employment (75 percent). An accompanying graph based on yearly responses to these questions since 1967 demonstrated a secular trend toward increased optimism about the future.[27] Under such conditions, it would seem tactically suicidal for an opposition movement to base itself on prophecies of economic disaster and strategically erroneous to depend on some long-term contradiction between economic growth and authoritarian rule.[28]

Another question asked of the Paulistas, however, brings us to the really crucial, long-term political issue: the distribution of

26. Cf. Lloyd A. Free, *Some International Implications of the Political Psychology of Brazilians* (Princeton, N.J.: Institute for International Social Research, 1961). Also, Frank Bonilla, "Brazil," in *Education and Political Development*, ed. J. S. Coleman (Princeton, N.J.: Princeton University Press, 1965), pp. 195–221.

27. "Por que se ufanam de 1970," *Veja*, 6 January 1971, pp. 20–24. A more recent (1972) survey reported by Gallup shows this optimism has persisted and perhaps increased. Compared with respondents in eight other countries, Brazilians had by far the highest expectations that 1973 would be a year of economic prosperity (68 percent), peace (72 percent), and full employment (67 percent). With the exception of Greeks, Brazilians also felt most strongly that 1973 would be free of strikes and industrial disputes. Interestingly, Greece was the only country to even approach the pattern of expectations in Brazil. The structural and policy similarities of the two regimes hardly need underscoring. "Americans now happier about economy — Gallup," *Chicago Sun-Times*, 7 January 1973.

28. Cf. Celso Furtado, *Obstacles to Development*, passim. A portion of the original text was published in Brazil under the more explicit title, *Um projeto para o Brazil* (Rio de Janeiro: Editôra Saga, 1968). For an excellent case study in policy change under authoritarian rule which led to sustained high rates of economic growth, see Charles Anderson, *The Political Economy of Modern Spain* (Madison: University of Wisconsin Press, 1970).

this apparent bonanza. When asked if their personal level of living had gone up, fallen, or continued the same, 48 percent said it had gone up, 7 percent said it fell, and 45 percent said it had remained the same. This was higher than 1969 when 41 percent thought their living standard had risen (the comparable figures in 1968 and 1967 were 33 percent and 30 percent), but it illustrates a key weakness of this pattern of "hothouse," authoritarian-sponsored growth: its great inequality. To a certain extent and for a limited time, Brazilians may feel a vicarious pride in their country's obvious dynamism, but eventually they must begin to ask, "What's in it for me?"

Data on income distribution in Brazil are, to put it mildly, not easy to come by — especially on a consistent time-series basis.[29] Fortunately, however, the Intersyndical Department of Socioeconomic Statistics and Studies (Departamento Intersindical de Estatística e Estudos Socio-Econômicos, DIEESE), an independent, trade-union financed research organization in São Paulo, has been collecting data on the standard of living of the working class there. Their rigorously compiled estimates show a very large decrease in purchasing power during the first two years of military rule, mitigated by very slight gains in 1968 and 1969. The cumulative total for the five-year period declined 31.5 percent. But this alarming calculation was based only on a formal juxtaposition of cost-of-living indicators and governmentally decreed wage increases. According to this, the average monthly salary in 1969 should have been NCr $430.83. DIEESE's survey research showed the actual mean salary to have been only NCr $345.06. Apparently, employers taking advantage of the weakness of working class syndicates and certain new legal wrinkles offered them by authorities have successfully avoided paying the increases. The result may be a decline in worker purchasing power in the major industrial center of the country of 64.5 percent since 1958.[30] A parliamentary commission of inquiry in November 1969 also documented this deterioration.[31] Even the United States ambassador to Brazil at that time admitted that "four and

29. For better, more up-to-date data on income distribution, see the essay by Albert Fishlow in this volume.

30. *DIEESE em resumo*, ano 4, no. 3 (March 1970).

31. "CPI conclui que salário fugiu a plano econômico," *Jornal do Brasil*, 14 December 1970. Three years later yet another parliamentary commission concluded that the real value of the minimum wage had decreased 43.5% since 1959 and that the salaries of government workers had fallen even more drastically in terms of purchasing power. Júlio Cesar Montenegro, "Uma espera sem ilusões," *Opinião*, no. 8 (25 December 1972–1 January 1973), p. 4.

a half years after the revolution, the real wages of labor [were] less than in March 1964." [32]

This issue of the very unequal impact of rapid economic growth finally broke into the open in 1971 and 1972.[33] The published results of a sample of the 1970 national census results, when juxtaposed to more-or-less comparable data for 1960, revealed an extraordinary increase in income concentration, most of which can safely be attributed to the post-1964 period. As table 6.6 indicates, the real income of the lowest 50 percent of the population barely increased while their proportional share of the gross national income fell very sharply. The more skilled components of the manual working class, constituting in crude terms the next strata of 30 percent of the total economically active population, also lost proportionately, while the *mesoi* (here defined as those receiving salaries higher than 80 percent and lower than 5 percent of the population) barely held their own in terms of gross national income. The only clear winners were the top 5 percent of wage earners whose real income rose 72 percent and whose share of the GNP advanced from 27 to 36 percent. Overall, Brazil's index of income inequality, as underestimated by the Gini coefficient, rose from a modest .488 in 1960 (relatively low by Latin American standards) to a whopping .574 in 1970 (the highest ever recorded at the national level in Latin America).[34]

There are also indirect proximate indicators of the impoverishment of lower classes. The per capita consumption of meat dropped from 41 kilos in 1961 to 39 kilos in 1967. Sugar consumption also decreased while consumption of the "people's staples," rice and beans, rose.[35] The only bright spot in the dismal dietary picture was a substantial rise in milk consumption. According to the government's own cost-of-living estimates, the percentage of total income spent on food rose from 40.3 to

32. John W. Tutthill, "Economic and Political Aspects of Development in Brazil," *Journal of Inter-American Studies* 11 (April 1969): 208.

33. This issue of income distribution has provoked the closest approximation to a genuine public debate to have occurred in Brazilian political life since 1964. For an account that captures much of its flavor and reviews several publications which have appeared on the topic, see "Milagre Brasileiro: O grande debate," *Opinião*, no. 4 (27 November–4 December 1972), pp. 11–14.

34. Rodolfo Hoffman and João Carlos Duarte, "A distribuição da renda no Brasil," *Revista de Administração de Empresas* 12, no. 2 (June 1972): 46–66.

35. Euphemistically, the official economist suggests that the decline in meat and sugar were due to "reasons of a medical nature!" *Conjuntura Econômica* 17, no. 1 (1970): 12.

Table 6.6. Social Classes, Income Groups, and the Distribution of Wealth, 1960–70

Social Class and Income Groups[a]	Average Real Income in Deflated Cruzeiros 1960	1970	Increase in Real Income per capita (%) 1960–70	% of Total Gross National Income 1960	1970	Total Population Increase 1960–70
Lowest 50% of the working population: Nonpropertied rural population; marginally self-employed urban workers; lowest strata of industrial and commercial workers	3,62	3,64	1	17.7	13.7	+12,000,000
Next 30% of the working population: Urban salaried and wage earner in industry and services; some rural proprietors	9,17 [bottom 2/3 of 15% strata]	10,27 [bottom 2/3 of 15% strata]	7	27,8	23,1	+7,200,000
Next 15% of the working population: Skilled workers; middle-level civil servants and administrators; small businessmen; liberal professionals; rural landowners (*mesoi*)	15,99 [bottom 2/3 of 15% strata]	19,65 [bottom 2/3 of 15% strata]	23 [bottom 2/3 of 15% strata]	27,1	27,0	+3,600,000
Top 5% of the working population: Industrialists; merchants; higher civilian and military personnel	56,02	96,16	72	27.4	36.2	+1,200,000

SOURCES: Rodolfo Hoffman and João Carlos Duarte, "A distribuição da renda no Brasil," *Revista de Administração de Empresas* 12, no. 2 (June 1972): 46–66; "Milagre Brasileiro–O grande debate," *Opinão*, no. 4 (27 November–4 December 1972), pp. 11–14.
[a] The social class and occupational categories placed in each of the income strata are my rough estimates, not groupings based on independent census data.

41.2 percent since the Revolution. By Engel's law, it should have fallen if the population's overall prosperity had risen.[36] Instead, in an increasingly restricted financial situation, families were compelled to spend more proportionately on merely staying alive. Like Alice, they were running harder simply to stay in the same place.

There are other holes in this post-1968 "boom" (job openings and admissions actually declined until 1970 and job offerings remained stagnant; electricity consumption did not increase as much as overall production — indicating, perhaps, the importance of purely financial and speculative manipulation). Most seriously, however, the so-called boom has contributed significantly to aggravating another disparity — that between regions within Brazil. As table 6.7 demonstrates, between 1960 and 1970

Table 6.7. Regional Distribution of Gross Domestic Income, 1939–68

	1939	*1950*	*1960*	*1966*	*1968*
North	2.66	1.71	2.23	2.11	2.08
Northeast	16.73	14.65	14.78	14.36	14.52
Southeast (Minas Gerais, Espirito Santo, Rio de Janeiro, Guanabara, and São Paulo)	62.91	65.56	62.77	63.06	63.20
South	15.56	16.29	17.77	17.32	17.43
Center West	2.14	1.79	2.49	3.12	3.28

SOURCES: "O sul cresce depressa, o norte devagar: Qual é a diferença," *Realidade*, special supplement (July 1970), p. 87; APEC, *A Economia brasileira e suas perspectivas, Ano IX-1972* (Rio de Janeiro: APEC Editôra, 1972), p. 113. Original source: Centro de Contas Nacionais, IBGE/FGV.

there was a reversal of the trend of the preceding decade toward a greater share of national income for the Northeast. Granted, some of this might have resulted from the practices of earlier regimes, but there is not much indication that the postrevolutionary management of the Superintendency for the Development of the Northeast (SUDENE) was successful in reversing the tide. In fact, one minister of the interior, General Albuquerque Lima, resigned in (ostensible) protest over the low priority given the Northeast in the regime's developmental program. A special tax

36. Ibid., p. 11. This article observes that the increase would not have been due to the change in food prices, which actually *declined* relative to other prices.

write-off scheme was successful in channeling some private investment northward.[37] But with the opening of equally attractive tax write-offs for other regions and sectors and the stock market boom in capital issues for industries in the most developed areas of the country, even this palliative will become less important. The regime's eventual solution for the Northeast is "peasant removal" by way of the Transamazonic Highway. This has already begun with the formation in 1970 of large labor gangs composed of drought victims.

The single most alarming indicator of policy outcome I have seen concerns the evolution of income distribution in Northeastern state capitals. According to research by the Bank of the Northeast, the percentage of total income going to the lowest 40 percent of the Recife population declined from 16.5 percent in 1960 to 11.5 percent in 1967. The data on Maceió show even more clearly the "responsibility" of the Revolution. In April 1964, 15.4 percent of its income went to the lowest 40 percent and in March 1968, only 11.2 percent. In only one of the eight cities did real monthly per capita income rise for this oppressed sector of the population in this oppressed region of the country.[38]

Brazil's present general-cum-president has admitted that "the economy may be going well, but the majority of the people still fare poorly." There is, unfortunately, no evidence of a concerted regime effort to redress these growing disparities in regional and class income. The only policy response has been a Program for Social Integration (PIS), which set up a compulsory, restricted access savings bank for all the nation's industrial and commercial workers. This ingenious scheme, while it costs the workers nothing, also is not charged to the employers. It is indirectly financed through various tax rebates. Money can be withdrawn only when the worker marries, buys a house or dies, and in the meantime the state controls the resources and redistributes them to employers as working capital at low rates of interest — further accelerating the growth of income disparities. In addition, this "all winners, no losers" scheme preempts any future claim on the

37. Cf. Albert O. Hirschman, "Industrial Development in the Brazilian Northeast and the Tax Credit Scheme of Article 34118," in *The Journal of Development Studies* 1 (October 1968): 5–28. Of course, the scheme, proposed in 1961–63, antedates the military seizure of power by several years.

38. Banco do Nordêste, "Distribuição e níveis da renda familiar no Nordêste urbano," as reported in APEC, *A Economia brasileira e suas perspectivas* 9 (July 1970): 137–38. Elsewhere it was reported that in Recife the top one-fifth of income earners increased their share from 47.1 percent in 1960 to 56.4 percent in 1967.

part of workers to profit-sharing or participation in management.[39]

THE STRUCTURAL COMPONENTS OF AUTHORITARIAN RULE

The major premise underlying my introductory remarks is that there exists a distinctive "authoritarian response to modernization" — a consistent, interdependent, and relatively stable set of political structures and practices that permit existing elites to manage, guide, or manipulate the transformation of economic and social structures at minimal cost to themselves in terms of power, wealth, and status. These regimes seek not so much to arrest change — in fact, they often promote it — as they seek to control its consequences from above. By changing, they avoid change. My second contention is that Brazil has long been firmly ensconced in this pattern of defensive modernization from above (this "let's do the revolution before the people do it" response on the part of elites) and that there are good (but speculative) reasons for believing that the context of delayed-dependent development favors such an outcome. Beyond identifying it generically with its Bonapartist prototype, however, I have as yet said little about what constitutes this "consistent, interdependent and relatively stable set of political structures and practices."

In this task, I and many other analysts of Brazil politics have found the pioneering formulations of Juan Linz very useful. Here, in summary, is Linz's delineation of the distinctive traits of this type of political system:

> Authoritarian regimes are political systems with limited, not responsible political pluralism; without elaborate and guiding ideology (but with distinctive mentalities); without intensive or extensive political mobilization (except during some points in their development); and in which a leader (or occasionally a small group) exercises power within formally ill-defined limits, but actually quite predictable ones.[40]

Although I have respecified and renamed some of the components, perhaps imposed empirical referents different from those

39. The President's statement, occasioned by his visit to the drought-stricken areas of the Northeast, can be found in *Jornal do Brasil*, 11 March 1970. On PIS, see "Um programa à Brasileira," *Veja*, 26 August 1970, pp. 28–30 and "O PIS e seus milhões," *Opinião*, no. 3 (20–27 November 1972), p. 4.

40. Linz, "An Authoritarian Regime," p. 255. See also Philippe C. Schmitter, "Paths to Political Development in Latin America," *Proceedings of the Academy of Political Science* 30, no. 4 (1972): 83–108.

Linz would have used, and added a new major characteristic ("die verselbständigten Machte der Executivgewalt," which I treat as a sort of summation of all the preceding ones), I will generally follow Linz's specifications. At this point I will ask briefly: What have Brazil's military rulers since 1964 done to alter the specific "Getulian" variant of authoritarian rule, the sistema that Brazilian intellectuals refer to so often? How do the policy outputs and outcomes discussed above relate to this attempt to perfect and, thereby, to institutionalize a new, purer, more "Portuguese" variety of authoritarian rule?

Corporatism or Limited Pluralism

Regimentation from above of interest representation into a preordained set of hierarchical categories; official recognition and control over internal finance, leadership selection and demand articulation; formal monopoly on representation; imposition of a symbiotic relationship between such "semivoluntary" associations and the central bureaucracy — this is corporatism. Corporatism is the "cornerstone of the sistema" [41] and a key element of authoritarian rule in general. The revolutionaries of 1964 quickly recognized this. Despite protests from liberals within their ranks, one of their first "guarantees" was the maintenance of the Consolidation of the Labor Laws (CLT) and, specifically, the syndical system enshrined in it.

Clearly, one of the signs of the decay of the previous sistema was the growing inability of the president and minister of labor to enforce the restrictive provisions of the CLT. Parasyndical workers' organizations had sprung up outside the officially imposed framework; leadership selection and demand articulation were getting out of hand; the power relations between ministry and syndicates seemed to be reversing. On the employer side, new "civil entities" were formed alongside syndicates, old private associations were revived; even officially recognized syndicates and federations began openly opposing the government and/or engaging in conspiratorial activities.

Literally without changing a line of existing law, but by applying a very different practice, the 1964 revolutionaries restored the syndical movement to its former status as cornerstone of the system. By first conducting massive purges and then controlling

41. The quoted phrase is from Oliveiros S. Ferreira, "Estado e Liberdade," *O Estado de São Paulo* (12 September 1965). For a more extensive discussion of this point, see my *Interest Conflict and Political Change in Brazil*, esp. pp. 383–86.

subsequent leadership recruitment to workers' syndicates, they got the enforced "social peace" they needed for their restrictive wage and investment policies. By less direct means, they removed undesirable "radicals" from employers' syndicates. Many of the more militant civil entities either faded or turned to more quiescent practices. Subsidies, clientelistic favors, and memberships in a multitude of new consultative councils were sufficient to co-opt the rest.

Hence, the burgeoning institutional and ideological pluralism of the early 1960s was abruptly and effectively halted, and the system returned to its unitary, central-imposed, corporatist configuration. Table 6.8 shows some of the consequences. The total number of workers' syndicates rose briefly (1965–67) then declined to earlier levels. The urban working class has now been *enquadrado* (literally, "framed") and growth in the number of formally syndicalized (but by no means participant) members has been purely vegetative. Growth in the number of urban employer syndicates has also stagnated, but membership in these syndicates has been increasing significantly.

The almost complete prohibition on strikes or even less aggressive but public means of articulating demands has resulted in a noteworthy bureaucratization of class relations as is exemplified by the rapidly increasing case load of the Juntas de Conciliação e Julgamento (lower-level labor courts). Wages are determined by a complex and thoroughly "technocratized" process, involving monthly coefficients decreed by the president, an inflationary residual estimated (at rates considerably inferior to the general rate of increase of cost of living) by the National Monetary Council, and, finally, a productivity quotient mysteriously calculated by the Ministry of Planning. Increases bargained for by syndicates cannot surpass these "maximal" rates.

Of special importance, however, is the rural sector. After closing down almost all of the rural syndicates and all of the peasant leagues formed under the Goulart regime, the military have proceeded continuously and gradually to extend a new associational coverage to this unrepresented sector. It is important to note, however, that the rate of formation of rural employers' syndicates has vastly outstripped that of rural workers — partly as a result of a simple legal switch from the already existent *associação rural* status to that of *sindicato rural,* partly as a matter of deliberate governmental policy. Nevertheless, there is no reason not to expect that within a relatively short time, every *município* will be tied into this sponsored network and that

Table 6.8. Brazilian Corporatism, 1959–70

	1959	1960	1961	1962	1963	1964	1965	1966	1967	1968	1969	1970
Number of syndicates												
Urban workers	1,582	1,608	1,669	1,776	1,883	1,948	2,049	2,158	2,137	1,991	1,987	1,991
Urban employers	992	1,005	1,039	1,057	1,092	1,119	1,170	1,235	1,222	1,186	1,181	1,190
Rural workers	—[a]	—	7	—	270[b]	2,268[b]	490	449	478	625	745	829
Rural employers	...[c]	...	...	...	...	...	...	294	381	845	1,225	1,268
Number of members (thousands)												
Urban workers	1,148	1,125	1,204	1,395	1,448	1,604	1,602	1,628	—	1,874	1,953	—
Urban employers	126	105	111	110	119	171	162	173	—	191	211	—
Labor courts cases (thousands)	138	136	155	190	272	267	307	322	363	416	463	465

SOURCE: Unless otherwise noted, Fundação-IBGE, *Anuario Estatístico do Brasil*, 1960–71.

[a] Dash indicates no data available.

[b] Estimates found in Neale J. Pearson, "Small Farmer and Rural Worker Characteristics in the Emergence of Brazilian Peasant Pressure Groups, 1955–1958" in *Cultural Change in Brazil* (Muncie, Ind.: Ball State University Press, 1969), p. 99.

[c] Prior to 1965, rural employers were organized in *associações rurais*, publicly subsidized entities attached to the Ministry of Agriculture.

some minimal panoply of social services will accompany it.[42] The last remaining uncorporatized arena that caused so much anxiety during the Goulart regime will then have been preempted and, presumably, placed beyond the reach of any future radical mobilization.

A Single, No-Party System

Linz does not include a single, no-party system in the summary description quoted earlier, but from the content of his lengthier analysis, it seems to be an important structural component of the mature Spanish (and by extension, the Portuguese) system. One official party must formally occupy a dominant position but it does not monopolize all access to power. "A considerable part of the elite has no connection with the party and does not identify with it. Party membership creates few visible advantages and imposes few, if any, duties." [43] In fact, one could argue that the primary function of party in a stable authoritarian regime is to do as little as possible but to occupy a particular political space in order to prevent less subservient, more competitive organizations from forming.

The Estado Nôvo was something of an oddity among interwar authoritarian regimes in its failure to maintain even the pretense of a dominant-party system. As the necessity for "redemocratization" emerged in the 1940s, Getúlio responded ingeniously by creating the basis for a two-party dominant coalition that functioned reasonably well until 1960. Jânio's victory and the subsequent (if short) transfer of control over the state apparatus to another and not yet institutionally dominant coalition placed severe strains on the system. Proliferation in the number of parties, rapid changes in strength, and constant shifting of alliances in the Jango period was heightened by the growing ambiguity surrounding the prospective presidential elections of 1965. The ingenious Getulian formula, which permitted local-level competition on the basis of coalitional shifts but which ensured a stable dominance at the national presidential level, was falling apart and something more ideologically and socially polarized was emerging around the parliamentary fronts. From semicompetitive, the sistema had become truly competitive.

42. Cf. "Décréto ámplia a previdência rural," in *O Estado do São Paulo*, 24 July 1969. In 1970, a "Program for the Assistance of the Rural Worker" (Prorural) was inaugurated to cover retirement and health benefits, "Programas de impacto já estão institucionalizados," *Jornal do Brasil*, 22 October 1972.

43. Linz, "An Authoritarian Regime: Spain," p. 264.

The 1964 golpistas did not, at first, grasp the implications of this. The First Institutional Act implied the continuance of the existing competitive system, and the speeches of leading revolutionaries supported it more explicitly. The relatively free elections of 1965 immediately revealed to the military their error in calculation and were followed by the Second Institutional Act, which abolished all previous parties. The military set about constructing a party system more appropriate to their longer-term political ambitions and settled upon a one-and-a-half party system. The predominance of the official party Aliança Renovadora Nacional (ARENA) over the opposition Movimento Democrático Brasileiro (MDB) had to be guaranteed by periodic purge and manipulation by the executive. Interestingly, they continued the practice of permitting local level conflict through the device of *sublegendas* (competitive lists) within the same party for state and municipal elections. However, they sought to reduce competitiveness at the national level by insisting on strict partisan voting discipline in the parliament.

Even this measure seemed inadequate to cut out the "pernicious" roots of partisan struggle. In a gesture of defiance — after years of compliantly acceding to executive *diktat* — the government party split, in December 1968, on the issue of divesting one of the opposition deputies of his parliamentary immunity so that he could be prosecuted for crimes against "the honor of the armed forces." The prompt reply was the Fifth Institutional Act, which closed down Congress and inaugurated a new wave of repressive acts (5 senators and 88 deputies immediately lost their political rights) that continued until 1970.[44] The Act is still in force at the present time although it has not been invoked actively during the Médici regime.

Despite occasional suggestions by military figures to the effect that a more tightly organized single party should be established *a la Mexicana* (the name Partido Revolucionário Nacional has been bandied about), the ARENA-MDB system was eventually called back into service after a protracted recess. It rolled up impressive (and apparently honest) majorities for regime-picked candidates in the November 1970 elections for the national Congress and the state legislatures and again in 1972. Only one state legislature (Guanabara) is not controlled by the ARENA, which

44. English translations of these and other institutional acts, as well as a partial translation of the 1967 constitution can be found in Bradford Burns, *A History of Brazil* (New York: Columbia University Press, 1970), pp. 390–413.

has a comfortable 222 to 88 dominance in the federal House[45] and a 38 to 6 majority in the Senate.

Although it has become increasingly difficult to recruit candidates to run (especially for the MDB) and newspaper editorials continue to decry the "unnatural" nature of both parties,[46] this artificial and unrepresentative party system is quite appropriate to protracted authoritarian rule. It provides the institutionally democratic façade and the domesticated semiopposition cultivated by such regimes without imposing any serious restrictions upon executive power.[47] The essential party functions of interest aggregation, candidate selection, and succession management have all been usurped by executive security institutions. The military are Brazil's real monopoly party.

Political Demobilization and Apathy

Unlike a pluralist democracy where support is sought through extensive voluntaristic participation in autonomous political associations or a totalitarian regime where intensive and enthusiastic devotion is promoted through a pervasive set of party and party-run organizations, a stable authoritarian system "often expects — even from office holders and civil servants — passive acceptance, or at least [that] they refrain from public anti-government activity." [48] As Linz further points out, this is a characteristic on which empirical cases show a wide range of variance — from the bureaucratized elitism of Spain (and Portugal) to the personalistic populism of Peron's Argentina or Vargas's Brazil. Nevertheless, by the late 1950s and early 1960s, Brazil's political mobilization had probably exceeded the limits of tolerance of stable authoritarian rule, especially because the rate and

45. See *Jornal do Brasil*, 21 December 1970, for a list and description of the victorious candidates. Also "Os 2 partidos e suas cadeiras," 25 November 1970, pp. 24–25. The formation of a third party is hardly likely, despite occasional "threats" to that effect. According to the present electoral system it would take 864,271 signatures of registered voters or 5 percent of those voting in the last election. Cf. *Jornal do Brasil*, 28 March 1970.

46. The two parties we have hardly manage to promote the minimal political activity necessary to keep alive the illusion of democracy." "Quarto Minguante," *Jornal do Brasil*, 24 March 1970. In the 1972 municipal elections, the MDB ran candidates in less than 2,000 of the 3,500 electoral districts. In the major cities, such electoral contests have been abolished on the grounds that they constitute "zones of national security."

47. Juan Linz, "L'opposizione in un regime authoritario: il caso della Spagna," in *Storia contemporanea* 1 (March 1970): 63–102.

48. Linz, "An Authoritarian Regime: Spain," p. 259.

scope of this burgeoning attention to politics seemed to be out-
running the assimilative co-optative capacity of state institutions.

Many of the measures taken by the revolutionary authorities
have already been mentioned or alluded to above: purges in the
syndicates; dissolution of peasant leagues and other paralegal
"subversive" organizations; loss of political rights for popular
(as well as populist) politicians; postponement of elections; careful control by the military over candidate selection at all levels;
media censorship of all political information; destruction of the
former party system and its replacement by artificial entities
with no roots in popular identification. Certainly, the major
structural change was to make the election of the president and
all state governors indirect — the deliberative product of purged,
domesticated legislative bodies. Not much opportunity or need
to build mass support or to appeal to disenfranchised clienteles
exists under such conditions. The *reductio ad absurdem* occurred
in October 1969 with the "election" to select a replacement for
the then-ailing Costa e Silva. The electorate consisted of a "Sena-
dito" of 118 generals, 60 admirals and 61 *brigadeiros* (air force
generals) in consultation with a "House" of colonels and the
eventual *pro forma* approval of the federal Congress. That is
quite a decline from the 12 million who had voted in the last
presidential election!

And yet, elections persist. They are held irregularly at the will
and whim of the executive, but the electorate has been permitted a voice. There is nothing peculiar about this in authoritarian regimes. Portugal has elections as regular as clockwork.
Table 6.9 indicates that, proportionately speaking, the voting
population changed very little from the late 1950s to 1966,
varying between 18 and 20 percent of the total population, but
rose significantly in 1970 to 24 percent. The formally registered
electorate more than doubled from the 1960 presidential contest
to 1970, but abstentions seem to have risen (despite the obliga-
tory nature of voting and stiffer penalties). So, apparently, have
the percentage of blank and mutilated ballots. Exact figures on
the 1970 congressional elections are not yet available, but the
magazine *Veja* reported that between abstentions and nullified
ballots, 50 percent of those eligible had not voted. In some states,
the proportion of nullified ballots exceeded 35 percent and was
apparently a factor in the poor showing of the MDB.[49] Blank
ballots were so numerous in the 1972 elections that some ARENA
candidates for municipal office were "defeated" by them.[50]

49. "O pesado dos votos brancos e nulos," *Veja*, 25 November 1970, p. 23.
50. "Eleições," *Opinião*, no. 2 (20–27 November 1972), p. 2.

Table 6.9. The Brazilian National Electorate, 1955–68

	1955	1958	1960	1962	1963[a]	1965[b]	1966	1970	1972
Actual voters (thousands)	9,097	12,721	12,586	14,747	12,286	6,574	17,286	22,436	32,000
Registered electorate (thousands)	15,243	13,780	15,543	18,563	—[c]	8,591	22,387	28,966	
Total population (thousands)	58,456	62,725	69,720	74,096	76,409	34,859	83,890	93,204	
Abstention (actual voters as % of registered electorate)	59.7	92.4	81.0	79.4	—	76.5	78.2	77.4	
Participation (actual voters as % of total population)	15.6	20.3	18.0	19.9	16.4	18.9	20.8	24.1	

SOURCES: Fundação-IBGE, *Anuário Estatístico do Brasil*, 1968, pp. 43, 589; *Anuário Estatístico do Brasil*, 1970, p. 758; *Anuário Estatístico do Brasil*, 1971, pp. 39, 815.
[a] National plebiscite on the presidency.
[b] By-elections in 10 states.
[c] Dash indicates no data available.

Unfortunately, no panel-type survey data are available to measure the extent to which Brazilians have simply retreated from all attempts to relate their problems, interests, and attitudes to the public political process and either withdrew into "privatized" apathy or resigned themselves to utilizing purely bureaucratic channels.[51] The attitudes of youth — especially those with little experience or even memory of a more open competitive political life — as indicated by recent research (admittedly of dubious reliability) on first-time voters, does suggest that depoliticization has affected them. Asked "Why are you voting?", 55 percent replied simply "by obligation" and another 28 percent said "to fulfill a duty." Only 10 percent thought they were exercising a right and only 4 percent were voting "due to interest in the future of the country." Qualitative probes revealed a deep sense of estrangement from politicians as such and low levels of political information: "Even when they complain about public men and generalize in their accusations, the youths do not demonstrate even a reasonable knowledge of political activity or a position consciously against the regime that permits the survival of these men." Only a few of them (6 percent) were in favor of a blank or nullified vote (but this increased to 11 percent in São Paulo), and their projected party preferences were similar to those of adults (even if they showed no enthusiasm for the parties as such).[52]

The aggregate and the survey evidence is incomplete but concordant. Whatever tendencies might have emerged in the early 1960s toward greater political participation — toward the transfer of interests and aspirations from privatistic or bureaucratic channels to more public and competitive ones, toward a growing confidence in the authenticity and representativeness of politicians — six years of military rule have reversed them. The approximately one-fifth of the populace that votes or joins syndicates does so out of a vague sense of duty, fear of sanctions, and lack of alternatives. But they participate with a profound sense of cynicism, little respect for the quality of their leaders, and a complete lack of enthusiasm.

51. "This preoccupation with procedure . . . may prevent political problems from being perceived as such, irreducible to administrative problems and not soluble by legislation. Legal procedures are often seen . . . as an adequate equivalent of more collective, political expressions of interest conflicts." Juan Linz, "An Authoritarian Regime: Spain," p. 273.

52. "A jovem maioria silenciosa," *Veja*, 18 November 1970, pp. 20–25.

The Role of Mentalities

In my study of interest politics, I argued at length that the Getulian sistema depended upon and developed from the peculiarities of Brazilian political culture. These predispositions toward consensual, negotiated solutions of conflicts (*pactualismo*) based on pragmatism, tolerance, procrastination, self-limitation of objectives, paralegal arrangements (*jeitos*), and legal formalism (*bacharelismo*) had their roots in previous republican practices, but were brought to full flowering under the post-1930 "soft" dictatorship (*dictablanda*). I also discussed the disintegration of these operational norms after 1960; the glowing intra-elite intransigence, popular impatience, decisional *immobilisme*, demagogic formalism, ideological rigidity, and polarization. It might have been a bit premature to claim the demise of the traditional *homem cordial* and his replacement by the more class-conscious, aggressive *homem radical*,[53] but clearly a political cultural transformation of considerable magnitude was underway.

Equally clear was the intent of Brazil's new military rulers to put a stop to this transformation. Their first acts were essentially negative: persecution of leading radical ideologues, closing down of such "subversive" institutions of elite indoctrination as the Higher Institute of Brazilian Studies (Instituto Superior de Estudos Brasileiros, ISEB),[54] depoliticization of such programs of mass literacy as the Movement for Basic Education (Movimento de Educação de Base, MEB),[55] and imposition of a diffuse, somewhat erratic, censorship on all media.

But gradually a more positive response began to emerge. For years, conservative women's associations and patriotic societies such as the League for National Defense had been complaining that the Brazilian citizen did not receive a proper "moral and civic education." In the absence of an indoctrination in such values as order, obedience, responsibility, respect for hierarchy, patriotism, family, community, and solidarity, they argued, in-

53. Cf. Pessoa de Morais, *Sociologia da revolução brasileira* (Rio: Editôra Leitura, 1965).

54. Cf. Frank Bonilla, "A National Ideology for Development: Brazil," in *Expectant Peoples*, ed. K. Silvert (New York: Random House, 1963), pp. 232–64.

55. Cf. Emanuel de Kadt, *Catholic Radicals in Brazil* (London and New York: Oxford University Press, 1970), esp. pp. 190–211. Recently, it was reported that MEB had closed down completely. Cf. *Times of the Americas*, 21 April 1971.

nocent young people were falling prey to the temptations of "alien ideologies" stressing, needless to say, contrary values. During the 1960s many of these organizations began running programs of civic and moral education on their own,[56] but with limited resources and effect.

As early as 1966, the military began expressing an interest in converting these private initiatives into a concerted public venture, but beyond statements of verbal encouragement and a few conferences, nothing was accomplished. On 19 September 1969, however, without prior fanfare and in the midst of the crisis over Costa e Silva's successor, Decree-Law 869-69 was promulgated. It established a comprehensive program of moral and civic education for all levels of the educational system, supervised by a special National Commission on Morality and Civics (CNMC). The decree also left no doubt about the ideological content of what was going to be taught in the "school civic centers" (lower and middle grades) and the "higher centers of civics" (university level). It set out its purposes in lengthy detail: "defense of the democratic [sic] idea, through fostering of the spirit of religion, the dignity of the human person, and the love of liberty *with responsibility*, under the inspiration of God . . . the building of character, rooted in morality, through dedication to family and community . . . honoring the fatherland, its symbols, traditions and institutions . . . equiping the citizen to exercise civic activities, in accord with morality, patriotism and constructive action for the common good." [57] To ensure compliance, "professors" in this subject must produce a "written attestation that they agree with the philosophical bases of the decree" and it is even suggested that, when civilians are not available, military officers should be called in as visiting lecturers. An emergency plan was immediately drawn up and, to my knowledge, all Brazilian students, public and private, have been receiving two hours a week of this political-religious indoctrination since the second semester of 1970.

Although there is no apparent overlap with the program of moral and civic education, the regime began (very hesitantly at

56. Cf. Norman Blume, "Pressure Groups and Decision-Making in Brazil," in *Studies in Comparative International Development*, vol. 3, no. 11 (1967–68), for details on one association, the Institute for Social and Economic Research (IPES), active in this area.

57. The text is quoted from Hugo Assmann, "When God Is Used to Legitimize the Dictatorship," as translated and reproduced in Latin American Bureau, USCC (LADOC), vol. 1, no. 47C (December 1970). The original appeared in *Perspectives de Diálogo* (Montevideo), August 1970.

first in December 1967 but massively after September 1970) to "alphabetize" the Brazilian populace. An enormous and well-financed military-style campaign (Brazilian Movement for Literacy; MOBRAL) was put into motion with the aim of enrolling 2 million illiterates by 1971 and 5 million by 1973.[58] Prudently, the campaign is beginning in the urban areas of the South. It will expand to cover "priority areas" designated by the Ministry of the Interior and will work through selected local authorities. Private firms are being asked to cooperate and the usual tax incentives are being offered for donations. There is no evidence of a manifest political content to this effort (as there clearly was during the literacy campaigns of the Goulart period), but the latent political intent is fairly obvious: let us make these people literate and thankful for it, before someone more subversive comes along and does it. Nevertheless, MOBRAL does represent one of the more calculated risks of an otherwise very cautious regime. As its director, Mário Simonsen, observed, "literacy does create new necessities in an individual, increasing the stimuli and horizon of one's life ambitions."[59] Whether a political system based on a deliberate reduction in political stimuli and horizons can satisfy these new needs is a challenging question.

To ensure that these new literates and those already literate will not hear or see anything too intoxicating, censorship has become increasingly strict and systematic. According to the "doctrinary norms" of the Federal Censorship Service, only programs and publications that "awake civic responsibilities, combat egoism, rebellion and disobedience or which exalt loyalty, heroism, and fulfillment of duty, respect for the aged and love of country and national historic events" can be offered.[60] With only that sort of drivel to read, illiteracy might not be such a bad idea!

The capstone to the regime's attempt to provide itself with a firm conformist mentality is its extraordinary manipulation of patriotic and chauvinistic symbols. Capitalizing on the soccer victory in the Jules Rimet World Cup, the state has deluged the country with flags, hymns, parades, jingles, bumper stickers, and pamphlets exalting the grandeur of Brazil. On National Independence Day (Sete de Setembro) in 1970 a special team of presidential advisers planned a week-long orgy of patriotic events (545 "solemnities" were held in Rio alone). The culmination,

58. "A derrota da ignorância," *Veja*, 9 September 1970, pp. 40–46. Also, *Jornal do Brasil*, 28 December 1970, which reported that 500,000 had been enrolled by that date.

59. *Veja*, 9 September 1970, p. 43.

60. "O Código do corte," *Veja*, 9 September 1970, p. 24.

however, came in 1972 when the sesquicentennial celebration of the country's independence offered the regime a convenient excuse for a year-long orgy of nationalistic celebrations. There are indications that Brazilians, traditionally not given to such *ufanismo* (petty chauvinistic, flag-waving displays of patriotism), enjoy these spectacles and that the regime intends to feed them a steady diet of such "circuses" in the future.[61]

Most of the general accounts of Brazil since 1964 have emphasized the dramatic ideological changes at the elite level. In particular, they have emphasized the preponderant role of a single set of values known as the "doctrine of national security" as elaborated by a clique of military intellectuals, the Superior War College (ESG). I have chosen to emphasize attempts at mass indoctrination, as I see these as more crucial to Portugalization in the long run. In any case, numerous exegeses of the ESG doctrine have appeared elsewhere and other essays in this volume discuss it and its ramifications in greater detail.

I would only make a few general interpretive observations. Despite its impeccably authoritarian substantive content, especially in its assignment of an exclusive hegemonic role to the state in the identification and promotion of "national objectives," the doctrine may well be antithetic to stable authoritarian rule. It is too rigid in fixing system goals and hence, may be incompatible with the goals of the economic, religious, and social elites whose interests it seeks to protect. It is too exclusivistic and self-righteous in assigning complete decisional responsibility to the military and this may prove frustrating to the mobility and participational aspirations of other elites, such as propertied groups. It is too extensive in its definition of opponents to national security and this may restrict the regime's capacity for co-optation and for shifting its coalitional basis in the face of changing parameters. Lastly, it is too narrow in basing the regime's legitimacy on a single criteria: the defense of Brazil against godless communism. The repressive elimination of all internal resistance and/or an external *detente* in Great Power tensions have removed much of the plausibility of that justification. All of the above is predicated upon the assumption that the doctrine of national security is as elaborate, rigid, comprehensive, and "binding" as it appears to be, not just a façade for the after-the-fact rationalization of whatever expedient course the military

61. "O dia do Brasil," *Veja*, 9 September 1970, pp. 16–19. Also, "O nôvo ufanismo," *Realidade*, September 1970, pp. 98–105.

chose to follow.[62] In the latter event, it would be an appropriate elitist mentality for the institutionalization of authoritarian rule — and a valuable complement to its efforts at the mass indoctrination of a subject political culture.

Constitutionalization

Stable authoritarian regimes are neither arbitrary nor capricious. No political system can persist without some minimal constitutionalization of its decision-making procedures, but the nature of procedural regularity and the degree of self-limitation will vary by regime type. Democratic regimes accomplish a good deal of this predictability and control by a juxtaposition of functional and/or territorial "powers"; totalitarian regimes manage less of it through a parallel set of interpenetrating party and state organizations. Authoritarian regimes characteristically seek to establish a centrally manipulated balance between more-or-less equal institutional hierarchies. Each of these "corporations" — the classic ones are the military, civil service, church, business, and perhaps party bureaucracies — is accorded a substantial degree of autonomy within its respective policy arena (policy segmentation). Centralized control is asserted and maintained by the careful balancing activity of a "neutral" sovereign who resolves emergent disputes between corporations. Ideally, he or they (rule by junta is by no means uncommon) will only have to intervene infrequently and can normally rely on hierarchical control within the subordinate corporate "pillars." Only in moments of crisis must he assert his supremacy. In the populist variation the leader may be quite publicly visible by virtue of his "direct pact with the masses," but in the more traditionalist (and more stable) Portuguese variation, executive power becomes virtually invisible but quite predictable. This aloofness from the daily struggle of politics is useful. It permits the leader

62. While the doctrine of national security may continue to enshrine the ultimate goals and wisdom of military tutelage at the highest level of abstraction, there are hints that the Superior War College (ESG) may be diverted to more concrete tasks. In his speech to the ESG, Médici suggested he "wants it less preoccupied with theoretical conceptualizations . . . and more engaged in the elaboration of real and objective projects." This conversion into what he called a "veritable school of statesmen" would be much more compatible with the prevalent mentality of stable authoritarian rule. Cf. *Jornal do Brasil*, 11 March 1970. For an interpretation of the doctrine that stresses its wide permissiveness vis-à-vis specific policies, see the essay by Alfred Stepan in this volume.

to assign responsibility for mistakes to subordinates, economize resources for use in crisis situations, and shift the basis of his supportive coalition with greater impunity.

Brazil's military rulers have been unable so far to constitutionalize their procedures in this or any other manner. They have not found that special formula for institutional stability which would remove them from direct responsibility for decisional outcomes, provide them with a greater margin of coalitional maneuverability, and reduce the overhead costs of terror and repression through greater reliance on voluntary compliance. Lacking legitimacy and predictability, the regime exaggerates the magnitude of threats to its existence and overreacts to crisis situations. This, in turn, makes future constitutionalization even more difficult.

Speculatively, I would suggest that two important political changes must precede an authoritarian institutional stabilization: intensive concentration of decisional resources at the center and extensive penetration by government agencies of the periphery. Brazil since 1964 has moved a long way toward filling both prerequisites.

Centralization in postgolpe Brazil has reached heretofore unprecedented levels through the gradual but systematic subordination of all potential countervailing powers, functional or territorial. Table 6.10 shows that in terms of aggregate amounts collected and dispersed, the ratio of federal to state to município (county) authorities has altered rather slightly. What the table doesn't show is that the entire tax schedule has been changed to favor the federal government, which then subsidizes (and so controls) the operations of state and local governments.[63] The 1967 constitution makes it illegal for the latter to pursue policies incompatible with the former, requires them to account in detail for all expenditures, and greatly extends the formal grounds for federal intervention. These legalities have been frequently used to purge state and local levels for a variety of motives. Police functions have passed almost completely to the military ministries, which now control all secretaries of security and militias at the state level. Other state secretaries find their activities coordinated by imperative visits to Rio or Brasília. When coupled with the close controls exercised by the president on the party-

63. In late 1968, these "tax-sharing" provisions were changed by reducing the quotas due to *municípios* and *estados* in the Participation Fund by 50 percent. This drastic cut was slightly mitigated by the creation of a Special Fund (2 percent of tax revenues). However, this fund is to be allocated at the political discretion of central authorities.

Table 6.10. Structure of Public Expenditure by Level of Government, 1960–68
(In percentages)

	1960	1961	1962	1963	1964	1965	1966	1967	1968
Federal government	34.3	37.0	37.0	36.3	36.9	32.8	31.7	28.4	25.9
Federal government corporations	20.3	21.2	21.6	20.3	21.5	24.0	25.9	28.4	30.8
Subtotal	(54.6)	(58.2)	(58.6)	(56.6)	(58.4)	(56.8)	(57.6)	(56.8)	(56.7)
State governments	39.2	35.8	35.4	35.3	34.1	35.2	33.9	33.9	32.6
Municipal governments	6.2	6.0	6.0	8.1	7.5	8.0	8.6	9.3	10.7

SOURCE: *Conjuntura Econômica* 17, no. 1 (1970): 6.

nomination process, especially at the state level,[64] one is hard put to imagine what, if any, autonomy is enjoyed by these "decentralized" political bodies. The formerly powerful states have been reduced to units of administrative convenience for central authorities and the municípios have been converted into easily manipulated dependencies.[65]

Nor have the functional countervailing powers fared much better. The Congress, as we have seen, has been repeatedly purged and simply shut down by force (as have some state assemblies). Under the 1967 constitution, as amended extensively and restrictively in 1969, deputies no longer are guaranteed legal immunity from prosecution, may hold only a limited number of inquiry commissions (and none will be financed outside Brasília), will be expelled for practicing "acts of partisan infidelity," that is, voting or speaking against the expressed will of the party directorate, or for missing one-third of the sessions. They must "appreciate" executive proposals and vetoes by special treatment in short order (45 days) or these become law automatically. They cannot tack on any amendments involving new expenditures or fixing new administrative positions or salaries. For a vast list of issues, only the president may take the legislative initiative.[66] Under these conditions it comes as no surprise that, after having had 10,000 of its proposed amendments rejected, the Congress approved the original executive budget in one half-hour.[67]

Recent research on the Congress has convincingly documented this loss of influence. In 1960 and 1963 (before the golpe) from 66 to 58 percent of the projects obtaining legislative approval were initiated from within the Congress. By 1971 this had fallen

64. Cf. Joseph Novitski, "Brazilian President Names Gubernatorial Candidates," *New York Times,* 9 July 1970. Novitski notes that all 22 selected candidates were "conservatives, committed to authoritarian government in Brazil and willing to use the techniques of planning in government. Nine of the future governors are technocrats who have not been active in politics."

65. "The municipal level is essentially a captive system. . . . The role municipalities are to play in executing the post-revolutionary national development plans, and indeed their very survival, now depends on the attitude, plans, and objectives of the executive branch of the federal government. By manipulating the percentages or delivery of the federal revenues shared with municipalities, and the fiscal control mechanisms, the federal government is not unlike a puppeteer in its control over approximately 4,000 municipalities." Ivan L. Richardson, "Municipal Government in Brazil: The Financial Dimension," *Journal of Comparative Administration* 1 (November 1969): 339.

66. "Os novos limites do Congresso," *Veja,* 22 October 1969, pp. 16–19.

67. "Meia hora," *Veja,* 7 October 1970, p. 23.

to 27 percent and virtually 100 percent of the proposals "suggested" to the legislature by the executive were approved.[68]

The courts have done no better. They have been purged, enlarged, circumvented, and simply browbeaten to the point that they offer no resistance to the manifestly extraconstitutional actions of the executive. In any case, virtually all political matters have been transferred to special military courts, but even these have yet to place a stamp of predictable legality upon the government's continual repressive actions.[69]

Another possible source of functional resistance to administrative centralization might have been, ironically, the federal bureaucracy itself.[70] Bloated, difficult to manage, nepotistically recruited, clientelistically dependent, and internally competitive, it presented the victorious military with a serious obstacle to implementing their austerity program effectively and to establishing their uncontested hegemony over the polity. After purging large numbers of *funcionários*, the military began a systematic program of administrative reform, especially after 1967. But more important than their efforts at rationalized management has been the extensive, direct penetration of the public civil service by military officers. Always moderately important in specific fields, they can now be found scattered throughout the federal and state governments. A recent survey of the 60 top national administrative posts showed that 28 of them were occupied by high-echelon military officers. Some state governments have been virtually militarized.[71] Current (1972) plans call for the creation of a special national training center for civil servants modeled on the military staff schools.[72] The important point is not necessarily that they possess special professional training and identity, but that they are chosen by the military hierarchy and from within the ranks for their post, remain in the armed services for career

68. Sérgio Henrique Hudson de Abrauches and Gláucio Ary Dillon Soares, "As funções do legislativo," unpublished manuscript, Universidade de Brasília, Brasília, 1972, and Clóvis Brigagão, "Poder e legislativo no Brasil" (Tese de mestrado, Faculdade Cândido Mendes, IUPRJ, Rio de Janeiro, 1971).

69. See Henry J. Steiner and David M. Trubek, "Brazil — All Power to the Generals," in *Foreign Affairs* 49 (April 1971): 464–79.

70. For a fascinating analysis of administrative resistance to a radical authoritarian regime, Nazi Germany, see Edward N. Peterson, *The Limits of Hitler's Power* (Princeton, N.J.: Princeton University Press, 1969).

71. "Os militares," *Veja*, 1 April 1970, p. 21. For example, the state of Ceará had 35 officers in "commanding posts" in its government.

72. "Funcionalismo," *Opinião*, no. 2 (14–21 November 1972), p. 2.

purposes, and often return periodically to field command positions. In short, the past pattern whereby military officers were "civilianized" by their protracted exposure to the public is being consciously reversed.

Coupled with these centralizing tendencies is an enormous expansion in the capacity for penetrating the periphery of the polity. The most important innovation in this regard has been the creation of a vast, efficiently organized National Information Service (SNI). Run by a cabinet-ranking general (the present president is the ex-chief of the SNI), it penetrates virtually all aspects of Brazilian political life from personal investigations of all prospective administrative officials and electoral candidates to mass surveys of public opinion. More than 200 active-duty officers "serve" in the SNI and are regularly rotated into other civilian and administrative posts. A recent magazine article cheerfully noted that 98 percent of the denunciations it handled came from "voluntary informants who do not receive remuneration," and concluded that, while comparable agencies such as the CIA and the KGB consider it excellent if 20 percent of their suggestions are accepted by the national executive, the SNI has had more than 80 percent of its recommendations approved by the government.[73] Its activities are duplicated, triplicated, and quadruplicated by other espionage agencies run by each of the military services as well as the civilian equivalent of the FBI, the infamous Department of Political and Social Order (DOPS). The result has been the creation of a vast information-gathering network, using both the most modern techniques of data processing and retrieval and the most medieval methods of "data extraction," that penetrates all private institutions and levels of government.[74]

At another level, there is reason to suspect that the central authorities may be establishing important links directly with compliant municipal or county officials, bypassing and downgrading the states, which ironically provided the political bases for their revolt against the Goulart regime. A recent monograph on a purportedly representative município in the state of São Paulo details how the Revolution has resulted in further entrenching local notables in power and purging local systems of competitive,

73. "Um ministério invisível," *Veja*, 15 October 1969, p. 24.

74. When I was interviewing in Brazil in 1965–66 — before this apparatus had been fully elaborated — several of my interviewees spontaneously informed me that as matter of patriotic duty they reported confidentially on the internal deliberations of their respective associations to the SNI. Many of these were themselves graduates of the Superior War College (ESG) and active in its alumni association (ADESG).

populist practices.[75] By combining extreme concentration of power at the center with local control through selected oligarchs in the periphery and tying the two together through the military command structure and a comprehensive intelligence system, Brazil's military autocrats may be able to accomplish the sort of stable authoritarian domination that Napoleon III did through the police and the prefect system.[76]

Despite the accomplishment of these two hypothetical prerequisites for authoritanian constitutionalization, the decision-making system continues erratic and capricious. Subordinate actors do not know where decisions originate, how they are elaborated, or what the bounds of permissible demand articulation are. Superordinate actors face few countervailing powers, yet seem insecure in their legitimacy and persistence in power. The constitution of 1967 was revised before it was applied and the military have refused to set aside the Fifth Institutional Act that permits them arbitrarily to override the flimsy legal structures they themselves have erected.

Why have they failed to provide even this minimal predictability and legality? If we accept the old adage, that only power can check power, then the first reason is obvious. The military's very success in the monopolization of power has eliminated all potential contending "corporations." Business, divided internally, regimented into unrepresentative corporatist institutions, and dependent upon state licensing and credit, was in no condition to share power. For reasons suggested above, the civil bureaucracy could hardly have been expected to sustain the traditions of legal-rational authority in the face of military usurpation. The church, a "corporation" frequently allied with traditional authoritarian regimes, has always been institutionally weak in Brazil. Even so, a faction of it has put up the strongest resistance to arbitrary rule.[77] Since the policy consolidation and improved outcome per-

75. See Fanny Tabak, "Desenvolvimento econômico sem desenvolvimento político na espera do poder local" (Paper presented at the International Political Science Association (IPSA) Round Table, Rio de Janeiro, 27–31 October 1969).

76. Cf. Theodore Zeldin, *The Political System of Napoleon III* (London: Macmillan, 1958); Howard C. Payne, *The Police State of Louis Napoleon Bonaparte* (Seattle: University of Washington Press, 1966).

77. Rowan Ireland, "The Catholic Church and Social Change in Brazil: An Evaluation," *Brazil in the Sixties*, ed. R. Roett (Nashville, Tenn.: Vanderbilt University Press, 1972), pp. 345–74 and Emanuel de Kadt, "Religion, the Church and Social Change in Brazil" in *The Politics of Conformity in Latin America*, ed. C. Veliz (London: Oxford University Press, 1967), pp. 192–220.

formance of the Médici regime, along with its more limited use
of arbitrary arrest and torture, there are signs of a growing clerico-
political accommodation. Nevertheless, a steady stream of criticisms continues to issue from progressive elements of the church
opposing wage constriction, usurpation of indian lands, and repression. Ecclesiastical authorities were patently absent from the
"civic orgy" of the Sesquicentennial.[78]

Party structures were totally incapable of any concerted resistance and were dissolved without protest or lament. In the absence of any competing corporate, hierarchic pillars upon which
to build, Portugalization is difficult, if not impossible. "Mexicanization" — the deliberate creation *de novo* of a single party apparatus designed to compete with and eventually to reduce the
military establishment to a subordinate status — might be one
possible route to constitutional order, but one that depends on
the prior emergence of a charismatic military statesman and of
a collective desire on the part of the armed forces for withdrawal
from politics. In addition, any form of constitutionalization, rest-
ing as it must on some form of countervalence of power, is likely
to involve the issue of amnesty. Purged and persecuted leaders
of corporate pillars will have to be permitted to enter the fold
in order for some pacified consensus to be established. Any such
move would immediately raise the specter of *revanchisme* — of
disorderly competition between returning outcasts and those who
usurped their positions and prerequisites. Having far exceeded the
bounds of civility observed by previous Brazilian regimes (including the "fascist" Estado Nôvo), the military and police have good
reason to fear the recriminations and disclosures such an amnesty
would inevitably bring.

Perhaps the most obvious barrier to a new normalcy is that
many people in Brazil, even in the Brazilian military, continue
to believe in pluralist, competitive democracy. Overtly authoritarian rule, especially its fascist variety, no longer rests on a popular, modern mass ideology, as it did during the 1930s. A manifest
and permanent shift away from the symbols of liberal democracy
would probably exacerbate factional tendencies within the military, as well as resistance on the part of intellectuals and some
bourgeois elements.

Lately, there have been repeated signs that the regime intends
to correct that "unfortunate" historical legacy. Government
spokesmen have stated authoritatively that *liberalismo* or *demo-*

78. Genilson Cezar and Waldecy Tenório, "A Igreja e sua ação," *Opinião*,
no. 9 (1–8 January 1973), pp. 4–5.

cracia liberal is a thing of the past, or that in any case, "real democracy is an ideal which, if it has ever been realized any place, certainly wasn't in Brazil." [79] The answer, they hint, lies in some new, authentically Brazilian, "estado revolucionário" that will guarantee "social" rather than "individual" rights and will introduce a "new democratic style [aimed at] the integration of all in the Government's efforts toward the realization of social objectives." [80] So far, there have been no clear indications of what institutional novelties lie in store, or when they will be initiated, only the promise that "the Revolutionary State will last the time indispensable for the implantation of the political, administrative, juridical, social and economic structures capable of promoting the integration of all Brazilians at minimal levels of well-being." [81] Devising a formula that is not manifestly fascist[82] and that respects at least the minimal participatory aspirations of the Brazilian people, yet one that establishes consensual procedures for the resolution of interest conflict and predictably regulates the problem of succession, will be no mean task — even for the inventive legal technocrats who eagerly serve their military masters.

79. "O Presidente e a democracia," in *Jornal do Brasil*, 11 March 1970. The citation is a direct quote from a press conference of President Médici on 27 February 1970.

80. *Jornal do Brasil*, 1 April 1970. The quoted remarks are from a speech of President Médici before the opening session of Congress. In the ominous words of the Minister of Justice, "The objective of the Revolution in disciplining individual liberty is not that of limiting its legitimate use, only that of organizing it according to the needs of national security." *Jornal do Brasil*, 2 April 1970. He also spoke of a "state of justice" as replacing the former "state of law." For an interesting discussion of how these new ideological themes have emerged, see "A Democracia," *Veja*, 8 April 1970, pp. 18–25. See also "O coquetel da reforma," *Veja*, 3 December 1970, pp. 17–19.

81. *Jornal do Brasil*, 11 March 1970. This is an excerpt from Médici's speech before the Superior War College.

82. Incidentally, there has been a considerable resurgence of *integralismo*, Brazil's native fascist movement of the 1930s. Its leader, then and now, Plínio Salgado, after hyperbolically claiming 700,000 members, 100 of which were federal deputies (in a chamber of some 400!), was asked if *integralismo* had representatives in the executive. He answered: "It does, but I prefer not to cite specific names. We are still not in the government but as things are going . . . (What do you mean?) . . . I mean the mentality. The mentality is being formed." "A volta do 'Chefe,'" *Veja*, 13 May 1970, p. 23. Salgado is presently a federal deputy for the São Paulo ARENA. By 1972, the integralistas had formed a "Crusade for National Renovation" and were attempting to form local-level associations appealing to "workers and peasants" in the state of São Paulo. Durval Guimarães and Jary Cardoso, "Os velhos senhores," *Opinião*, no. 1 (6–13 November 1972), p. 3.

Conclusion

The generals, colonels and *técnicos* who have governed Brazil since 1964 have gone a long way toward institutionalizing authoritarian rule. They have done so not by making many changes in formal political structures[83] but by purging existing ones of "semi-competitive" and "populist" practices and inserting a new policy content determined from above. Nor have they dramatically expanded the scope of state action[84] or extended the basis of state resources at the expense of privileged and propertied groups. Instead, they have "merely" diversified its financial base, centralized the decision-making process, and made much more rational and authoritative use of existing policy instruments.

They appear to have largely accomplished the two paramount goals of stable authoritarian rule. *They have rendered the power of the executive progressively more autonomous* — independent of any enforceable accountability to organized social classes or competing institutions. In so doing, *they may have effectively eliminated all plausible alternative rivals to their hegemony.* Paraphrasing Marx, all social classes and political groups seem to lie prostrate before the rifle butt and the national plan.

Ironically, the military continue to insist on their "salvationist" role and their ultimate commitment to the establishment (under their tutelage) of an open competitive society. If one ignores the chiliastic rhetoric of the *Doctrina de Segurança Nacional* to the contrary, there is little to suggest that the golpistas of 1964 anticipated or desired the outcome they have produced. They seem sincerely to have believed that they were taking the first step toward demolishing, rather than perfecting the Getulian sistema. I see no "grand design" in what they have done during the ensuing six years, merely a series of interrelated reactive responses to

83. The major exception is the forcible dissolution of the former multi-party system and the imposition of a one-and-a-half party system. But even here, when viewed from the local level, the changes have been more apparent than real. Cf. Fanny Tabak, "Desenvolvimento econômico," for evidence on continuity in Araraquara, São Paulo.

84. One major exception here is the creation of the Companhia de Pesquisa de Recursos Minerais (CPRM), which extended governmental control over mineral prospecting and exploitation. On the other hand, the regime did sell the National Motor Factory (FNM) to private (foreign) interests and has created a number of joint public-private consortiums in the petrochemical field, a presumed monopoly of the State Petroleum Agency (PETROBRAS). CPRM greatly alarmed the private business sector, which protested its establishment vigorously and to no avail. "Private v. State Enterprise," *Brazil 1969* (New York: Center for Inter-American Relations, 1970), pp. 100–04.

emergent crises, each of which further diminished the probability of any return to civilian democratic rule. In this sense, labels like Portugalization, Spanification, or Mexicanization can be misleading, if they are taken to mean that Brazilian authorities have a prototypic regime model in mind toward which they are consciously and concertedly striving. They have gotten where they are institutionally "by the force of things" rather than by specific intent.

Complete Portugalization, whether intended or not, has not yet occurred. As we have seen, two key structural elements have still to be institutionalized. Through "civic and moral education," the rulers are busy trying to create a set of compliant "mentalities," but there is reason to suspect that the effort will be as fruitless, perhaps as counterproductive, as were similar indoctrination attempts during the Estado Nôvo.[85] As cynical and disillusioned as they may be, there is no evidence that Brazilians have a permanent desire to withdraw from all participation in decisions affecting their collective life or to deliberately turn away from their historical quest for democracy. Similarly, the military may hint darkly that liberalism and individual civic rights are dead or *dépassé*, but they have yet to devise some new, "authentically Brazilian" formula for the estado revolucionário that they themselves are willing to rule by, much less one the populace as a whole will accept as legitimate. Unsure of their own decision rules and uncertain of their popular support, the military overreacted to real and imagined threats with increasingly arbitrary and repressive measures making constitutionalization all the more impossible.

Even if its rulers could accomplish these final authoritarian feats, I doubt whether Portugalization can become a permanent solution to Brazil's political development problems. The most obvious sources of difficulty lie in the external environment. Brazil's great power pretensions, sensitivity to its foreign image, and increased dependence on continuous flows of foreign capital and technology make it exceedingly vulnerable in this quarter. Most authoritarian regimes consolidate themselves by following neomercantilistic, autarchic policies, sealing themselves off as much as possible from external perturbations by promoting the image

85. See my *Interest Conflict and Political Change in Brazil,* pp. 59–69 for a discussion of the weakness of past attempts at deliberate indoctrination in Brazil. For some Spanish and Italian analogies, see Gino Germani, "Political Socialization of Youth in Fascist Regimes: Italy and Spain," in *Authoritarian Politics in Modern Society,* ed. S. P. Huntington and C. H. Moore (New York: Basic Books, 1970), pp. 339–79.

of a hostile world incapable of understanding their special national *Zeitgeist*. Brazil since 1964 has opted for the contrary —
for deliberately cultivating international contacts and resources,
public and private. Should foreign capitalists, international civil
servants, or United States officials lose confidence in the Brazilian
military's capacity to guarantee stability or, conversely, should
these outsiders decide that long-term authoritarian rule will not
protect their economic or political interests, the system could be
in trouble. It would be interesting, for example, to observe the
reaction of Brazil's military if the United States military were
publicly to retract the de facto concession they have granted the
Brazilians as guardians of the "Free World and Western civilization" in the Southern Hemisphere. There is not much chance of
this occurring — but the prospects are well worth simulating,
even worth stimulating.

Paradoxically, the regime itself has deliberately created one potential element of its own future instability. Lacking the legitimacy accorded to political systems that are accountable to freely
organized and expressive publics or even to those which operate
under regular and predictable norms of legal-rational process,
Brazil's military rulers have sought to cover over their fundamental illegitimacy with a heavy emphasis on symbolic identification
and vicarious participation.[86] They have made an attempt, temporarily successful by all accounts, to fuse the ends and means
of the country's military establishment with those of the state and
those of the nation as a whole. As long as the people-subjects do
not tire of vacuous orgies of patriotic happenings and endless
repetitions of civic jingles, as long as the national soccer team
continues to win and racing-car drivers pile up well-publicized
victories, those in power can expect to enjoy a substantial degree
of voluntary compliance with their policies — however arbitrarily
and autocratically defined.

But this element of mass affect is not likely to persist forever.
In the terms used by Marx to refer to Napoleon III, there are
limits to the regime's capacity to act "like a conjurer, under the
necessity of keeping the public gaze fixed on himself," especially
when its leader is likely to be a not very magnetic or appealing
person selected from within a highly routinized and bureaucratized military establishment. The regime, therefore, must produce
fresh, popular (but apolitical) heroes and heroic acts, and exe-

86. Referring to this heavy reliance on ritualistic identification and ersatz
participation, Fernando Henrique Cardoso coined the felicitous expression:
"programmed euphoria." "A Esfinge fantasiada," *Opinião*, no. 3 (1–8 January
1973), p. 3.

cute "constant surprises . . . *coups d'état en miniature*" in public policy.

But, after all, soccer teams do lose — even brilliant Brazilian teams. While there seems to be no end to the number and variety of imaginative-sounding, new "impact programs" that can be invented or catchy acronyms that can be assigned to them (MOBRAL, PRORURAL, PROTERRA, PODOESTE, TRANSAMAZONICA, PIN, PIS), the inflated rhetoric, insufficient resources, inadequate planning, confused purposes, overlapping competences, legal chaos, poor performance, and unexpected consequences are likely eventually to shift the public gaze from the conjurer's intended direction. A few spectacular failures in popular pastimes or public policies would, no doubt, jeopardize this carefully cultivated patina of affective legitimacy, as well as lift the mystic veil of technocratic efficiency.

The other major potential source of vulnerability lies in the global performance of the economy. The last four years demonstrate that authoritarian rule, even arbitrary authoritarian rule, is not incompatible with considerable and sustained economic dynamism. Nor have the exhaustion of easy import substitution, excess productive capacity, income concentration, stagnant to declining living standards in the "popular classes," limited import capability, continued inflation and structural underemployment yet produced insuperable contradictions. There is, however, little indication that the regime's policies are eliminating these characteristics of Brazil's delayed development. A decline in overall growth — triggered, for example, by lagging export performance — might burst the current bubble of unrealistic optimism and exaggerate regional disparities, class tensions, and sectoral conflicts. Nevertheless, with its financial resources, technical capacity, and relative autonomy from special clientelistic dependencies, there is little reason to expect that such problems will threaten the regime as such. Its margin of maneuverability for policy change is considerable and there is good reason to expect that much of this will occur "preemptively." Social indicators, survey research, and a comprehensive intelligence network will provide the needed information formerly supplied by more public and collective means of expression, and enlightened technocrats can be expected to make the necessary marginal adjustments.

The most acute element of vulnerability lies within the regime itself — not in its dependence upon external powers, its heavy reliance on mass ritualistic identification, or its accountability to specific internal publics. With the almost complete atrophy of all political associational channels of representation and conflict resolution, all groups that wish to influence policy must address themselves directly to the military and, to a lesser extent, the higher civilian bureaucracy. Unless organizational discipline and ideological unity remain extraordinarily high, these appeals can be expected to elicit differential responses from regime factions. As cleavages become more cumulative, the system may find it less and less possible to shift policy incrementally and expedientially or to respond as a unit to crises or declines in global performance. Presidential succession and the regime's persistent inability to constitutionalize it brings all these tensions and factional tendencies to bear on a single, overriding issue.

There is ample evidence that such factionalism already exists. It became manifestly acute during the tense and protracted negotiations over Costa e Silva's succession and certainly lies behind the current government's rigidly enforced censorship on all public references to the issue.[87] It is difficult to tell whether its basis is still shifting and overlapping according to such factors as age set, region, and level of expertise or whether it has begun to jell into relatively stable, cumulatively based segments professing distinct policy approaches, for example, "nationalist," "corporatist," "internationalist," "professionalist." [88] A golpe or peaceful transfer of executive power from one of these factions to another, say the present "internationalists" to some more "nationalist" group, would not of itself be destructive of authoritarian rule, but it would further delay institutionalization. Perhaps in the intraelite factional struggle one of the contestants might begin to appeal "populistically" to disenfranchised extraelite groups for support. Ironically, since the military has worked so hard at depoliticizing the citizenry, it seems that only by politicizing the military can the citizenry begin to recuperate its lost political role. Sadly, I admit that this is not much protection against the ossification of political choice and free inquiry which is the price that Portugalization or any other model of authoritarian rule seems to exact for its nonrevolutionary response to the strains of modernization.

87. Interestingly, the replacement of Médici is scheduled to take place in 1974, the same year that many of the initial ten-year suspensions of political rights are scheduled to lapse.

88. For a discussion of these factions and some wishful thinking about a reconciliatory democratic outcome, consult Luiz Alberto Bahia, "Apontamentos para discussão de um modêlo de reconciliação," *Cadernos Brasileiros*, no. 60 (July–August 1970), pp. 5–12. Also Nelson Werneck Sodré, "O regime conservado," *Opinião*, no. 9 (1–8 January 1973), pp. 4–5.

7 The Future of an Authoritarian Situation or the Institutionalization of an Authoritarian Regime: The Case of Brazil

JUAN J. LINZ

Though I am not a specialist in Brazilian politics, I have been encouraged to contribute to this volume because of the use Brazilianists have made of a model of authoritarianism that I developed originally for Spain.[1] The work of the Brazilianists has helped refine my original model, as well as contribute to the important theoretical task of constructing a typology of authoritarian regimes.[2] With some reservations, there seems to be a consensus among the contributors that in Brazil many aspects of the

I want to acknowledge the discussions I had with the other participants in the conference and to thank in particular Alfred Stepan and Cândido Mendes for their useful comments and suggestions during the revision of my paper.

1. The most complete statement of the model is found in Juan J. Linz, "An Authoritarian Regime: Spain," in *Mass Politics: Studies in Political Sociology*, ed. Erik Allardt and Stein Rokkan (New York: Free Press, 1970), pp. 251–83, 374–81. This first appeared in *Cleavages, Ideologies, and Party Systems*, ed. Erik Allardt and Yrjö Littunen (Helsinki: Westermarck Society, 1964), pp. 291–342. Specific aspects of the model are elaborated in my "From Falange to Movimiento-Organización: The Spanish Single Party and the Franco Regime, 1936–1968," in *Authoritarian Politics in Modern Society: The Dynamics of Established One-Party Systems*, ed. Samuel P. Huntington and Clement H. Moore (New York: Basic Books, 1970), pp. 128–203; and in my "Opposition In and Under an Authoritarian Regime: The Case of Spain," in *Regimes and Oppositions*, ed. Robert A. Dahl (New Haven: Yale University Press, 1973), pp. 171–259. Also see Juan J. Linz and Amando de Miguel, *Los empresarios ante el poder público: El liderazgo y los grupos de intereses en el empresariado español* (Madrid: Instituto de Estudios Políticos, 1966).

2. In addition to the essay by Schmitter in this volume, see Ronald M. Schneider, *The Political System of Brazil: Emergence of a Modernizing Authoritarian Regime, 1964–1970* (New York: Columbia University Press, 1971), pp. 342–43, 345–48; Philippe C. Schmitter, *Interest Conflict and Political Change in Brazil* (Stanford: Stanford University Press, 1971), pp. 373–83, 387, 467–68. See also Susan Kaufman Purcell, "Decision-Making in an Authoritarian Regime: The Politics of Profit-Sharing in Mexico" (Ph.D. diss., Columbia University, 1970), for an application and elaboration of the model.

regime developed by Getúlio Vargas during the Estado Nôvo of
1937–45 persisted into the period of competitive politics from
1945 until the military assumed power in 1964. A more uneasy
consensus seems to exist, as well, that no immediate return to
competitive politics is in sight for Brazil. Concerning the degree
and type of institutionalization achieved by Brazil's authoritarian
regime and the capacity of the regime to become stable, consensus
seems to falter. It is in regard to these latter points that I wish
to raise some questions and offer some tentative answers.

The overthrow of a regime does not assure the consolidation,
and even less the full institutionalization, of the successor regime.[3]
In Brazil, since many of the partisans of the 1964 coup viewed
the subsequent military rule as only an interim process whose
goal was to prepare the way quickly for a return to democracy,
the entire question of creating new authoritarian political institutions was, in particular, fraught with ambiguity and contradictions. Nonetheless, some might argue that after eight years of
rule by the military under three military presidents, the regime
can be considered consolidated. This assessment gains further
plausibility in view of the limited capacity of the old political
classes to present any effective opposition, and the failure of the
new Left to move from small-scale terrorism to large-scale insur-
rection. Indeed, those whose attention centers on the socioeconomic policies of the Brazilian military governments might even
argue that the regime is already institutionalized because it has
demonstrated staying power and the capacity to formulate and
execute programs.[4] Those who see the ideas of the Superior War

3. In contrast to the extensive theoretical literature on rebellions, insurgency, revolutions, and breakdowns of regimes, there are few studies of
the process by which rulers proceed to consolidate power, once they have
gained it. An exception is Karl Dietrich Bracher, Wolfgang Sauer, and Ger-
hardt Schulz, *Die Nationalsozialistische Machtergreifung: Studien zur Errich-
tung des Totalitären Herrschaftssystems in Deutschland 1933–34* (Cologne:
Westdeutscher Verlag, 1960). See also Otto Kirchheimer, "Confining Conditions and Revolutionary Breakthroughs," *American Political Science Review*
59 (December 1965): 964–74.

4. The reader of this chapter might be surprised that a sociologist should
focus less than other contributors on the class structure, interest groups,
sectors of the economy, regional differences of economic and social development, social composition and ties of the armed forces. This is in part the
result of an implicit division of labor among the contributors to avoid
repetition. It is also a reflection of a theoretical orientation that emphasizes
the more strictly political factors: the relative autonomy of the military in
making their choices and the long-run implications of decisions they have
made in response to their mentality (and *ressentiments*) that could not be

College (Escola Superior de Guerra) as forming a coherent program, conceived even before the military assumed power, will tend to consider the regime even further down the road toward full institutionalization.

However, when we focus on the more strictly political actions of the successive military governments since 1964, such as the periodic issuance of drastic institutional acts, the making and breaking of constitutions, the constant changing of the rules of the game in regard to elections, and most importantly, the profound internal military struggles that marked the two succession crises, we sense a void in political institutionalization. It is true that, despite internal tensions, the military has been able to exercise power, but their hesitant efforts to "civilianize" their rule have had only limited success. Power has basically remained with the armed forces, except for economic policy making, which is shared between the military, selected technocrats, and, to a lesser extent, businessmen. Institutions outside of the armed forces have been created and disregarded constantly, leaving the military with ultimate power. Even those political figures selected by the military are thus dependent, almost day by day, on the internal consensus of the officer corps. When we examine the Brazilian national security doctrine, with its basically negative character and its ambivalent commitment to democracy, we must question its ultimate capacity to serve as the foundation for "legitimate" and stable authoritarian political institutions like those that have emerged in Spain under Franco.

All this leads me to suggest that the Brazilian case represents an authoritarian *situation* rather than an authoritarian *regime*. Furthermore, the nature of the regime that might eventually emerge is still largely undefined. That after eight years of rule there is an authoritarian situation, rather than an authoritarian regime, is evidence of the difficulties faced in the institutionalization of such regimes (difficulties compounded in the Brazilian case for reasons to be explored). It is also evidence that consolidation of power and even considerable success in specific policies do not in themselves ensure institutionalization and that the weakness of regimes is not determined only by the strength of the opposition. The Brazilian case in all these respects poses particularly

explained in traditional sociological categories. It also reflects my concern in this essay with the process of institution building rather than with the formulation of specific policies. Furthermore, I have limited myself to an analysis of the alternatives open to the present rulers and particularly the officer corps. The constraints set by the social bases of the 1964 Revolution are taken as given and therefore not the object of our analysis.

interesting and important problems for the comparative study of the dynamics of authoritarian regimes.

In Brazil, even though fully competitive democracy (with freedom for all political actors and social groups) has now definitely been excluded through a variety of means, such as control of the press and the cancellation of the political rights of the most prominent politicians, the present government is still only in the constituent stage. What alternative models of authoritarian regimes are available to the present military leaders in Brazil, which ones have they considered, and what are the prospects of successful institutionalization of each of them? These are the basic questions.

Unfortunately, we are still far from an adequate typology of authoritarian regimes. For some answers to these questions we therefore have to turn to regimes found in certain countries, in order to see what parallels they suggest for Brazil. This explains the references in this volume to the "Mexicanization" or "Portugalization" of the Brazilian regime.[5] In addition, since my original model of an authoritarian regime was developed largely by contraposition to both competitive democracies and strictly defined totalitarian systems, the inquiry into the prerequisites for stable authoritarian regimes still demands much work.

As a first (far from satisfactory) approximation, we may say that authoritarian regimes are likely to emerge wherever the conditions for stable democratic or totalitarian systems are absent.[6] However, such a "residual" explanation does not tell us much about the conditions for their stable institutionalization and even less about the prerequisites for different types of authoritarian regimes.

In my original presentation of the model, I tried to distinguish between two main types of authoritarian regimes.[7] The first type is characterized by the *controlled mobilization* of a population that by and large had not previously been mobilized and is thus reasonably available. The second type is one characterized by the *deliberate demobilization* of a population that had previously been mobilized within a more competitive political situation, but in which the political institutions did not possess the capacity either to satisfy the demands created by mobilization or to guarantee stable processes of political and social change. Using this

5. See in particular the essay by Philippe C. Schmitter in this volume.

6. See Robert A. Dahl, *Polyarchy: Participation and Opposition* (New Haven: Yale University Press, 1971), in addition to the contributions of Harry Eckstein and S. M. Lipset, among others.

7. See Linz, "An Authoritarian Regime: Spain," pp. 260–62.

frame of reference, the basic question the present rulers of Brazil have to face is whether they want and can create a mobilizational, authoritarian regime. If the answer to either part of this question is no, then the next question is whether a regime based on the demobilization of the population activated in the populist period before the 1964 coup is possible without excessive repression, and whether, if repression is necessary, it will assure stable rule.

I will now endeavor to examine in some detail the complex series of obstacles in Brazil to the institutionalization of either the mobilization-populist-fascist subtype of authoritarian regime, or the demobilization-bureaucratic-military subtype that Schmitter has in mind when he writes of the Portugalization of Brazil. In the comparative analysis of authoritarian regimes particular attention must be given to the immediate political circumstances surrounding the origin of the regime and the way in which these circumstances condition the evolution of the regime. Attention must also be paid to the way in which the country's social and political development, the international ideological climate of the time of the assumption of power, and the nature of the country's international links and dependencies combine to constrain or facilitate the legitimacy formulas and the political-party systems that are feasibly available to the builders of the authoritarian regime. It is in these areas that some clues must be sought for understanding the institutionalization of authoritarian structures.

THE FORMATIVE STAGE OF BRAZIL'S AUTHORITARIAN REGIME: BRAZIL'S AMBIVALENT LEGACY

Let us start with the circumstances surrounding the creation of the current Brazilian regime. In contrast to some of the most stable authoritarian regimes in the world today, whether left-authoritarian or right-authoritarian, the present Brazilian rulers did not come to power in the course of a bitter civil war nor after a serious national crisis accompanied by foreign threats, such as occurred with Atatürk in Turkey or Nasser in Egypt. Nor did Brazil experience a prolonged period of widespread terror, as did Spain and Yugoslavia, terror that helped assure the allegiance of those who participated in the formative stages of the regime, based on their fears and/or shared guilt, whatever their subsequent disillusionment. In Brazil, in contrast, despite the mobilization of some conservative middle- and upper-class groups, the active support of some Catholic conservative masses, and the collaboration of some leading politicians, the birth of the regime was fundamentally the result of a successful coup by the army.

There is another important contrast between Brazil and many

of the fascist or semifascist regimes and even some of the leftist-nationalistic authoritarian regimes of the Third World. In Brazil, a civilian political party aspiring to fully noncompetitive rule did not exist before the beginning of authoritarian rule by the military. This obviously limits the possibility of creating a single party composed primarily of committed civilians who could link the current military-technocratic regime with a political movement of richer symbolic content or provide the military with a more widely recruited political cadre. In the absence of such a party, when the military felt the need of politicians to work with them, they have had to recruit these politicians from among the remaining members of the old political parties, particularly from the ranks of the União Democrática Nacional (UDN) and the Partido Social Democrático (PSD). This situation creates a variety of problems for the regime's evolution. On the one hand, the bulk of the officers have a visceral dislike of the style and record of the old-school politicians. On the other hand, these politicians, though willing to cooperate in the official dominant party, Aliança Renovadora Nacional (ARENA), are more likely to feel at ease in a political system that is at least semicompetitive. They are not the kind of men that other authoritarian regimes have used to forge either a fairly disciplined bureaucratic-elitist cadre party, or a real or pseudo mass party.

Paradoxically, the relative ease and rapidity of the 1964 coup also created difficulties for the current rulers in Brazil. The fact that the coup was virtually unopposed makes the rationalization of "saving the country from communism and subversion" questionable. Samuel Huntington has noted that one of the characteristic forms of authoritarian rule is the "exclusionary one-party system" based on a clear identification of the "enemy." [8] The lack of a credible "enemy" in the Brazilian case makes such a basis for exclusion less clear. In any case, the destruction of much of the political class cannot be legitimated on the basis of their identification with the "subversive" government of ex-President Goulart. Many of the most prominent centrist or conservative politicians, such as Juscelino Kubitschek, Adhemar de Barros, and Carlos Lacerda, all of whom later had their political rights taken away, were strong supporters of the coup against Goulart.

This raises the crucial question of symbols. Among the many important factors in the analysis of the formative stages of an

8. Samuel P. Huntington, "Social and Institutional Dynamics of One-Party Systems," in Huntington and Moore, *Authoritarian Politics in Modern Society*, p. 14.

authoritarian regime are the slogans, phrases, and symbols that accompany its birth. Whatever policies authoritarian regimes may later follow, it becomes difficult for them to overcome the image they have initially created. This image inevitably limits their freedom as they strive for political institutionalization at later stages. When the military assumed power in Brazil in 1964, some prominent officers articulated attachment to their "salvationist" mission to "clear up the mess" and restore democracy. Though many of the regime's later policies made carrying out such a mission increasingly unlikely, the constant restatement of the intention to restore competitive liberal democracy (whatever ambivalence these statements contained), was and still is a drawback for the legitimation of permanent authoritarian elitist rule. Only — and in this the hard-line wing of the military may be right — complete discontinuity with the initial leadership and ideas of 1964 and a displacement of the present ruling groups would open the door to an unabashed, self-confident authoritarian regime.[9] However, such a reversal would undoubtedly be viewed by many officers as endangering the already perilous unity of the military institution. Furthermore, the negative component that justified 1964 would not be sufficient almost a decade later to justify such a step toward pure authoritarian rule. A large part of the population and even significant sectors of the military would legitimately ask why now, if not then. Only a greatly stepped-up campaign by urban guerrillas might rationalize permanent authoritarian rule.

There are thus contradictions and obstacles inhibiting the early establishment of a fully elaborated authoritarian regime. However, after the salvationist claims are finally renounced, as they are likely to be, the question then becomes what types of symbols or institutions might serve to rationalize permanent authoritarian rule. We will first examine the question of alternative legitimacy formulas, particularly charismatic or corporatist formulas, and then turn to the possible subtypes of authoritarian political-party systems available to the Brazilian military regime.

9. This analysis is confirmed by the self-criticism of the "Castellistas" as reported by Schneider, *The Political System of Brazil*, p. 339. One of them said that Castello in his desire to preserve as much democracy as possible had "improved his place in history at the cost of sacrificing chances for more thoroughgoing changes in the old system," and that many civilian backers of 1964 "hold that the entire political class should have been dismantled in 1964 and the groups actively backing the coup utilized as the nucleus for a new political force."

THE NEED FOR A LEGITIMACY FORMULA

As Alfred Stepan has noted, the Brazilian doctrine of national security, developed in the military milieu as an intellectual elaboration of responses to insurgency and as a result of the new professionalism, is too limited to provide a legitimacy formula because of its essentially negative character.[10] To say that the military espouses anticommunism tells us too little about the kind of society the rulers want to create and the kind of social and economic policies they want to implement. It tells us even less about the kind of political institutions and legitimacy formulas they want to use. Certainly, some repressive policies can be derived from an anticommunist stance. Some manipulation of interest conflicts by controlling and changing the leadership of labor and peasant groups and even some technocratic social reform and economic development policies can be justified by a doctrine of anticommunism. The success of such a combination of policies based on repression and development can assure some stability in periods of prosperity, but it can never satisfy those who ask questions about legitimacy, except perhaps in purely subject political cultures, with traditional rulers in the most narrow Weberian sense of the term. In any society that has developed beyond this stage, as Brazil clearly has, questions about legitimacy will inevitably be asked. They will be asked by intellectuals and those under their influence, by those concerned with religious values, and ultimately by some of those who have to use coercion, like judges or army officers confronted with subversion or public disorder. Only praetorian guards or the lowest ranks of a police force do not ask such questions. Anyone in a position of responsibility, one who must die or kill to defend a regime, must ultimately ask questions about why he should do so and whether he should obey in a crisis situation.

THE AVAILABILITY OF THE CHARISMATIC LEGITIMACY FORMULA

In the modern world, all legitimacy formulas refer in some way to the authority coming from the *demos,* the people. Who "the people" should be and how they should transfer their authority to the rulers are the great questions of politics. The number of answers is not unlimited, nor is it a matter of indifference which one is chosen. One "answer" that has had considerable psycho-

10. See his essay in this volume and his *The Military in Politics: Changing Patterns in Brazil* (Princeton, N.J.: Princeton University Press, 1971), pp. 172–87.

logical power to demand obedience is the establishment of an identity between the people and an extraordinary man who represents the people, who feels that he can speak for them, and who is accepted by the people as their leader in view of his unique quality. This is charismatic authority. Never mind that in many societies which are led by such a leader large minorities do not believe in the leader's charisma. The majority believe in his authority. More important, he too believes in his mission to lead.

Despite the widespread and often loose use of this term by social scientists, such authority appears rarely and only under very special circumstances. It cannot be produced "on order." The military organization, particularly (as in the Brazilian case) when bureaucratic seniority rules are adhered to and when achievement of the highest office requires corporate consensus of the officer corps, is not the best breeding ground for charismatic rule. Normally it is only after an international or civil war that something like charismatic authority appears within the regular channels of the army. Certainly, none of the presidents of post-1964 Brazil fit the role of charismatic leader, and probably none of them aspired to it. The officer corps, in fact, seems hostile to and fearful of the emergence of a "caudillo."

Even when charismatic authority cannot serve as a long-term and sufficient basis to institutionalize an authoritarian regime, it can serve to give it a lease on life and provide the leader with the opportunity to create an institutional framework out of other materials. This has probably been the role of Cárdenas in Mexico, and possibly that of Nasser in Egypt and Franco in Spain. Brazil, on the other hand, because of the circumstances surrounding the military's assumption of power and the bureaucratic nature of the military organization, has no charismatic leader in the making. Indeed, any officer with clear political skills and potential for populist charismatic appeal is vetoed by the military organization. Thus any use of the charismatic formula to help institutionalize and legitimate authoritarian rule is very unlikely in the Brazilian case.

THE CORPORATIST, NONPARTY LEGITIMACY FORMULA

Another option that might give a more democratic base to such an authoritarian regime is to reject "individualistic" democracy and substitute for it some form of corporatist organic representation. Organic democracy "in theory" offers a legitimate alternative to competitive-party democracy to assure the participation of people in their government. In practice, as Max Weber noted, it serves to exclude from political participation large numbers of people or whole sections of the society and to manipulate the composition of representative assemblies.[11] This would be fully congruent with the idea of limited pluralism that is a key characteristic of the authoritarian-regime model and the realities of Brazilian politics since 1964. Furthermore, as the articles by Skidmore and particularly Schmitter in this volume demonstrate, corporatist institutions, ideologies, and policy-making processes have a certain tradition in Brazil.[12] If the current regime decided to go further in this corporatist direction, the Portugalization of Brazil would certainly be achieved with such a formula. As in Portugal, corporatist ideology and institutions would be combined with republican institutions like a directly elected national parliament. This formula would avoid the appearance of a complete break with Brazil's long history of commitment (despite lapses) to the form of direct and liberal democracy.

There are, however, some difficulties with this solution. The link established in the public mind between corporatism and fascism (whatever misunderstanding of many fascist regimes, particularly of the Nazi case, this involves), gives such a solution dubious attractiveness. It could, however, be argued that corporatism has been more important for Catholic conservative social doctrine than for fascism, and therefore would be congruent with the sentiments of those segments of Brazilian society identified with a conservative church. Certainly, if Brazil were to move in this direction, some of the ideologies of corporatist institutions would come from conservative clerical and lay groups. However, the traditional weakness of lay Catholicism in Brazil as well as the development since the late 1950s of progressive and even radical Catholic lay movements are obstacles to such a development. Even if these obstacles did not exist, international Catholicism has undergone significant changes since the late 1920s and 1930s, when corporatist authoritarian regimes of Europe were instituted as a new alternative to liberal, individualist democracies. The ideas of the early social encyclicals, quoted by Salazar in Portugal, Dollfuss in Austria, and important segments of the Franco regime, are still available, but their legitimacy within the Catholic tradition has been seriously weakened by Vatican II. Not only have large sections of Belgian, German, Dutch, and French Catholicism abandoned such ideas, but so have recent popes, whereas in the past many of the popes could be interpreted as preferring, if not prescribing, such a corporatist approach to

11. Max Weber, *Economy and Society,* ed. Guenter Roth and Claus Wittich (New York: Bedminister Press, 1968), 1: 297–99.

12. Also see Schmitter's *Interest Conflict and Political Change in Brazil.*

politics. The Brazilian church is today divided over the position it should take concerning the authoritarian military regime. A militant minority would like to see the church systematically confront and oppose the regime, and they appeal to the "prophetic mission" of the church. On the opposite wing is a militant group of Catholic conservatives who actively urge the military to impose a corporatist state. A large part of the institutional church, however, is uneasily but passively acquiescing to the authoritarian regime — partly because of financial dependency, partly because of the church's historic caution in regard to major church-state conflicts.

In light of this political, ideological, and theological division within the contemporary Brazilian church, it seems reasonable to argue that the Brazilian military regime will not be able to persuade the church hierarchy to take an enthusiastic, unified, and active role in the construction of a corporatist state. Another limitation of a corporatist solution is its lack of appeal to intellectuals and even to those military officers who may feel that Brazil, as a potential world power, should be offering new political formulas. Corporatism, furthermore, would not provide Brazil with an appealing image abroad.

A further difficulty with a corporatist solution in Brazil is that it would be difficult (though not impossible) to harmonize it with the federal structure of the country or the traditional role of state governors. Over the long run, it might be useful to have some kind of party system for election of the state governors, and it might be too severe a break with tradition to have the governors elected by corporatist chambers. To have them permanently appointed by the central government would be an even greater break, although the centralizing tendencies and the weakening of the federal tradition have gone very far in recent years.

The combination of these national and international factors, plus the military's attachment to their "salvationist mission" to reestablish United States–style democracy, helps explain why the military rulers have not openly decided to use corporatist structures and ideologies to institutionalize the authoritarian regime or to give it an ideological façade to date.

As we have argued before, the initial circumstances surrounding the founding of the regime influences the feasibility of subsequent steps. In the Brazilian case, the fact that the military governments have already created new electoral and political party laws, as well as a new constitution, means that the subsequent creation of corporatist institutions would entail a break with their own recent past and would alienate even more those who

collaborated in experiments such as the creation of the government party, ARENA, and the half-controlled opposition parties
such as the MDB.

ONE-PARTY ALTERNATIVES — FASCIST AND POPULIST

Thus the two nonparty legitimacy formulas — charismatic and
corporatist — do not seem to be readily available to Brazil's current rulers. This section will explore the possible party-system
solutions.

A single-party system at first impression would seem to be the
simplest solution. It is important to repeat here that the present
regime was not created by a coalition between the military and
civilian political parties or politicians committed to the idea of a
single party. In this, Brazil in 1964 was quite different from
Spain in 1936. Obviously, many authoritarian regimes have used
their power to create single parties even when such parties have
been far from satisfactory for the long-run institutionalization of
these regimes. In the Brazilian case the difficulties are compounded by a number of international and national circumstances.

The antirevolutionary, and largely antipopulist, initial thrust
of the Revolution was supported by the upper and middle classes.
Its appeal to symbols of order and tradition would inevitably tend
to associate a resultant single party with fascism, an ideology and
system of the past, viewed negatively by most people, probably
even by many of the same people who support the regime on
social or economic grounds. Single parties are far from being out
of favor in the world, but a fascist single party is certainly not
fashionable. The cultural acceptance of the United States' liberal political forms by many of the Brazilian elites also makes
a single party that would inevitably be labeled as fascist undesirable.

What of the populist single-party option? In contrast to other
military coups and regimes, whatever policies the Brazilians may
pursue, they will have great difficulty avoiding the label "rightist."
Military organizations that take power today in traditional societies, in which competitive or semicompetitive regimes are perceived as having failed by significant segments of society, have a
chance to create a single party. But their rhetoric must be leftist;
they must speak of socialism, of agrarian reform, sometimes of
secularization, and above all, of nationalism, anti-imperialism,
and (best of all) anti-Americanism. Some of these themes are not
out of the question in Brazil. In fact, some members of the military might feel closer to them than corporatist formulas or to the

defense of a dynamic capitalism linked to the Western capitalist world economy.

A coup by some segment of the army attempting to turn the country toward such a left-authoritarian regime cannot be excluded, but it would have to overcome resistance both within and outside the military. Many within the military would fear it because it would risk dividing the military institution. Just as importantly, the economic policies of recent years, which many credit with contributing to the very high growth rates since 1968, would have to be abandoned. The successor policies would come into conflict with strong vested interests that would not tolerate such policy reversals passively. The recent success of Brazilian capitalism — national, mixed national, international, public and private — and the complexity of the financial, industrial, and commercial structure of São Paulo and Rio, as Stepan notes, is one among many factors accounting for the differences between the attitude of the Brazilian military and the more populist Peruvian officers toward the socioeconomic system.[13] To reverse the ongoing Brazilian economic system would require a broader impetus than a faction of left-authoritarian officers in the army could provide.

A populist authoritarian regime with a single party created by the army in coalition with some intellectuals, searching for support among labor and seeking legitimacy by assuming an anti-United States stand in world affairs, with ties to the Soviet Union is not out of the question. Many factors would stand in the way of such a project, however. Not only the capitalist structure of Brazilian society, the conservative middle-class segments of Brazilian Catholicism, public and private pressures from the United States, but historical developments in recent years stand in the way. The fact that the populist appeal had already been made and to some degree organized prior to 1964 by politicians now in exile or deprived of their political rights, or dishonored and persecuted by the army, makes it difficult to shift to such an appeal without endangering very seriously the unity of the armed forces. In addition, it is doubtful that men who have experienced such defamation would collaborate with a segment of the army, even should some of the officers try to plot with them. After the last eight years it is very questionable whether the intellectuals, the students, and the Catholic Left would unite with a sector of the army in the building of an authoritarian regime with a left-oriented single party to which they would provide ideas but only

13. See Stepan's essay in this volume.

a minority of leadership. Too many have undergone a process of radicalization and put their hopes in more revolutionary solutions, whatever the chances of success, or have become cynical if not outright hostile toward the military in general.

Populism is not a flag that the present rulers, or a segment of them, can appropriate easily, even though it is certain that they will do their best to appropriate some of its issues and some of its rhetoric in the coming years. The Brazilian military is far from institutionalizing the regime on the basis of a large-scale, manipulated single mass party like the one Nasser created in Egypt. The Peruvian military, on the other hand, given the anti-United States, antioligarchical "signs" under which their rule was born, and the social and economic structure of the country, as well as the more limited success of populist mobilization before the takeover, have some or perhaps many chances to do so. Their Brazilian peers have more limited and dangerous options.

THE HEGEMONIC OR PREDOMINANT-PARTY ALTERNATIVES

If a fascist-type single-party regime or a socialist-populist single-party regime is not an entirely feasible alternative for the military in Brazil (as well as being of dubious appeal to the technocrats working with them and of even less appeal to some of the old-time politicians that they have co-opted), it would seem that some kind of multiparty system with a hegemonic party would be the most realistic option.[14] In a sense, the hesitant efforts of "constitutionalization" and "civilianization" have been moves in this direction.

It seems probable that the present rulers find this a much more feasible alternative, and one less divisive for the armed forces. The Mexican solution comes immediately to mind. Here I must stress that I do not accept the argument that in Mexico the minor parties are completely free to organize and that the country is thus democratic. Nor do I find compelling the theoretical model of internal party democracy through the sector structure, which was initially formulated by Robert Scott.[15] I see Mexico rather as having an authoritarian hegemonic party

14. We use "hegemonic party" in the sense given to it by Giovanni Sartori, "The Typology of Political Systems — Proposals for Improvement," in Allardt and Rokkan, *Mass Politics*, pp. 322–52 and 382–88; in particular see pp. 326–31, where he discusses the distinction between predominant party, hegemonic party, single party, and their subtypes. See also his forthcoming book, *Parties and Party Systems*.

15. Robert E. Scott, *Mexican Government in Transition* (Urbana: University of Illinois Press, 1964).

system which has some of the formal structures that make it appear to approximate a competitive democracy or at least give the appearance of moving toward a polyarchy. Though I define the Mexican system as authoritarian, I acknowledge that most participants see the hegemonic party, Partido Revolucionario Institucional (PRI), as legitimate and popular. If Brazil could create such a party, while reducing other parties to irrelevant opposition roles (if not to manipulated allies of the hegemonic party) and outlawing subversive parties, this solution would undoubtedly be welcomed by much of the Brazilian military. It would also be welcomed by the United States as a face-saving solution that would be preferable to either the straightforward single-party solution or the corporatist path toward Portugalization. The great question is, can it be done?

Certainly the manipulation of electoral laws can go very far in assuring the emergence of a de facto hegemonic party, but given the recent history of Brazil and its level of development, the successful transformation of ARENA into a Brazilian PRI will be very difficult. The semicompetitive period of Brazilian politics has left a heritage of leadership identifications that interferes with the creation of such a party by the present ruling group. As the state elections in recent years have shown, there is more of a tradition in favor of a competitive party system than would be desirable for the inauguration of such a pseudodemocratic, authoritarian formula. The passage of time, together with continuous economic prosperity, some appealing structural reforms, and effective patronage might make it possible to forge such a government party and limit and exclude other parties. At present, however, the memory of a more open party system, the potential appeal of some of the political figures of the past, the links established between the old parties and some interest groups like the trade unions make the task of creating a broadly popular hegemonic party much more difficult. One of the greatest difficulties is likely to be the unwillingness of powerful factions within the armed forces to give an official, controlled government party sufficient autonomy and a large enough share in power. Past military intimidation of Congress, interventions in the nominating process, and withdrawal of political rights from ARENA leaders who show any independence have frustrated many of those willing to cooperate in such an experiment.

Past military pressure from one or another segment of the army has resulted in the withdrawal of political rights from a large number of politicians who had, in essence, been very willing to cooperate with the regime. This has limited the range of politicians still available to build a civilian-led hegemonic party. In addition, the loss of power within the military of those officers who appeared to be most eager to search for a nonmilitary social base (e.g. Passarinho and most noticeably Albuquerque Lima, who during the struggle over the succession to Costa e Silva attempted to make himself known to the country) points to another limiting factor in any attempt to forge a broad civilian base for a hegemonic party.

The major trouble for the Brazilian ruling circles is that the Revolution of 1964 was not the Mexican revolution. Its heroes are villains for those who admire the Mexican revolutionaries. Its myths and symbols are the opposite of those of the Mexican revolution of 1910, and no similarity in actual government output can correct these birth defects. No achievements in economic development, stability, or even in any possible future selective redistribution policies can compensate for them. A Brazilian sympathetic to such pseudodemocratic but actually authoritarian solutions might ask why he should expect the reaction to a hegemonic party to be so different in Mexico and Brazil. It is necessary to stress once more that the political problems of authoritarian regimes, given their ambiguous status in the struggle for the minds of people in the twentieth century, are not exclusively nationally determined. The opinion of foreign intellectuals, scholars, and journalists are an important reality with which they have to contend. The birth of the Brazilian regime antagonized intellectuals at home and abroad. Revolutionary violence by peasants is very different from police terror that is tolerated if not encouraged by the government. Rightist symbols do not have the same legitimacy for most intellectuals as those of the Left. In addition to such difficulties, which we should never underestimate, there are practical ones. The creation through power of a predominant or hegemonic party of the Mexican type is not easy for a group of officers with a basically bureaucratic mentality, nor for technocrats with a commitment to apolitical, rational economic and social policy making. It is perhaps feasible if there were a charismatic leader working with them, but no such leader exists yet in Brazil, and for reasons stated previously his appearance is not likely. Such a process of party creation also would require a "civilianization" of segments of the army so that they could assume more strictly political functions. The performance of these functions, however, would tend to split the military, for they still perceive such acts as "politicking" or "demagoguery."

If the military government could associate itself with nationalistic-populistic policies it would aid the process of building a hegemonic party. Some attempt in this direction will undoubtedly be made, but the stage of Brazilian development makes this more difficult than it was in Mexico in the 1930s or, as we have noted, even in Peru today. Some of the more successful authoritarian regimes, such as those that came to power in Turkey after the fall of the Sultan, in Egypt after the overthrow of King Farouk, or in Mexico after the revolution against Porfirio Díaz, *created* for the first time in their society nationalist symbols and populist structures. These regimes inherited a great ideological and institutional space in which they could build. In Brazil, however, the first step of the current military government was to disinherit the nationalist leaders and to repress the already growing populist mobilizational structures of the trade unions, the peasant leagues, and the ideologically inspired literacy campaigns. Thus, even if the military government were later to successfully implement nationalist-populist policies, it would be doubtful that these policies would win for them the legitimacy and support they won for their executors in Egypt, Mexico, or Turkey.

Consideration of these factors leads me to conclude that it will be a very difficult task to create a broadly popular hegemonic or predominant party in Brazil. These same factors will also make the creation of the "preferred mix" of the minor parties even more difficult if we keep in mind that the goal is to achieve at least the façade of competitive politics. Thus even a pseudo-predominant party must allow other parties a relatively free existence, while assuring itself dominance by a combination of success in economic policies, manipulation of electoral laws, gerrymandering, indirect pressures, and co-optation or corruption of emerging leaders of other parties. In a country where a variety of parties had already achieved a certain maturity, the creation of a credible predominant party by such Machiavellian methods is not easy. The alternative would obviously be the creation of a hegemonic party that by legal, rather than by de facto, obstacles would allow other parties a subsidiary role. The model of hegemonic parties in pseudo-multiparty systems like those in communist countries in Eastern Europe ideally requires in the last analysis a historical, ideological justification of the hegemonic party that is difficult to provide in the Brazilian case. In the absence of such justification, considerable legal and/or illegal limits would have to be placed on the many opposition parties that potentially could emerge spontaneously. If the existence of such parties is to win the regime any legitimacy, the level of obvious coercive restriction against the parties must not be too high. However, given the degree of political freedom and politicization that prevailed in Brazil before 1964 and the degree of the country's development, an extremely high level of coercion apparently would be necessary in order to create and maintain the docile, manipulated, semiopposition parties that the hegemonic party formula calls for.

In any case, even were the domestic conditions for the creation of a hegemonic or predominant party system more favorable than we think, in Brazil the symbolic ideological birth defects of the system would still persist. While radicals in the world have no difficulty in calling the PRI in Mexico fascist, a populist hegemonic or even predominant ARENA would be labeled fascist by a much broader spectrum of opinion, thus destroying its function of legitimizing the system. ARENA's basic policies of dynamic capitalism — partly private, partly public — rapid economic development with stability, and the maintenance of good relations with the United States would not differ much from those of the PRI, but this fact would not cause many to change their minds.

AUTHORITARIAN REGIMES IN THE CONTEMPORARY WORLD

Ultimately, authoritarian regimes, despite their pragmatism, their lack of ideological rigidity, the similarities across a wide spectrum of systems in terms of their institutionalization and uses of power, are very dependent on their symbolic identification when they face the problems of political institutionalization. Politics is not simply a question of policies and administration, but of appealing to politically interested segments of society. Millions of passive supporters and obedient citizens are insufficient, as are, also, numerous groups who see a coincidence of their interests with those of their rulers and are thus willing to abdicate political power for the sake of minding their own affairs — whether these affairs be business, personal social mobility, or welfare policies for certain groups. I agree with Philippe Schmitter's intriguing observation that in this respect the authoritarian-regime model is very similar to the Bonapartist model of Marx.[16] Authoritarian regimes normally flounder about because they lack an appealing ideological stance. In the contemporary world large segments of society still believe, rightly or wrongly, in the desirability of an open, competitive, democratic political system or in the desirability of an ideologically driven, possibly totalitarian society whose elites provide some sense of historical mission

16. See Schmitter's essay in this volume.

to the nation, and thereby satisfy some of the more politically involved citizens. In this setting an authoritarian regime has serious weaknesses. Ultimately all authoritarian regimes face this legitimacy pull toward the polyarchical model, with political freedom for relatively full participation, or toward the committed, ideological single-party model. To resist those two pulls is possible de facto, but none of the authoritarian institutionalization attempts we find around the world have been fully satisfactory. The fact that the United States, Japan, England, the Soviet Union, and China are the models for those two polar alternatives and at the same time are the greatest powers of the day, makes the institutionalization of authoritarian regimes, notwithstanding the considerable achievements of some of these regimes, all the more difficult. There is ultimately no authoritarian regime in the world comparable in economic, technological, intellectual, or social weight to the major democratic countries or the major mobilizational one-party systems. The most important and successful authoritarian regimes, in the past Turkey, and now Mexico, Egypt, Spain, or Yugoslavia, are only imperfect models for those who want to bring their nation to the height of their times, to use Ortega's expression.

In essence, despite their variety, all the authoritarian solutions are dependent through symbiosis, mimicry, or transformation on the three basic great models of political systems — the liberal competitive democratic model, in any of its varieties; the communist, ideological single-party or hegemonic model; and the now defeated, but in the past appealing, fascist, nationalist pseudoconservative single-party rival. With great reservations, one might add the corporatist model. This fourth alternative has never been very appealing to intellectuals, and on a world scale has not succeeded to the same extent as the other three, perhaps because it is much more closely tied to the pragmatic bargaining or balancing of material interests rather than to ideas of a just and ideal society. As the group theory of politics has tried to show, largely successfully, elements of such corporatist politics are present in liberal, democratic systems and increasingly in complex communist single-party regimes, particularly Yugoslavia. In all of them, however, corporatism is, in reality, in conflict with the idea of some clearly perceived common good. Authoritarian-corporatist political regimes have a strong component of reality and pragmatism that makes them work, but the search for ultimate meaning, purpose, legitimacy, and justice demands something beyond the adjustment of interests conflicts through bargaining. That is the ultimate difference between systems with and without political parties. Parties, while representing interests, also stand for a certain type of social order, or at least make that claim.

In political systems which do not have either political parties that grow more or less spontaneously from the demands and aspirations of the people or a vanguard party that mobilizes the society the decisive actions will be taken by the bureaucratic elite controlling the state apparatus. This is so whether the bureaucratic elite is largely from a military, civil servant, technocratic, or managerial background. Almost by definition, such bureaucratic systems entail the rule of the state over the society. The state establishes the permissible limits of freedom and spontaneity in the society and attempts to control the ground rules by which groups can interact with the state. Such authoritarian rule works in many parts of the world. However, nowhere does it seem to have attained the degree of institutionalization achieved by systems characterized by competitive democratic parties or even by large-scale ideological mass parties. Ultimately, authoritarian regimes are condemned to constant experiments with other alternatives, to processes of institutionalization incorporating elements, symbols, and mechanisms, developed in those other political forms considered in line with modern historical development. The success in this process depends, as we have continuously stressed, on historical situations, on specific national constraining factors, on international situations, and on specific policies. All this leads to a strange combination between freedom of choice for the group wanting to institutionalize such a regime and constant limits to its choices. This situation introduces complex elements of unpredictability, uncertainty, ambivalence, and thereby lack of appeal.

Within these limitations, the authoritarian solutions linking leftist symbols, and to a lesser degree policies, with leftist allies on the international scene are today at an advantage over those justly or unjustly perceived as being on the right. This has not always been so. In the past, the great fascist powers gave to those creating authoritarian regimes — that were often not, strictly speaking, fascist — an aura of legitimacy similar to that which socialism gives to those who are not, in the strict sense, socialist, in the Third World today. A link of identification, dependency, or whatever relationship we might posit with the United States makes the successful institutionalization of authoritarian regimes even more difficult. The United States, despite the economic or military support it provides to many authoritarian regimes, often, on an ideological level, implicitly or explicitly contributes to the delegitimization of such regimes. Key members of the Congress, the press, or even the executive branch question the regimes' attempts to institutionalize themselves along authoritarian lines. This introduces ambivalence because the leaders of the authoritarian regime often feel compelled to pay at least lip service to democratic procedures by promising the eventual return to free elections and polyarchical competitive democratic institutions. Thus, like the nineteenth-century bourgeoisie that Marx was describing in his *Eighteenth Brumaire,* the United States often creates the condition for authoritarian rule elsewhere, but at the same time contributes to its moral erosion.

In addition, the United States, and to a lesser extent the European democratic societies, by their emphasis on the free choice of individuals in political, religious, aesthetic, ethical, sexual, even consumer values and styles, are a threat to the very idea of a society in which one or another elite knows better than the individual choosing in isolation what a good society should be like. This accounts for the paradox that conservative, religious, anticommunist authoritarians — whether they be army officers, bureaucrats, technocrats, or managers — often admire Soviet-type societies and feel disgusted with the United States and other Western polyarchic democratic societies with which they are closely tied by an infinite number of relations of interdependence. In the present world context, and particularly in Latin America, this paradox is a strong incentive for anti-American, pseudo-left, authoritarian solutions appealing to those who at another moment might be the allies of the United States.

This line of argument leads us to conclude that the institutionalization of an authoritarian regime by groups within the present ruling circle of Brazil, independently of their success in economic and even social policies, is unlikely to be fully successful without a turn to nationalist, anti-imperialist, anti-American rhetoric, if not actual policies.

Ultimately, the present ruling group faces serious stress whatever road to institutionalization it chooses. Without a charismatic leader making decisions, without a deep and bitter crisis comparable to a civil war in the recent past, the unifying element behind any of the choices made by the authoritarian leaders will be weak.

Even though in my analysis I have expressed grave doubts about the viability of all the various alternatives by which the current rulers in Brazil might seek to institutionalize an authoritarian regime, this does not imply the fall of the present authoritarian situation and the return to open competitive politics or the turn toward full totalitarianism. A possibility that cannot be excluded is a constant and indecisive experimenting with various alternatives, and a sequence of military coups or quasi-coups. At best this might mean that successive governments administer the society and the economy, but postpone almost indefinitely any serious and consistent political institutionalization. Pragmatically speaking, such a process, combining administration, manipulation, arbitrary decisions, false starts, and frequent changes in personnel, might be successful as long as the economy goes well. It could assure the continuity of the present situation, while leaving a frightful political vacuum for the future.

Contributors

FERNANDO HENRIQUE CARDOSO held the Chair of Political Science at the University of São Paulo before his teaching rights were revoked by government decree. He is now director of the Centro Brasileiro de Análise e Planejamento in São Paulo. His books include *Empresário industrial e desenvolvimento econômico no Brazil* and *Escravidão e capitalismo no Brasil meridional.* He is currently working on the theoretical and political problems of "dependent development" and has coauthored *Dependencia y desarrollo en América Latina.*

ALBERT FISHLOW is professor of economics at the University of California at Berkeley and chairman of the Economics Department. He was formerly head of the university's Brazil Development Assistance Program. His publications include *American Railroads and the Transformation of the Ante-Bellum Economy* and "Origins and Consequences of Import Substitution in Brazil," in Luis Di Marco, ed., *International Economics and Development.* He was awarded the Schumpeter Prize in 1971 for his methodological contributions to the study of economic history.

JUAN J. LINZ is professor of sociology and political science at Yale University. His theoretical model of authoritarian regimes is reprinted in Erik Allardt and Stein Rokkan, eds., *Mass Politics.* His other essays on authoritarian politics appear in Huntington and Moore, eds., *Authoritarian Politics in Modern Society* and in Robert A. Dahl, ed., *Regimes and Oppositions.* He is the author of monographs on Spanish business and local elites, published in Spain, and articles on parties and elites.

SAMUEL A. MORLEY is associate professor of economics at the University of Wisconsin and a former member of the University of California's Brazil Development Assistance Program. His articles on Brazilian development have appeared in such journals as *Review of Economics and Statistics, Economic Development and Cultural Change, Oxford Economic Papers* (coauthored with Gordon W. Smith), and in Howard S. Ellis, ed., *The Economy of Brazil.*

PHILIPPE C. SCHMITTER is associate professor of political science at the University of Chicago and the author of *Interest Conflict and Political Change in Brazil.* His other publications include quantitative analyses of political development and public policy in Latin America and several studies of regional integration processes. He recently completed a monograph on corporatism and public policy in Portugal.

THOMAS E. SKIDMORE is professor of history at the University of Wisconsin and was president of the Latin American Studies Association in 1972. He is the author of *Politics in Brazil, 1930–1964,* and his articles on Brazil have appeared in such journals as *Journal of Contemporary History* and *Comparative Studies in Society and History.*

GORDON W. SMITH is assistant professor of economics at Rice University and a former member of the University of California's Brazil Development Assistance Program. His works include *Marketing and Economic Development: A Brazilian Case Study* and *Brazilian Agricultural Policy, 1950–1967.*

ALFRED STEPAN is associate professor of political science and chairman of the Council on Latin American Studies at Yale University. He is the author of *The Military in Politics: Changing Patterns in Brazil,* coeditor with Bruce Russett of *Military Force and American Society,* and the author of various articles on political development in Latin America.

Index

Brazilian personal names are indexed under the final name; for example, Silva, Arthur Costa e, although he appears in the text as Costa e Silva. Page numbers in *italics* refer to tables.

alization, 21n, 159; foreign investments in, 144, *145*, 146; growth patterns, 129, *130–32*, 133; Kubitschek's policy, 143–44; monopoly by large firms, 77; output, 72; pricing of manufactures, 77–78; public ownership (*see* Public enterprises); sales growth, 106–07; total output of key goods, *150*

Inflation, 6n, 197, *198*; Castello Branco policy, 6–10, 12, 20, 71, 75, 80–81; "corrective," 80; cost, 81; Costa e Silva policy, 12–14, 81; excess-demand, 71, 73, 74; growth cycles and, 104–06; Médici policy, 13; models, orthodox and heterodox, formulas, 114–18; money supply and, 8, 13, 73; in 1964, 4, 71; price determination and, 73–74; stabilized, 69, 71. *See also* Stabilization programs

Institutional Acts, 190; First, 6, 38, 210; Second, 9, 165, 210; Fifth, 14, 38, 40, 69, 169–70, 210, 225; Sixth, 15

Institutionalization, 168, 170, 181, 186, 191, 228, 234,

Instituto de Pesquisas Estudos Sociais-Guanabara (IPES-GB), 6n

Instituto Nacional do Livro (National Book Institute), 42

Instituto Superior de Estudos Brasileiros (ISEB), 215

Integralists, 37, 227n

Intellectuals, 42, 245

Inter-American Development Bank (IADB), 23, 24

International corporations, 144, *145*, 146, 156–57, 161–63

International Monetary Fund (IMF), 7, 23, 71

Intersyndical Department of Socioeconomic Statistics and Studies (DIEESE), 200

Investments: foreign, 21–23, 40–41, 99, 102–03, 133–37, *134–36*, 144, *145*, 146, 149; industrial, 30, 144, *145*, 146; international corporations, 144,

145, 146; U.S. in Brazil, 21–23, 103, 144, *145*

IPES-GB (Instituto de Pesquisas Estudios Sociais-Guanabara), 6n

Iron ore, 24, 161

ISEB (Instituto Superior de Estudios Brasileiros), 215

Italy, fascism, 40, 41, 42, 154

Jaguaribe, Hélio, 143, 162, 167; economic determinist model, 150, 153–57

Janowitz, Morris, 53, 60

Japan, 251

Juntas de Conciliação e Julgamento, 207

Kemal Atatürk, 237

Kennedy, John F., 46

KGB, 224

Kubitschek, Juscelino, 4, 8, 46, 70–71, 161, 191, 238; industrialization policy, 143–44

Labor: government plans opposed by, 112; in growth-rate study, 121, 138–39; income distribution and, 138–39; PIS program for, 171, 204; purchasing power, 200–01; syndicates, 206–07, *208*

Labor Code (Consolidação das Leis do Trabalho, CLT), 33, 42, 206

Labor unions. *See* Unions

Lacerda, Carlos, 238

Latifundiários (agrarian sectors), 147

League for National Defense, 215

Lebret, Father, 63

Left: authoritarian opposition to, 39; Catholic, 245; criticism by, 99; internal security threatened by, 58; new, 234; technocrats and military against, 16–17

Lima, Afonso Albuquerque, 11, 167, 170–71, 203, 248

Lima, Negrão de, 8

Linz, Juan J., 205–06, 209, 211, 214n, 233

Literacy: campaign for, 217